REBECCA HUXLEY-BINNS
LEON RILEY
CHRIS TURNER

UNLOCKING
LEGAL LEARNING
SECOND EDITION

SERIES EDITORS:
JACQUELINE MARTIN & CHRIS TURNER

Orders: please contact Bookpoint Ltd, 130 Milton Park, Abingdon, Oxon OX14 4SB. Telephone: (44) 01235 827720. Fax: (44) 01235 400454. Lines are open from 9.00–5.00, Monday to Saturday, with a 24 hour message answering service. You can also order through our website www.hoddereducation.co.uk

If you have any comments to make about this, or any of our other titles, please send them to educationenquiries@hodder.co.uk

British Library Cataloguing in Publication Data
A catalogue record for this title is available from the British Library

ISBN: 978 0 340 96836 9

First Edition Published 2005
This Edition Published 2008
Impression number   10 9 8 7 6 5 4 3 2
Year   2012 2011 2010 2009 2008

Copyright © 2005, 2008 Rebecca Huxley-Binns, Leon Riley, Chris Turner

Cover photo © Peter M. Fisher/Corbis
Typeset by Phoenix Photosetting, Chatham, Kent
Printed in Malta for Hodder Education, part of Hachette UK, 338 Euston Road, London NW1 3BH

CONTENTS ■

ACKNOWLEDGEMENTS

The series editors would like to thank the publishers for their support in making the project a reality. In particular we would also like to thank Alexia Chan for her continued faith in the project from its first conception, and Colin Goodlad and Matthew Sullivan.

The authors would like to thank Angela Donaldson, Liaison Librarian for Law at Nottingham Trent University, for her help and enthusiasm. In particular, we would like to thank her for her hard work on Chapters 4 and 5 of this book. We hope the readers find the chapters as clear and informative as we do. We would also like to express a belated thanks to Laura Pinkney and Andy Bell for their help and advice on the first edition (and our apologies for our omission in the first edition's acknowledgements).

Angela Donaldson would like to thank her colleague Terry Hanstock for helping her develop the knowledge to write the chapters and also Owen for proofreading and continual support.

The authors would like to dedicate this book to all their students past, present and future, without whom the book could not have been written.

The author and publishers would like to thank the following for permission to reproduce copyright material: © Justis Publishing Limited for Figs 5.7, 5.13 and 5.21; © Sweet & Maxwell Ltd for Figs 5.1, 5.3, 5.5, 5.6, 5.9, 5.11, 5.12, 5.14, 5.16, 5.17, 5.18, 5.19, 5.20, 5.22, 5.28, 5.29, 5.32, 5.33 and 5.38; Figs 5.4, 5.10, 5.15, 5.23, 5.24, 5.25, 5.26, 5.27, 5.30, 5.31, 5.34, 5.35, 5.36 and 5.37 reproduced by permission of Reed Elsevier (UK) Limited, trading as LexisNexis Butterworths; © Ministry of Justice for Statute Law Database, Figs 5.2 and 5.8; © Controller of HMSO and the Queen's Printer for Scotland for Crown Copyright material in Figs 4.2, 4.6 and 4.9. Some of the changes to the second edition reflect changes in the law, others reflect improvements suggested by teachers and students.

Parliamentary copyright material is reproduced with the permission of the Controller of Her Majesty's Stationery Office on behalf of Parliament.

The publishers apologise if inadvertently any sources remain unacknowledged and will be glad to make the necessary arrangements at the earliest opportunity.

PREFACE ■

The 'Unlocking' series is an entirely new style of undergraduate law textbooks. Many student texts are very prose dense and have little in the way of interactive materials to help a student feel his or her way through the course of study on a given module.

The purpose of this series then is to try to make learning each subject area more accessible by focusing on actual learning needs, and by providing a range of different supporting materials and features.

All topic areas are broken up into 'bite size' sections with a logical progression and extensive use of headings and numerous sub-headings. Each book in the series will also contain a variety of charts, diagrams and key fact summaries to reinforce the information in the body of the text. Diagrams and flow charts are particularly useful because they can provide a quick and easy understanding of the key points, especially when revising for examinations. Key fact charts not only provide a quick visual guide through the subject but are useful for revision purposes also.

Finally the books also include much formative 'self-testing', with a variety of activities ranging through subject specific comprehension, application of the law, and a range of other activities to help the student gain a good idea of his or her progress in the course.

This book is unlike the other titles in the 'Unlocking' series because it is not on a specific area of law. It is also probably unlike other books that you might see. It is not like a standard 'Legal Skills' book and nor is it like the usual 'Introduction to Law' type books. In fact in some ways it might be called 'Everything that you wanted to know about a law degree but were afraid to ask'. The three authors are all experienced teachers and examiners with many years of experience of both between them. We have all created courses and exams and developed skills programmes. Importantly each author is also very student focused and has listened to students over many years and learnt about the problems that they face when taking law courses.

The purpose of the book is to give you a taste, not just of the new things that you will have to learn on a law degree or similar course involving law, but also of the kind of difficulties that you may encounter in a study of law. We hope it will give you some insight and some encouragement as you embark on your law degree or similar course. There is no reason of course why you should not return to it whenever you feel unsure about a particular aspect of your study.

Changes have been made from the first edition to reflect changes in the law, changes to various resources referred to in Chapter 4 and Chapter 5 and to reflect improvements suggested by teachers and students.

We hope that after reading it you will find your study of the law more relaxed, more informed and even more stimulating.

Rebecca Huxley-Binns, Leon Riley and Chris Turner

chapter 1 WHAT LEARNING LAW IS ALL ABOUT ■

AIMS AND OBJECTIVES

After reading this chapter you should be able to:

- Understand the basic definition and character and purpose of law
- Understand the specific character of the English Legal System
- Understand the various classifications of law within the English Legal System
- Understand the basic sources of the law in England and Wales
- Use accepted legal terminology
- Research aspects of law by using a legal dictionary

1.1 The character and purpose of law

What do you think 'law' means? A very important legal skill is being able to define concepts and topics. To start with, you may wish to write down as many different examples or types of law that you can. Then reflect on that list and see if you can come up with a definition of 'law'.

The term 'law' is very difficult to define because it is used to mean different things in different contexts. A comprehensive definition is therefore hard to provide as it would have to be very wide.

The majority of people use the term 'law' to describe the criminal law. This may be because of the media coverage given to crimes, such as assault, murder, 'joyriding' etc. Some people use the word 'law' to describe the institutions of the legal system, such as the courts, the police, prisons and so on. Other people associate it with the rules regulating our relationships with others. Every time we purchase goods or pay for a service (like a haircut) we are entering a contract and contracts are regulated by the law. Other people would think of the processes of law, its rules and procedures, such as the steps that have to be followed when beginning a legal action under the well-advertised 'no win; no fee' schemes. Alternatively, the word law may be used to describe the rules laid down by Parliament and/or the courts that govern our behaviour and thus refers to the sources of the law.

So, which of these options, in your opinion, is right?

In fact, none of the above can be said to be 'right' to the exclusion of the others. The better way of phrasing the answer would be to say that none of them is wrong.

Consult a good English dictionary, such as *The Concise Oxford Dictionary*, and notice the numerous different ways in which the word 'law' can be defined. You may find that your understanding of these definitions changes as your knowledge increases. Clearly the word alone can have very broad meanings, which will be seen by looking for the definition of law in any dictionary. Even in a dictionary as small as the *Collins English Gem Dictionary* we found the following:

> '*Law.* noun. Rule binding on community; system of these rules; legal science; knowledge, administration of it; general principle deduced from facts; invariable sequence of events in nature.'

Clearly there is quite a lot of scope within these definitions and there is obviously more than a single definition included here. One definition we like because it seems to identify all of the key elements of any type of law is in the *Shorter Oxford English Dictionary*:

> 'Any body of rules which is organised and structured and relates to a particular code of conduct.'

From this activity you will probably have realised that the word 'law' can be understood in many different ways, including those outlined above, but is very often defined in terms of **rules**. You are probably aware of many rules which people observe in their daily lives which regulate the way that they behave and yet these are not necessarily referred to as law. Many people also live according to moral rules and abide by religious codes and yet these are not laws either. So when is a rule regarded as part of the law? Rules are regarded as law when they originate from one of the recognised law-making institutions which you will learn about shortly. But that is not the whole story, for where does the system of law and its processes fit into the picture?

One way of defining the law so as to take account of all three aspects mentioned above, ie the rules of law, the legal system and its processes, is to say that law is a body of the rules of conduct formally recognised as binding or enforced by a controlling body. This definition is useful as a brief and simple way of explaining the concept of law. We could, however, say that the law is simply a way of regulating behaviour; it tells us what must be done, what may be done and what cannot be done.

ACTIVITY

From your reading so far and from your general knowledge, which of the following statements are true and which are false?

- There is no difference between moral rules and legal rules. TRUE/FALSE.
- Procedural rules, for example, how to begin a breach of contract action in court, are not part of law. TRUE/FALSE.
- The concept of law is not the same as the concept of justice. TRUE/FALSE.
- Law is an instrument of social control. TRUE/FALSE.

These questions should have given you some food for thought! You will probably have realised that although many of the rules which we regard as laws are based on moral codes (for example, people must not commit murder), not every moral rule is part of the law of this country. For example, envy, though forbidden by moral codes, is not forbidden by law. Therefore the first statement in the exercise above is false, as law and morality are not the same, although they may overlap.

There is a great deal more to law than this, however, and you will probably realise by now that the law also comprises many procedural rules which must be followed in order for legal issues to be dealt with by the courts. The second statement in the question above is therefore false, as these procedural rules are also part of the law.

When legal issues are considered by the courts, or when Parliament creates law, one of the aims of those involved in the process is to do justice between people who are affected by the law. Sadly, we know that this aim is not always achieved and therefore it has to be said that law and justice do not always coincide, so the third statement above is true.

You should by now have a good idea of what law is and what it is not and you should also have a good working definition of the law, a suggestion of which appears in the final statement in the exercise above. This statement is true. You might wish to reflect on the following definition given by Glanville Williams in his book *Learning the Law*:

'law is the cement of society and an essential medium of change'.

(12th edn, London: Sweet and Maxwell, 2002, p 2)

1.1.1 Lawyers' definition of law

When we begin to study 'the law' on a law degree or other law course we need a specific definition because we are talking about law in a very specific context. Legal philosophers would say that 'the law' is quite hard to define because again it has so many aspects and must be used in so many different contexts.

3

A clear and straightforward one is provided by Sir John Salmond in his book *Jurisprudence*:

> '. . . the body of principles recognised and applied by the courts in the administration of justice.'

He even goes on to explain what he means:

> 'In other words the law consists of the rules recognised and acted on by the courts of justice.'

So, when we study 'the law' we are not talking merely about any body of rules that has some type of organisation and some type of structure. Hopefully, the law is both organised and structured but what we are specifically looking for is law that can be enforced in a system of courts.

1.1.2 The character of a legal system

There are many different legal systems in the world. In the UK we obviously study the English legal system, although it is possible, usually as an elective module or option, to study comparative law or sometimes even to do degrees in the law of other jurisdictions such as American law or French law.

Whatever legal system we study there are common characteristics. Understanding what all legal systems share as common characteristics goes a long way towards helping us understand what it is we are studying and in recognising what may be expected from a particular branch of the law.

Professor Hart in *The Concept of Law* identifies five things which he suggests that all legal systems must include:

1 Rules forbidding certain behaviour on forfeit of some form of penalty or sanction for non-compliance (we would recognise this in English law as the criminal law).

2 Rules that make people compensate other people that they have wronged for the damage caused by the wrong (in English law we would refer to this as civil liability or often, in very specific circumstances, as the law of torts).

3 Rules that regulate the conduct of and that enforce agreements, arrangements and relationships between individuals (these could be contracts or wills or even involve the rights and duties within a marriage – and in a more modern context it could involve the regulation of businesses – so we could see these as contract law, the law of succession and company law respectively).

4 There must be a system of courts in which to enforce all of the above rights and obligations.

5 There must also be a legislature of some form to make new laws to fit new situations and also to get rid of or repeal outdated laws (in the UK this role is carried out by Parliament).

Hart called this body of rules to regulate conduct the 'primary rules'. He also recognised that on their own these rules are insufficient for a system of law to work effectively. There must also be 'secondary rules':

(a) **Rules of recognition** – we have identified a number of separate branches of law above; crime, tort, contract, succession, matrimonial, company – each individual body of rules must have a character allowing it to be distinguished from any other body of rules.

(b) **Rules of change** – we have recognised the need above for Parliament to change the law to be relevant but there must, therefore, be superior systems of conduct which will authorise alteration of the rules to accommodate social and economic changes in society but which themselves operate according to law.

(c) **Rules of adjudication** – the courts are identified as the place where disputes are heard but they also must have rules regulating the methods by which those disputes are resolved, otherwise the law would be administered in an arbitrary way and may be seen as unfair.

These 'secondary rules' are equally essential and the presence of both types of rules is what separates a legal system from a more primitive code of behaviour or indeed from a dictatorship.

1.1.3 The character of the English Legal System

There appear to be two main types of legal system. One is based on what we sometimes refer to as 'Roman Law'. The other system, the one that we are used to in the UK, is known as a 'common law' system. The English legal system is the most well-known common law system and many other countries have followed it.

Roman law developed during the era of the Roman Empire and the many conquests made during that period. Because of the extent of the empire this type of law influenced a wide area that came under Roman rule. Examples would be found throughout western and southern Europe and indeed in North Africa. Interestingly, Britain was also under Roman rule for many centuries but still developed its own very particular type of legal system at a later stage.

The common law of England is usually traced back to the Norman Conquest and King William I. However, much of the law that developed during that period can also be traced back into Saxon society. The significant difference was that, even though the Norman and Angevin Kings adopted much of the existing local law and custom following the conquest, the nature of their rule meant that it became the law that was 'common' to the whole of Britain. Previously the country was made up of many separate kingdoms and so local laws might differ. Because Britain was over a number of centuries a colonial power and there was a British Empire, the common law of England was also the law that was used in the various countries of the Empire during British rule. As a result, following independence, many of these countries have retained a common law system. These are identifiable today as the Commonwealth countries, such as Australia, Canada, India, and many African or Caribbean countries. It also includes the USA.

The basic difference between Roman and common law legal systems can be identified as follows:

- Roman law is codified:
  - codes tend to be written in very broad terms and it is then the role of the judges to interpret these broad terms in specific situations
  - many modern countries have adopted a codified law following changes to their constitutions, for instance following a revolution as in France.
- English common law, on the other hand, has developed over a long period of time:
  - it is at least in part based on precedents that emerge from an accumulation of case decisions and so the law is based on real situations and has been built up principle by principle
  - in more recent times parliamentary law, through Acts and delegated legislation, has become more important.
- The English common law is said to have had an uninterrupted and continuous growth from the time of the Norman Conquest in the eleventh century.
- Some codified systems, on the other hand are relatively recent – France, for instance, had a revolution as recently as 1789 and French law develops from that point.
- The English legal system is preoccupied with rules of procedure. In other systems the broad spirit of the law may be more important.
- The English legal system depends mainly on an adversarial resolution of disputes:
  - this means that most law is settled in a form of contest between two parties claiming different or competing rights
  - this is true of criminal law and in most instances it is also true of civil law, although there are processes such as arbitration, conciliation and mediation now available.
- Continental systems of law, however, are often more inquisitorial in character:
  - instead of the judge acting as a sort of referee between the parties in dispute he will intervene and ask his own questions and will often try to find a compromise position.

1.2 The various classifications of law

In order to study the law in more detail you need to be able to appreciate how it can be broken up into a number of different component parts. One method of dividing the law into different categories is to classify it as substantive law or as adjectival law.

Substantive law is the term which is used to refer to the rules which govern our rights and duties under the law, for example, the cases and statutes which create criminal offences, or the cases and statutes which define contractual obligations. Adjectival law prescribes how those substantive rules can be used within the legal system, for examples the rules of evidence, procedure and costs which are to be observed when bringing a case to court.

For example, the Civil Procedure Rules 1998 contain the detailed procedural steps and guidance on commencing civil proceedings (eg suing another party). This should therefore be classified as adjectival law. By contrast, by way of another example, s 4 of the Bail Act 1976 describes the rights and duties of those involved in criminal proceedings and this is therefore substantive law.

An alternative way of classifying the law is by reference to its subject matter. From the point of view of lawyers and those involved in the legal system, this is the most useful way of dividing the law into categories.

The broadest distinction which can be drawn is between international law and domestic law. International law is concerned with the external relationships between different States and is based on treaties and conventions. A good example here is the Treaty on European Union (also known as the Maastricht Treaty). Domestic law comprises the laws of a particular State, that is the cases or statute law which govern relationships within that country and can be divided into public law and private law.

Public law cases are those cases in which one of the parties to the dispute is the Crown, usually acting through a government department. Public law can be further sub-divided into the areas of criminal law and civil law.

Criminal law is concerned with conduct of which society disapproves so strongly that the State must punish the wrongdoer; for example, murder, theft and driving offences. The major objective of criminal proceedings is to punish the perpetrator of the crime, not to compensate the victim. The Crown Prosecution Service, acting on behalf of the Crown, prosecutes the accused, who will be found guilty of the offence charged if the prosecutor can convince the court beyond reasonable doubt that the accused did commit that offence. Public civil law cases, by contrast, are concerned with problems in constitutional and administrative law. For example, these cases may challenge the legality of actions carried out by central or local government, or may bring test cases on individual freedoms which have been infringed by the government, such as telephone tapping.

As mentioned above, the other branch of domestic law is private law. This involves civil law and is concerned with the rights and duties which private individuals have in relation to each other. There are many different categories of civil law, for example the law of contract, the law of torts (wrongs such as negligence or slander) and the law of property. The major objective of an action which involves private civil law is to compensate the person who has suffered the wrong, usually by payment of money (damages). A civil action is commenced by the victim, that is, the claimant, who sues the defendant in order to obtain a remedy. The claimant must prove his or her case on a balance of probabilities, in other words it must be more likely than not that the defendant harmed the claimant in the manner alleged.

The following diagram (overleaf) illustrates the basic classifications of English law.

SUBSTANTIVE LAW	and	ADJECTIVAL LAW
This term refers to the actual areas of law and represents different groups of rights and obligations as we have seen above – so it could refer to contract law, tort, matrimonial law, succession, company law, property law etc.		This term refers to the rules of evidence and procedure – these determine how the case is conducted – in English law they originated from the medieval writ system but have undergone many changes.
PUBLIC LAW	and	PRIVATE LAW
This term refers to the law governing the relationship between individuals and the State – usually two types of law are included in this definition: criminal law and constitutional and administrative law.		This term refers to the law governing the relationship between individuals and includes many of the areas already identified under substantive law.
CRIMINAL LAW	and	CIVIL LAW
This term concerns the rules of law concerning behaviour that the state proscribes against and will punish.		This term refers to the rules of law concerning the settlement of disputes between parties which may be individuals but may include businesses and other corporate bodies.

Figure 1.1 The basic classifications of English law

The last two, criminal law and civil law, need to be distinguished because there are many differences in the way that the law is administered and even in the language used when either type is in question. The main distinctions are classified below.

	CRIMINAL LAW	CIVIL LAW
Involves	Offences against the State – behaviour which is classed as unacceptable.	Disputes between individuals.
Purpose of the action	To preserve order in the community and to deter unacceptable behaviour by punishing offenders.	To regulate relationships between individuals, to allow individuals to organise their affairs, to remedy the wrongs suffered by individuals.

CONTINUED ▸

	CRIMINAL LAW	CIVIL LAW
Parties to the action	A prosecutor (who prosecutes the offence) and the defendant(s) (who answers the charges).	A claimant (who sues in respect of the damage suffered) and a defendant (who answers the claim).
Burden of proof and standard of proof	The prosecutor must prove the case beyond a reasonable doubt. There is no strict obligation on the defendant to prove his or her innocence.	The claimant must prove his or her claim on a balance of probabilities.
Resolution of the action	The defendant may be convicted, if found to be guilty of the offence, or acquitted, if found to be not guilty.	A defendant will be found to be either liable or not liable for the claim.
Outcomes of the action	The defendant may be sentenced to a penalty which can range between a custodial sentence and a discharge.	The claimant may be awarded a remedy against the defendant, which can be in the form of a money compensation – damages – or an equitable order of the court, such as an injunction.
Courts	Magistrates' Court and Crown Court for trial. Divisional Court of the Queen's Bench Division of the High Court, Court of Appeal and House of Lords on appeal.	Magistrates' Court, County Court and High Court for trial. Divisional Courts of the High Court, Court of Appeal and House of Lords on appeal.
Examples	Murder, Theft, Drink Driving, Applying a False Trade Description.	Breach of Contract, Negligence in Tort, Wills, Conveyancing of property.

Figure 1.2 Classifying the differences between criminal law and civil law

ACTIVITY

Answer the following questions using the information in Figure 1.2. You will find the answers in the Appendix on page 300.

1. Who usually brings an action in a criminal trial?

2. Which courts have both civil and criminal jurisdiction?

3. In a civil action what is the burden of proof on the party making the claim?

CONTINUED ▶

4. What happens to a person accused of a criminal offence who is found not guilty?

5. What do we call the person who is being accused in a civil action?

6. What remedies are possible in a civil action?

7. What are the major purposes of criminal actions?

This system of classifying the law according to subject matter is not watertight, however. One set of facts can have multiple legal consequences and can straddle the various categories outlined above. For example:

Alf is riding his bicycle on a road one morning on his way to work. Becky drives past him at very high speed and knocks Alf from his bike. She does not stop. Charles is also cycling to work. He pulls over and calls an ambulance on his mobile phone. When the ambulance arrives, Alf is taken to the hospital where he is treated for serious injuries. After a long period in hospital, Alf is recovering, but Danny, a junior doctor, gives him an antibiotic to which Alf has already shown intolerance. Danny did not read Alf's medical notes before giving him the antibiotic. Alf falls into a coma from an extreme allergic reaction to the tablets. When he eventually wakes up, he has suffered brain damage and is told he will need full-time nursing care for the rest of his life.

Event	Consequences in criminal law	Consequences in civil law
Becky knocks Alf from his bike	Becky can be prosecuted for careless or possibly even for dangerous driving.	Alf (or in light of his injuries, some one on Alf's behalf) can sue Becky for personal injury. This action is part of the law of negligence. It means Becky owed Alf a duty of care and she breached it, causing personal injury to Alf.
Becky drives away	Becky can be prosecuted for failing to stop and report an accident.	
Danny gives Alf an antibiotic	Generally negligence is not actionable in the criminal law in these circumstances, but if Alf had died, Danny might have been prosecuted for manslaughter by gross negligence.	Alf or his representative could sue the doctor, the hospital or the NHS trust for negligence.

Figure 1.3 Example of multiple legal consequences

1.3 Legal terminology – and using legal dictic

One of the things that you will discover almost immediately about law is that it is full
terminology with which you may be unfamiliar but that you quickly need to understan
with your course.

This is not just because you will find a lot of Latin phrases used such as *ratio decidendi* (meaning
the legal reason for the decision in a particular case), or *obiter dicta* (meaning other things said by
the way by the judge that do not affect the outcome of the case). You will almost certainly also
come across the *de minimis* rule from the Latin *de minimis non curat lex* (meaning the law has no
remedy for anything that is too trivial). This is an appropriate phrase in the circumstances because
learning the appropriate terminology is important to you and you will be expected to know it and
to use it in different forms of assessment.

It is not only Latin that will confuse you to start with. There are plenty of technical words used in
text books and by teachers that you will also need to understand and get used to. It is important
that you do understand the technical language of law, otherwise you will struggle to follow lectures,
you will struggle reading many text books and you will struggle when you try to read the
judgments of cases.

1.3.1 Common law

One term that you are bound to hear used repeatedly from very early on in your course, and that
you will certainly see many times in text books, is the phrase 'common law'.

This can be a very confusing term for you because lawyers use the term in so many different
contexts and for quite different meanings. It is important then for you to have an appreciation of
the different meanings right from the start so that you can follow exactly what is being referred to.
Usually the precise meaning is taken from the context in which the phrase is being used and from
what it is being contrasted with.

In this way the phrase 'common law' can be used in the following ways:

1   Referring to the law that is common to the whole country – in contrast to the local laws and
    customs that existed before the eleventh century, a few of which survive in one form or another
    today, eg a byelaw introduced by local councils may impose a fine for your dog fouling the
    footpath.

2   Referring to remedies in particular (the major one being compensation in the form of damages)
    – in contrast with equitable remedies such as the injunction (an order preventing someone from
    doing something) or specific performance (an order for a contract to be carried out – usually
    the transfer of land that has been purchased).

3   Referring to principles of law developed in the judgments of decided cases – in contrast with
    statute law, created in an Act of Parliament (some law is mainly to be found in cases such as
    tort – while some areas are mainly statutory, such as crime).

11

4   Referring to the type of system itself (one that has developed incrementally over centuries through case law as well as other sources) – in contrast with civil law systems such as that in France where the law originates in a code.

There is a very comprehensive chart explaining in detail the various meanings of 'common law' in *Unlocking The English Legal System* in the same series as this book.

1.3.2 Using legal dictionaries

As we have said, you will come across many expressions that are new to you when you start a law degree or similar course. If you are lucky your teacher will remember that he once had to learn all these expressions too and will not assume knowledge on your part that you do not have. If so, you will find that the teacher will stop and give you an explanation of these terms.

Some you will use constantly, such as the term common law above. Others though you may not come across again for some time. So it is useful for you to keep your own little 'dictionary' of the terms and expressions that you were unfamiliar with. Go through your lecture notes after the lecture and extract these terms and transfer them to a booklet that is laid out alphabetically. Then you have it for reference every time you come across the expression again but may have forgotten it.

One of the ways that you can keep up with all the new terminology you come across is to make use of a legal dictionary. There are many examples on the market, including *The Complete A-Z Law Handbook* published by Hodder & Stoughton or *Mozley & Whiteley's Law Dictionary* published by Butterworths.

These legal dictionaries are never too costly, about a third of the price of the average law text that you have to buy. They have the advantage of lasting you for the whole of your course and even beyond. They are updated on a regular basis to include new expressions that come from changes to the law, but even so your copy is likely to be sufficient to last the course.

They can be very useful in helping you to keep up with things that are unfamiliar to you in lectures but left unexplained. They are probably even more useful when you are reading through law reports or through the 'weightier' text books, both of which tend to presume a level of knowledge which may be beyond a first year student.

1.4 Brief overview of the sources of law and where to find them

In the first year of your course, usually in the English legal system module, you will find out very quickly that English law is not to be found in a single place or a single document. English law comes from many different sources and it is important that you remember these since it will help you in following different types of substantive law later on. It is also important for you to know quickly and easily where to look for the law in particular areas.

Below is a table with brief explanations of the main sources of law and some explanations of what can be found in them.

Source	Illumination
Custom	Not a very important source in modern times. Early law before the creation of the common law system was generally based on local custom. Because of the saying 'custom hardens into right' some custom survives. Public rights of way and the modern byelaws are examples of custom being incorporated into law.
Case law	Case law is the law that is developed by judges in reaching decisions in actual cases. The law developed by judges is important in two particular contexts (explanations of which are given in Chapter 6): • **The doctrine of precedent** – Judges develop the law by applying existing principles of law to the cases in front of them. If the material facts of the case differ from those from which the existing principle was found then the judges will have to produce an extension of the principle to cover those facts. If no principle can be found which might cover the facts then the judges create what is known as 'original' precedent. Judicial precedent is important in many areas of law. The Law of Torts for instance is almost exclusively found in the case law, so you should be prepared to learn many cases when you undertake that module. (See section 6.2 for a detailed explanation.) • **Statutory interpretation** – Judges can have a major impact on the application of statute law when they are called on to interpret words contained in a specific part of an Act when the meaning of those words is in dispute in a case before them. Because the judges have so many quite different rules and aids to help them interpret the words of an Act there can be some very surprising results. (See section 6.3 for a detailed explanation.) Judges also play a major role in developing or even restricting the development of law when they reach so-called 'policy' decisions. An example of this is the imposition of restrictive controls on the ability to make a claim of a 'secondary victim' who suffers 'nervous shock' (psychiatric damage) resulting from a single traumatic event caused by another person's negligence. These can be found in the leading case of *Alcock v Chief Constable of South Yorkshire* [1992] 1 AC 310. Judges can also have quite an impact on the law when they take a particular moral stance. For instance in the case of *Shaw v DPP* [1962] AC 220, the House of Lords (the highest court in the country) decided that the publisher of a contact magazine (giving contact details for prostitutes) was guilty of an offence of 'conspiracy to corrupt public morals' even though no such offence existed in law. When the judges were criticised for this they defended themselves by saying that they had a residual right to protect public morality.

CONTINUED ▶

Source	Illumination
Equity	Equity basically means fairness. Originally equity was a separate system of law administered in separate courts and providing some relief for people who had been treated unfairly by the common law system. Equity is no longer a separate system of law but it is still an important concept. It was responsible for developing a number of remedies that were more useful to a claimant in an action than the standard damages (money compensation) allowed under common law. Examples include: • **Injunctions** – preventing a defendant from doing something that would interfere with the claimant's rights. • **Specific performance** – an order for the defendant to complete his side of a contract (usually meaning to pass over land that had been sold). • **Rescission** – putting contracting parties back to their precontractual position once one party had discovered defects in the contract. Equity was responsible for developing enforceable interests that had more flexibility than common law ones including: • **The trust** – a means of dividing ownership of property rights that could then be enforceable. • **The mortgage** – a means of lending and borrowing but with much more flexible rules and protections than the common law equivalent; the debt.
Legislation	Legislation is in two forms: • **Acts of Parliament** – Parliament is said to be the supreme law maker – it can make or unmake any law and the validity of Acts cannot be challenged by any court (but see the effects of membership of the EU and of the Human Rights Act 1998 below). Much modern law comes in statutory form and many areas of law are said to be mainly statutory, eg criminal law, company law etc. • **Delegated legislation** – This is subject to the control of Parliament and also can be challenged in the courts if it is *ultra vires* (beyond the powers given to the body making it) or offends the rules of natural justice. Delegated means that Parliament has given power to the body to make specific laws for specific purposes or in specific circumstances. Delegated legislation can be one of three types: – **Statutory instruments** – usually produced by Ministers in Government departments which have more specialist expertise than Parliament itself.

CONTINUED ▶

	— **Orders in Council** – introduced by the Privy Council and usually only used in times of emergency, eg wartime.
	— **Byelaws** – usually introduced by local authorities because they apply to particular local issues and the local bodies have more local knowledge.
EU law	The United Kingdom has been a Member State of the EU (originally the EC) since 1st January 1973 after signing the Treaties and passing the European Communities Act 1972, incorporating the Treaties into English law. On matters where EU law is relevant, the UK is bound absolutely by that law because the EU has supremacy on those issues, so the UK Parliament cannot make laws that conflict with EU law. Citizens can also enforce EU law in Member States through the process known as 'direct effect'. EU law is an important feature of English law, mostly at the moment in economic areas. It is vital to contract law, consumer law, employment law, company law and some other areas.
Human rights	The UK is also a signatory to the European Convention of Human Rights and citizens, once they have exhausted their national rights of action can make an application to the European Court of Human Rights. The Convention includes many very basic rights such as the right to life and the right not to be tortured, as well as freedom of expression and freedom from discrimination. In 1998 the Human Rights Act gave effect to the main provisions of the Convention into English law. Now a judge in a case can consider whether or not a provision of the Convention has been infringed. Judges may also declare that new legislation is incompatible with a Convention right, although it is only Parliament that can then alter the legislation.
International treaties	Like other countries the UK frequently signs up to international treaties by which it is then bound in international law. Generally the United Nations oversees much international law. An example of such a treaty is the Geneva Convention which proscribes certain codes of conduct in warfare and prohibits the manufacture and use of certain types of weapon.

Figure 1.4 Sources of law

The concepts and issues that have been explored in this chapter form the basis of knowledge for a law student commencing a law degree. It is, therefore, important to review this information. To assist in this, try to attempt the following questions:

ACTIVITY

1 Select the option that has the greatest validity:

(a) Law is an easy word to define;
(b) Law is a word that has universal meaning;
(c) Law is a word with a very broad meaning;
(d) Law is a word with no meaning.

2 Select the option that has the greatest validity:

(a) Hart suggests there are three key primary rules;
(b) A legal system needs primary and secondary rules;
(c) A dictatorship has primary and secondary rules;
(d) A legal system should have no rules.

3 Select the option that has the greatest validity:

(a) The English legal system is based on Roman law;
(b) There is no difference between the common law and Roman law;
(c) The English legal system is a common law system;
(d) The common law system is unique to the English legal system.

4 Select the option that has the greatest validity:

(a) There is no distinction between substantive and adjectival law;
(b) The law can be classified in terms of substantive and adjectival law;
(c) Adjectival law relates to the cases and statutes that give us our rights;
(d) Substantive law focuses on issues like rules of evidence.

5 From the statement below identify which are civil matters and which are criminal:

Beyond all reasonable doubt	Liable for a claim
Prosecutor	Balance of probabilities
Theft	Damages

6 Identify which of the following is not a source of law:

(a) Legislation
(b) EU law
(c) Case law
(d) Media.

See the Appendix on page 300 for the answers.

chapter 2 LECTURES AND SEMINARS ▪

AIMS AND OBJECTIVES ☐☐☐

After reading this chapter you should be able to:

- Understand how to listen effectively

- Understand the factors that might prevent you from listening effectively

- Understand the most effective ways of preparing for lectures

- Understand how and when to take notes in lectures

- Understand how to prepare effectively for seminars

- Understand what to do in seminars

- Prepare effectively for lectures

- Listen effectively and make useful notes in lectures

- Prepare effectively for seminars

- Participate effectively in seminars

2.1 Learning to listen

2.1.1 Listening

One of the key delivery methods used by universities is the lecture. A lecture involves the dissemination of a body of legal knowledge. Its aim is to give an overview of the major themes and cases related to a particular legal issue eg offer and acceptance. Lectures may last for one, two or possibly even three hours, and each will involve you listening to the delivery of set subject content. Your techniques in listening will have a dramatic effect on the amount that you will get out of lectures. If you are unable to master the techniques of listening effectively then it will affect your understanding of the issues under discussion and the quality of your lecture notes, which are a significant part of your later success in exams or in coursework.

It is important that you learn to listen and not just simply to hear. Effective listening will build your understanding while merely hearing may well cause misunderstanding.

2.1.2 Barriers to effective listening

Distraction

You need to have maximum concentration in a lecture. A few seconds of lost concentration could have a dramatic effect on your ability to absorb information. Common distractions include mobile phones, friends, day-dreaming and a lack of resources, eg stationery.

Lecturers inevitably get upset with disturbances and will try to put a stop to them so they can go on with the lecture. However, this in itself breaks the flow and breaks your concentration. So you should always be punctual for lectures and seminars, take the correct equipment with you (never go out without a pen), turn your mobile phone off before you go in, do not rustle sweet papers etc. More importantly, show that you have ownership of your own education by encouraging your friends to follow these simple rules; although if you are going to take them to task over disturbances that they have created, make sure that you do it outside of the classroom and after the lecture.

Tiredness and hunger

Make sure you are fully refreshed for your lectures. Take a bottle of water and make sure you have eaten if you are not allowed to take a snack into the lecture theatre with you. This will boost your energy and your attentiveness.

Concentrating on note-taking

If your focus is to try and write everything down, you will soon start to miss out key issues and concepts.

Lack of preparation

Law has a number of technical terms and some difficult concepts. If you go into lectures unprepared then these issues will confuse and distract you.

2.1.3 Improving listening

Prior preparation

Skim read the lecture material beforehand. This will give you an awareness of the concepts and allow the lecture to build upon your awareness – hence assisting the development of knowledge.

Develop a note-taking system

Use text language or a version of shorthand. This allows you more time to listen as opposed to writing. However, remember not to use sloppy language or shorthand of any type in your assessments. Your lecturers will tell you of any accepted legal abbreviations that you may use.

Actively listen

Sit in a good position to listen. Some lecture halls have poor acoustics. Avoid areas that make listening difficult. Write follow-up questions on areas of misunderstanding and ask lecturers or friends to explain. Also, if it is permitted, ask questions.

Practise

Listening is a skill. Like most skills it develops through practice.

2.2 Preparing for lectures

There are common features of law lectures:

2.2.1 Length and style of delivery

Law lectures normally involve one lecturer disseminating and explaining a legal area. Lectures can vary in length but could be as long as three hours. Different lecturers have different delivery styles. Some will give handouts at the beginning of the module or beginning of the lecture. Some may use information technology and refer to web or intranet areas. Others will give handouts at the end. Some will allow questions. Others will not tolerate interruptions. Knowing the individual styles of your lecturers will help you in your preparation.

2.2.2 Focus on the delivery of subject content

There will be a introduction by the lecturer to outline the subject content of each lecture. This may be done verbally or on, eg PowerPoint at the start of the class. Be on time so you can identify the topic area for focus. The lecture will not be a complete overview of a legal issue. It will be an insight into the major cases and concepts related to a particular legal issue. Make a note on the key areas for further reading that the lecturer recommends.

2.2.3 The common mistakes

Lectures are perceived by many students to be a vehicle to gain a complete set of notes on a topic. This may be because there are a number of competing demands placed on the student in a lecture:

- listen to subject content
- take notes
- understand subject matter
- relate this to tutorial tasks.

Many students make note taking the highest priority believing that by reviewing the notes they will be able to complete all of the other tasks above after the lecture. The danger with this is that they may fail to understand the legal issues being outlined and find the notes they have taken have gaps, which result in a difficulty in understanding the subject content. Never rely merely on lecture notes when preparing for tutorials because your knowledge and understanding will be incomplete.

If you think about the stages of learning that you have to go through to attain high marks, gathering the basic knowledge of a topic is the first rung on the ladder. After the essential knowledge is attained, the student then has to ensure he or she understands the area. This is called the comprehension stage. Following that, the learner must be able to apply the understanding to new scenarios and analyse it in relation to a factual problem. Next comes evaluation; making judgments on the strengths and weaknesses of the topic. Finally comes synthesis. This is where the student hypothesises on the area: he or she asks questions of the topic, and ponders 'what if we changed it to . . .?'

Each of these stages involves an activity, as shown in the grid below:

Stages to develop high levels of learning	Activity
Knowledge	Pre-reading Lectures
Comprehension	Lectures Research
Application	Research Tutorials
Analysis	Tutorials Reflection
Evaluation	Reflection Revision
Synthesis	Revision Assessment

Figure 2.1 Stages of learning

As you can see, the lecture is a vital part of the process. It is where you will build your foundation knowledge from which your higher learning stems. You therefore need to make the best use of the lecture.

2.2.4 Getting the most out of lectures

- **Select an appropriate place to sit** – Do not sit in a position where you cannot see visual aids or have difficulty hearing. This may necessitate you turning up slightly early to get a good position.

- **Pre-reading and note gathering** – Some lecturers give handouts or place their lecture notes 'online' or on the university intranet. Law courses are information rich; the lecture will cover many cases and issues for discussion. By skim reading the handouts or pre-available material you will gain an awareness of the issues for discussion and will improve your learning. It will also prevent you wasting time taking notes on topics that are covered in detail on the handouts or elsewhere. If materials are available take them into the lecture and supplement them with your own comments in a way suitable to your understanding.

- **Connections** – In the lecture focus on how the issues relate to each other eg what cases are linked and how they developed. This not only improves understanding but also aids listening. You may find it useful to keep a separate page of A4 to one side of you and draw a flowchart of how the lecturer progresses from one stage to the next. This will help you to build up a logical structure to your own notes.

- **Focus on listening** – Pre-reading will assist in gaining a broad awareness of the issues/topics which will allow you to focus on the lecture as opposed the note taking. As previously mentioned, you need to listen actively using the strategies given to improve your exam listening focus.

- **Use the lectures as guidance for your further study** – The lecture should provide a guide as to how much depth and what importance individual legal issues have. The lecture, therefore, is a guide to direct your subsequent research and also to highlight the importance of areas in terms of assessment.

- **After the lecture** – If you have listened actively you need to make further notes to support your understanding. It is important to do this as soon as possible after the lecture has taken place. You will quickly forget the issues discussed in the lecture. Within 48 hours, 80 per cent of the information that was presented to you will be forgotten unless reviewed within that period.

2.3 Taking notes in lectures

2.3.1 The reasons for taking notes

For many of you your degree course will be the first time that you have ever studied law. Even if you have studied and have been successful at A-Level Law, you will have studied two or maybe three subjects at most (English legal system plus one or two areas of substantive law such as contract law, criminal law or tort).

A major difference that you will find, or may have already found, from other subjects is the volume of information that you will need to understand and to be able to remember. You will also discover a great many new terms and expressions that you have never come across before. In many ways studying law is almost like studying a new language. Besides this, studying law demands that you develop a wide range of skills. You will not only need to learn huge quantities of information. You will need also to develop practical skills of applying the law to factual situations, and to develop critical awareness and be able to see how the law operates in context.

For these reasons it is important that you have a good set of notes that are easily understandable and can form the basis of your revision.

You have a number of resources available to you to help you to learn and indeed to help you when you come to revision. Your teacher or lecturer may have given you prepared handouts, but your own notes are best because you will understand them. You can take notes in class and when you read textbooks. Getting into the habit of reading and note taking will ensure that you are building up information to help your learning. The more you do it, the more familiar you become with the information and the more you get used to writing about law, so that you feel comfortable doing so in the exam. Note-taking promotes active learning and aids memory.

2.3.2 When to take notes

There are four different times when you are likely to need to take notes:

- when you are in lectures from what the tutor is saying or writing on the board or from discussion or even from watching videos
- when you are following up information given by your tutor
- when you have been asked to prepare for a seminar/tutorial
- when you are preparing the outline for assignment work.

The last three obviously apply to Chapter 3, but you should see the connection between building up your bank of learning resources both in lectures and in your outside reading and research.

2.3.3 Note-taking in lectures

As discussed, it is better to listen actively and not focus on trying to write everything the lecturer is stating. There are a number of different approaches to how notes should be taken. Although each approach has advantages and disadvantages, it is about finding the method that not only suits you, but also matches the lecturer's delivery style. Whatever approach is taken it is important that you do the following:

- date all notes
- paginate
- file as soon as possible
- title the work
- use highlighters to focus on cases and important issues
- question mark the parts of the subject content you do not fully understand
- make sure all notes are legible.

2.3.4 Note-taking methods

The traditional approach

This involves you trying to copy out what the lecturer is saying as he or she is delivering the subject matter. If you adopt this technique only use three quarters of a page as this allows you to add your own comment and analysis, either during the lecture or just after when reviewing the notes. (See Figure 2.2 below.)

Omissions

Definition:

An omission is a failure to act.

In criminal law there is no liability for a failure to act. However there are exceptions

  1) Statutory exceptions

These are normally strict liability offences, eg failure to provide a police officer with a breath sample . . .

Add your own comment here. This could be to highlight its importance to the exam or the tutorial or simply to aid in the understanding.

Figure 2.2 Traditional approach to note-taking

Advantages

- strong comfort factor because you believe you are walking away with a complete picture
- easy to do
- can be recorded quickly with shorthand writing techniques or abbreviations for words, eg $\therefore$ = therefore.

Disadvantages

- assumes you can write quickly and that the lecturer has an even/slow delivery speed
- you become a passive listener
- you can easily miss important concepts.

Taped lectures

This involves the use of a Dictaphone or digital recorder to record the lecture.

Advantages

- you can concentrate on listening
- negates the need for extensive note-taking
- can be used in revision and is particularly good for auditory learners
- if written up, repetition enforces grasp of the information heard in the lecture.

Disadvantages

- getting a good recording can be difficult
- not allowed by all lecturers
- can be expensive in relation to the volume of resources needed, eg tapes or VCDs
- time consuming to write up.

Summary sheets

This involves focusing on the main themes and issues in the lecture and making a brief note of them and using these as a springboard to make notes post lecture.

For example, see Figure 2.3 opposite.

Advantages

- reinforces active listening
- provides a framework for further note-taking
- focus is on the core important issues.

Disadvantages

- requires pre-lecture reading familiarisation with subject matter to be discussed
- requires post-lecture time for more detailed note-taking
- requires selection skills in breaking down what is important during the lecture.

Concept maps or spider diagrams

See Chapter 11 page 266 for an example.

Advantages

- gives a logical flow of the lecture from the perspective of the writer
- focus is on active listening
- gives a logical linkage and the inter-connections relating to a subject
- excellent for visual-based learners
- can be used as a revision aid.

Lecture:	Date:

Key cases:	Key comment and analysis:

Links to tutorial activities:	Academic references:

Figure 2.3 Example of a summary sheet

Disadvantages

- requires practice to produce effective diagrams
- needs follow-up work to produce detailed notes.

Cornell note system

This involves dividing your note-taking page into two columns. The second and bigger of the two columns is to make traditional notes or diagrams etc. The smaller column is there to write self-test questions regarding the notes. The areas should be interrelated in that each section of notes should have questions or comment attached. (See Figure 2.4 below.)

	Arrest
What powers of arrest does (the amended) s 24 PACE allow a police officer?	Section 24 lays down general conditions of arrest without a warrant for any offence. A police officer may arrest: Anyone who is about to commit an offence, who is in the act of committing an offence, or whom he has reasonable grounds to suspect is about to commit an offence, is committing an offence, or if he has reasonable grounds to suspect that an offence has been committed anyone he has reasonable grounds to suspect of being guilty of it, or where an offence has been committed, anyone who is guilty of the offence or who he has reasonable grounds to suspect is guilty of the offence.
What powers of arrest do citizens have?	(The amended) section 24 states that a citizen can only arrest where an indictable offence is being committed or he has reasonable grounds to suspect that the person is committing the offence or where an indictable offence has been committed and he has reasonable grounds to suspect the person is guilty of it, but only then when it is impracticable for a police officer to make the arrest and where the arrest is necessary.

Figure 2.4 The Cornell note system

Advantages

- an excellent technique for auditory learners
- can be used as revision prompts. By looking at the questions you should be able to explain the related notes
- encourages active learning.

Disadvantages

- can be difficult to keep pace
- questions may need to be done after the lecture
- some students find it difficult to relate the notes to a question.

ACTIVITY

Task

Below is a sample of traditional notes on precedent that could have been taken in a lecture. Alter these notes to the following note-taking methods:

- Summary sheet
- Cornell note system
- Spider diagram.

Examples of all of these are given in the Appendix on page 301.

House of Lords

This is the most senior domestic court. When matters do not involve Europe it has the final decision on the case. This court binds all courts below it. It does not bind itself due to the Practice Statement 1966.

House of Lords & the Practice Statement

Originally the House of Lords had flexibility and could change its mind about its own past decisions but in 1898 the court decided that certainty in the law was more important than flexibility so in *London Street Tramways v London County Council* the court decided that the House of Lords were bound by their own previous decisions.

This created a rigid system as seen in <u>DPP v Smith</u>

A man murdered a police officer. The House of Lords made a mistake by giving a poor definition as to the mental test for murder. Due to this mistake Parliament passed the Criminal Justice Act 1967 to replace the mistake.

1966 Lord Gardiner issues a Practice Statement. This allows the judges in the House of Lords to depart from past decisions when it is right to do so.

It was first used in *Conway v Rimmer*. This was not seen as a major use as it only involved a technical matter.

Examples Civil

<u>Herrington v British Railways Board</u> overruled <u>Addie v Dumbreck</u>

These cases concerned what duty of care was owed to a child trespasser. In *Addie* it was decided that there was only a duty when injuries to a child were caused deliberately or recklessly. *Herrington* overruled this due to the changes in social conditions and made the duty owed stronger. *Herrington* was the first major use of the Practice Statement.

<u>Pepper v Hart</u> overruled <u>Davis v Johnson</u>

These cases concerned the use of Hansard. In *Davis* the use of Hansard by a judge as an aid to statutory interpretation was not allowed. *Pepper v Hart* removed this limit.

CONTINUED ▸

> **Example Criminal**
>
> *R v Shivpuri* overruled *Anderton v Ryan*
>
> These cases concerned the criminal nature of attempting the impossible. *Anderton* decided that you could not have criminal liability if what you were doing was impossible. This was contrary to an Act of Parliament. *Shivpuri* therefore overruled *Anderton*. It can now be a crime if you attempt the impossible. This was the first criminal case to use the Practice Statement.

You will find some sample answers in the Appendix on pages 301–303.

2.4 Preparing for seminars/tutorials

The seminar/tutorial system in university education is very common. It involves independent research on a directed legal area followed by a timetabled group session to discuss your findings. The group size is normally small. The research task will take the form of a tutorial brief with a series of questions and activities for address/completion. Some tutorials may require presentations. A lecturer may lead the tutorial session and use the activities as a method of discussing the subject matter. The tutorial will involve answering the questions or adding to a debate leading from them.

NOTE

The lecture and seminar/tutorial system may be different from your previous educational experience where prior investigation or research has not been required as most learning occurred in the classroom. Developing knowledge and understanding should occur before a tutorial. Application and analysis should be practised before the tutorial and enhanced during it. An effective tutorial should build evaluative skills.

☐ ☐ ☐

Whether you are familiar with the tutorial system or not, there are key strategies that can be adopted to make the experience more successful.

Law students are commonly given a tutorial guide book that contains the activities and guidance for the tutorials which they will have. A typical layout might look something like Figure 2.5 below.

TORTS TUTORIAL 4:

Special Duty Situations: Psychiatric Damage (nervous shock)

Essential Reading: *Unlocking Torts*, Chapter 7.1

Cases and Commentary on Tort, Harvey & Marston, Chapter 2

CONTINUED ▸

Essential cases that you must know

Victorian Railway Commissioners v Coultas (1888) 13 App Cas 222
Dulieu v White & Sons [1901] 2 KB 669
Hambrook v Stokes [1925] 1 KB 141
Bourhill v Young [1943] AC 92
Chadwick v British Railways Board [1967] 1 WLR 912
McLoughlin v O'Brian & Others [1982] 2 All ER 298
Alcock & Others v Chief Constable of the South Yorkshire Police [1992] 1 AC 310
Attia v British Gas Plc [1988] QB 304
Taylor v Somerset Health Authority [1993] PIQR 262
McFarlane v EE Caledonia Ltd [1994] 2 All ER 1
Page v Smith [1996] 1 AC 155, [1995] 2 WLR 644 (HL)
White v Chief Constable of the South Yorkshire Police [1999] 1 All ER 1
North Glamorgan NHS Trust v Walters [2002] EWCA Civ 1792
Vernon & Bosely (No 1) [1997] 1 All ER 577
Sion v Hampstead Health Authority [1994] 5 Med LR 170
McLoughlin v Jones [2002] 2 WLR 1279
Greatorex v Greatorex [2000] 1 WLR 1970 QBD
W v Essex CC [2000] 2 WLR 601

Be prepared to answer the following questions

1   What is meant by the phrase 'nervous shock'? Is 'psychiatric damage' a preferable phrase?

2   What was the principle laid down in *Dulieu v White*?

3   How was the law developed in *Hambrook v Stokes*?

4   What was the test of liability laid down by Lord Wilberforce in *McLoughlin*?

5   What is meant by the phrase 'immediate aftermath'?

6   What are the essential requirements of liability for psychiatric damage in relation to secondary victims in *Alcock & Others v Chief Constable of the South Yorkshire Police*?

7   What is meant by the use of the word 'bystander'?

8   Following the decision of the House of Lords in *White v Chief Constable of the South Yorkshire Police*, what types of claimant are now treated as 'primary victims'?

9   What distinctions between primary and secondary victims are shown in the case of *Page v Smith*?

10 How does the Law Commission propose this area of the law should be reformed?

Problem-solving exercise
Because of the negligence of his employers, SLS Construction Ltd, Ron is badly injured when a large section of crane falls and lands on him as he is working below. He is taken to hospital and dies two hours later in hospital from multiple injuries.

CONTINUED ▸

Consider the possibility of each of the following succeeding if they claim for psychiatric injury (nervous shock) against SLS Construction:

(a) Gurdeep, Ron's close workmate, who is on the site at the time of the accident, and although he is in no danger from the falling crane, witnesses the accident from nearby, and suffers severe depression as a result.

(b) Bill, a firefighter who was called to the scene and freed Ron from the debris. Bill suffers post-traumatic stress disorder after seeing the extent of Ron's injuries. While Bill was freeing Ron there was always a danger that more metal from the crane might become dislodged and fall.

(c) Elizabeth, Ron's mother, is telephoned by Ron's manager immediately and gets to the hospital in time to see Ron as he is being carried out of the ambulance. Elizabeth suffers from grief and insomnia (cannot sleep) after the accident.

■ *Figure 2.5 An example from a tutorial guide book*

2.4.1 Start planning the tutorial before the lecture

The first step to successful tutorials is to attend lectures. Lecture content is normally highly related to tutorials which follow, and lecturers often direct you to the subject matter for discussion in the tutorials. Therefore, look at the tasks that are given for tutorials and relate them to specific lectures. For example, an EU law lecture on the institutions of the European Union will normally be followed by a tutorial related to that topic. By looking at the materials and tasks before the lecture you will gain an understanding of the key issues that are being directed in terms of your learning. During the lecture, these issues will be discussed and you can make notes next to the tasks, which will start helping you complete some of the activities. This process will also focus your attention during the lecture, improving your listening ability.

2.4.2 Use your lecture notes as a starting point

The next stage of the tutorial process is to utilise the lecture notes and the annotations that were made on the tutorial sheet. The lecture will provide answers to some of the tutorial activities. Use these notes to help complete as many tasks as possible. Reviewing the lecture notes will also improve and refresh your understanding of the issues that will be discussed in the tutorial.

2.4.3 Research

The next stage is to explore the recommended reading. You may need to explore further afield for these resources, eg the library for law journals, law reports etc. Law courses involve a significant amount of research and you will be required to research specific legal issues independently. It is therefore important to be organised – the key to a successful tutorial is the preparation. It is also important for you to manage your time effectively. There will be more than one tutorial each week and law courses traditionally involve significant research and reading.

Some students find it embarrassing when they have failed to prepare for the tutorial. An unprepared student cannot answer any of the questions and can offer nothing in the discussions that take place. It is impossible to understand the legal issues if you have not done the preparation beforehand. It may be useful to produce an action plan for the materials needed and to stick to it. For example:

Topics	Resource	Priority	Completed?
ELS/M	Walker & Walker CH 4.	Priority 1	Yes/no
Tort	*Unlocking Torts* C Turner & S Hodge, Chapter 7.1, pages 184–202 *Cases and Commentary on Tort* Harvey & Marston, Chapter 2	Priority 2	Yes/no
Crime	Smith & Hogan pages 56–88. D Lanser, 'Intention and Recklessness', *The Legal Executive Journal*, 1995, Nov. S Cooper, 'Summing up Intention', *New Law Journal*, 18 August 2000.	Priority 3	Yes/no

Figure 2.6 An action plan to help prepare for tutorials

This list is quick to prepare and is a methodical way to gain the materials for upcoming tutorials and makes library visits and research effective. There is nothing worse that trying to complete directed activities and realising that you have forgotten to get an article.

Once you have gathered the material you should be able to begin successfully completing the tasks assigned in your tutorials.

2.5 Getting the most out of seminars/tutorials

2.5.1 Study buddy

Tutorial research does not have to be a solitary activity. You can split the task of finding law reports, journals and relevant articles with a fellow student. This can be an invaluable method of saving time. Time can then be spent on digesting the information and completing the directed tasks. There is, however, a note of caution – the person you choose should be reliable and there needs to be a clear indication of who is gathering what, when it will be done by and when you will swap information. Without clear parameters like this, you or your study buddy may become frustrated through different priorities (eg your land law seminar may not be until the end of the following week. For you it is a low priority, but for your research partner the required resources will be a high priority if it is their first tutorial of the week).

2.5.2 Using textbooks

To gather the research you will either need to make photocopies from the sources, take notes or highlight relevant texts. You do not need to take copies of everything that many of the texts discuss, because they will include many of the same cases, although the analysis and comment may differ. Your priority after reviewing your lecture notes is to complete the essential reading. It is a waste of time making complete notes from this because you should already have gained a core of knowledge from your lecture notes. So, when making notes from the essential reading look for the following:

- different cases
- academic comment and analysis
- differences in interpretations of the law from your lecture notes
- materials that focus on the tutorial topics.

This process will allow you to build a stock of knowledge that not only allows you to complete a tutorial successfully but also gives you a complete set of materials that can be used for exam preparation.

2.5.3 The activities

Through study carried out during the lecture and research cycle you will have probably completed the majority of the tasks set. There may be activities that still require completing because they require your judgment, eg you are asked to assess the validity of a case which requires your own interpretation. These should be quickly achieved due to having all the requested materials. It may be that the answer is not clearly gained from the research. In this case make a list of the issues you do not understand and try to adopt one or more of the following tactics.

Explaining the difficulties that you are having in the tutorial

This approach is sometimes not favoured because of a sense of failure and self-consciousness in front of others. Some may decide to go along to the tutorial and hope the discussion gives elaboration, but there is danger with this approach because you may be asked to give a response to the topic causing difficulty.

The tutorial may not discuss in detail issues of uncertainty and if left until the time of the examination, this could be fatal. It may be useful to catch the tutorial leader before the commencement of the tutorial to explain that you had difficulty with a particular activity and that you are hoping the tutorial will aid you in your understanding.

Seeking your tutorial leader's support before the session

This will allow you to talk through specific difficulties and improve your understanding of the task. However, gaining access to support can sometimes be difficult as the availability of lecturers varies due to their individual commitments.

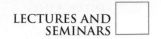
Peers

As mentioned previously, some students may find it beneficial to discuss issues with other students. This not only allows them to help each other with areas of difficulty but can also be used to confirm conclusions to other activities, which builds confidence.

2.5.4 The tutorial/seminar

If you have followed the tactics, the tutorial itself should be a rewarding experience as you will be able to share and discuss the concepts you have prepared. But remember:

- **Be considerate** – It is natural to be proud of your understanding but give others the opportunity to have an input.

- **Make notes** – There will be issues raised that you may not have considered. These may offer a different approach.

- **Ask questions** – If issues are raised with which you need help, seek clarification.

- **Positive body language** – Make use of positive body language. Make eye contact with the person talking, lean forward in your seat when you want to contribute.

- **Do not be afraid** – At first you may be unsure about the validity of your responses. Someone may offer a different interpretation of the law to what you have perceived. The law has many conflicting opinions and there is a vast amount of case law that can cause conflict. It is therefore usual, considering the range of activities set for tutorial, that there will be no right answer as the questions are there to form the basis for the discussion. You will find that the more you contribute the more confidence you will gain and the easier the tutorial experience will become.

2.5.5 After the tutorial

It is important to consolidate after each tutorial:

- put notes in order and file them

- research areas of poor understanding

- ensure all notes are legible and comprehensible. During a lecture you may have written a specific comment next to a task, but will you understand it in three months' time when beginning your revision?

AIMS AND OBJECTIVES

After reading this chapter you should be able to:

- Understand the purpose of reading legal materials

- Understand how to read effectively

- Understand how to use the supports to reading effectively – the contents table and index

- Read effectively

- 'Scan' read

- Make effective notes from reading

3.1 The purpose of reading

In Chapter 2 we focused on lectures and seminars. This interaction with your lecturers is one source of information available to you on your course. Lectures are an overview on a topic and seminars/tutorials are essentially practical sessions where you are called on to demonstrate your knowledge and understanding, whether through discussion, problem solving or simply answering short questions.

Reading is another and different source of information. A lecture on a particular topic area may last only two or three hours; you only have to look at the shelf in your library/learning centre to discover that there will be sufficient books on that particular subject to keep you reading for a very long time. This inevitably means that there is a great deal more information and understanding to be gained on the subject than can be gained in the lecture.

Reading helps you to build on the understanding that you have been given already. It may also help to clear up areas of confusion and is a vital means to follow up information that your tutor did not have time to tell you. The tutor in any case may want you to discover particular information for yourself and direct you to specific reading. This may be a way of building your skills, or he or she may want you to find that there are complications that could only be touched on in a tutorial, or indeed may want you to read ahead so that you are able to gain more benefit from a particular session.

There are a number of reasons why you should read and it is vital that you get into the habit of reading extensively and reading regularly.

3.1.1 Different legal materials

There is a wide range of reading materials available to read when you study law. These include:

- textbooks
- case books
- articles in academic journals
- the law reports themselves
- statutes and statute books
- periodicals and daily newspapers.

3.1.2 Where to find reading materials

You will find that there are many stimuli to reading and aids that will direct you to specific or relevant material:

- Your module guide will usually suggest specific textbooks and, if the guides are detailed enough they will even provide you with a breakdown of the chapters or pages that you need to read on relevant topics.
- Your lecturer may well refer to specific supplementary reading in lectures and give you appropriate references so that you can locate the material.
- Textbooks very often have references for further reading in footnotes or suggested extra reading indicated at the end of chapters or sections and many will carry bibliographies where other useful works are listed.
- Journal articles will usually make reference to source materials.
- If you look into law reports at the start of these there is always a list of cases that were suggested as being relevant.

So there are many places that you can look to find extra sources of relevant reading.

3.1.3 Assessing your existing skills

Reading is a skill that any student would naturally assume they are good at. But it is important you take stock of your reading skills. It is important to focus on two key skills, your reading rate and your recall rate. Your reading rate relates to how long it takes for you to read a set number of pages and your recall rate focuses on your ability to understand and retain the core information contained in the material.

ACTIVITY

Select a reading task from a seminar topic. Make a note of how many pages it asks you to read. Start reading the material, but time yourself on how long this takes. Once completed you should have an awareness of your reading time, eg if you are directed to read 15 pages and it takes you 15 minutes you are reading on average one page per minute.

Why is reading speed important?

- **It allows you to plan** – understanding your reading time will give you a good idea of how long reading tasks for tutorials and other reading tasks will take.

- **It allows you to monitor improvements** – law is a subject which requires the reading of significant amounts of material. For you to be an effective student your reading rate needs to be as strong as possible. By adopting the techniques and suggestions in this chapter you should notice an improvement in your reading rate. It is important to check this rate regularly, eg once every couple of months.

You also need to understand the key issues you are reading about. There is no point in having a fantastic reading rate if you cannot recollect any of the cases and concepts you have read. It is, therefore, also important to reflect on your recall rate. When you test your reading rate, write down the issues and cases that you have just read about. Again, by adopting the techniques in this chapter, your recall rate should improve.

3.1.4 Reading effectively

NOTE

Being able to read is not the same thing as being able to read *well*.

The important point is that you should read effectively. Law texts and other legal reading material are not like novels that you can read from cover to cover. In fact you should not be reading them from cover to cover because your reading must be both specific and relevant to what you are doing at the time. In any case you do not have time to read textbooks on your subjects from start to finish.

What you must do is to read those things that are relevant to you at the time. In order to achieve this you must develop certain skills.

First, so that you do not spend hours and hours reading the irrelevant, in order to find the relevant material in the quickest time, you need to build a familiarity with the textbooks and other materials that you use.

Many legal texts are written in a very prose-dense way without extensive use of headings or sub-headings to guide you to what you really need to know:

- So you must get used to using the contents page to find the specific area that you want to read and the index for the relevant aspects.

Many law reports are very lengthy, sometimes a hundred or more pages, although you are only really looking for the legal principle or comments that the judge had to make about it:

- So you must get used to using the brief information at the start of each report so that you do not read one unnecessarily.

Second, you must learn how to find the maximum amount of information in the shortest possible time:

- So you need to learn the skill of scan reading.
- This is so that you can look through books quickly to locate appropriate information.
- You can develop the skill by learning to focus on key words as you 'scan' down the page. For example if you were reading a law report on a negligence case you might focus on the words 'duty of care' or 'breach of duty' or 'cause' – these are the classic elements of a negligence action and whenever you see them you can be sure that the judge is talking about something important to you.

Third, you must be able to distinguish between reading to locate information and reading in depth:

- So you must get used to reading a little before and even a little after where aids, such as the index, direct you then you won't miss an important lead up to the point you are focusing on or where it developed.
- When you are reading to try to understand something that you are not clear on then you must read more slowly and comprehensively and at these times in particular you should always make notes on what you have read.

Fourth, you must be able to make use of the information that you have gained from your reading – so you must always have a way of going back to the specific points without having to read at length all over again:

- So you must get used also to making notes while you read.
- Or if that is too time-consuming you must get used to doing effective highlighting.

3.1.5 How you can benefit from effective reading

There are a number of positive benefits to be gained from regular reading:

- It increases your knowledge and understanding of the subject.
- It exposes you to a different perspective than you might get in your lectures.
- It develops critical awareness as you may find a wider range of analytical material in textbooks and articles than you may get from a lecture.

- It will improve your vocabulary and your appreciation of technical terms.

- It will develop your knowledge of how to structure your work in a logical and fluent way.

- It will benefit your course work as you are not just giving your lecturer back what he or she has already given you.

- It will increase your performance in exams by giving you a wider spread of knowledge and understanding from which to draw.

3.2 Using the shortcuts – the contents page and the index

If you want to make the most of reading textbooks then you need to be able to locate the precise piece of information quickly, rather than having to read half the book to find it.

For this reason you need to be familiar with finding your way round a legal textbook. One of the best ways to make your reading effective is to get used to using as many shortcuts to the information as are available to you. Key in these are the contents page and the index. If you know how to use them then they can save a lot of time and effort.

3.2.1 The contents page

Contents pages are located at the front of texts and are many and varied in style and format. What they hopefully do is to present you with a way of finding your way easily round the book so that you can get straight to the point that you want.

Below is an example of a contents page taken from the front of a standard textbook on tort and covering the area of 'Trespass to the Person'.

8 Assault and battery	203
Battery	203
Assault	214
9 False imprisonment	216
Definition	216
The meaning of imprisonment	216
Lawful justification or excuse	218

Figure 3.1 An excerpt from a contents page

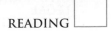

You will see that this contents page does not actually give a lot away. You can easily move to the section on battery, if that is what you are looking for. However, that covers 11 pages of the text. If you wanted to look more precisely at one of the defences available in an action for battery, say necessity, then you are going to have to read through those 11 pages until you find it.

Below is a contents page from another textbook on tort.

Figure 3.2 An excerpt from a more detailed contents page

This contents page is much more detailed and it breaks the subject down into many more specific aspects. This time if you wanted to read about the defence of 'necessity' in battery you would find it straightaway under the subsection on defences and it even has its own subsection which you can find at page 45, according to Figure 3.2.

The difference between the two different contents pages above also probably tells you something different about the styles of the two books. The second is trying to give the student as much information as possible right from the start of the book so that areas of interest can be instantly found. In fact the first book does have a small heading for 'necessity', where it is located, on page 209. As the chapter starts on page 203 you may still have read six pages before you come across 'necessity' as a defence to battery (see Figure 3.1).

When selecting a textbook it may be worth looking at how detailed or not the contents page is. The more detailed it is the easier it will be for you to find your way round the book and to the specific information you need at the time.

3.2.2 The index

A detailed index is just as important to you as the contents page. However, it serves a different purpose:

- The contents page should lead you quickly to the particular area that you are interested in at the time.
- The index should lead you inside that area to even more specific points of interest.

Indexes are usually prepared by professionals. They read through books and find key words that keep repeating themselves and put these in the index with a reference to all the pages where the word appears.

Some authors like to produce their own index, usually because they have an idea from their teaching of the words that students are likely to look up. Very often, the words are cross-referenced, and as well as appearing on their own they also appear under broader and more logical headings.

The difference between the two may well mean that you have to learn how to use the index by thinking more laterally. So sometimes instead of looking up the word that you are actually concerned with you will have to think of a broader heading and look there and see if it is included in a sub-list under that broader word.

Look at the extract from an index opposite taken from a book on the law of torts. Various words are highlighted to make valuable points on how to use the index.

Index

Figure 3.3 Excerpt from an index

This is a good index. It is well cross-referenced and the indexer has anticipated the words you may look for. For instance:

- The 'Anns test' appears both as an individual entry and under the 'Duty of care' reference (if more of the index was reproduced here then you would also find 'Duty of care' under a reference for 'Negligence').

- Many other words repeat the same point – 'Act of God' is also entered under 'Defences'; 'Breach of duty of care' appears on its own and also under 'Duty of care'; 'Reasonable man test' appears under 'Breach of duty' and also under 'Duty of care' and so on.

- You will also see that most of the words to the left side of the index have lists of other words underneath them and indented because they are important aspects of the broader word.

Do not be put off if you cannot go straight to the word that you want in the index. Use a bit of lateral thinking and you could use the words in the headings in the contents page as a guide. If you cannot find the word itself you may find it under a different heading.

However well referenced the index is, you should still be able to find what you need and the index is a quick way of getting to the information. One final point worth making is that you may use the index to find aspects of the particular area that you are researching in chapters other than the ones that are more obvious from the contents list.

Again, however, it may well be worth looking at the index in a book before you choose to buy it. If it is quite limited it tells you something about how easy it will be to use the book.

ACTIVITY

Imagine that you have looked at the whole of the index (the extract of which is provided above at Figure 3.3) but cannot find the words that you want. Use your lateral thinking and see if you can do the following:

1. You want to find the difference between 'special damages' and 'general damages' and you have no idea at all what 'exemplary damages' are but none of them is listed in the index under those phrases – see if you can find them in the above extract.

2. You need to do some research on 'guard dogs' but there is no entry under 'guard dog' – see if you can find them in the extract and spot more than one reference.

3. You have been told that a person will not be liable in tort if the damage has resulted from an 'inevitable accident', again there is no entry under those words – see if you can think under what broad heading you might find it.

A bit of practice in looking through indices from the start of your course will save you time as you become more efficient at your reading. The quicker you can get directly to the information you need, the more time you have for reading and the more widely you can read.

3.3 Scan reading

As we have already identified, you will soon run out of time if you try to read everything word by word, particularly where you are reading initially for research. There are times when you need to read in depth, but you must learn to focus on key aspects of your reading and be able to get very quickly to the particular information that you need.

One of the ways in which you can increase the speed of your reading is to scan read. Scan reading is about focusing in on key words in whatever you are reading so that you can concentrate on those parts that are particularly relevant and do not get bogged down with those parts that are not.

You may think that it is quite a hard skill to master to read something by actually missing out large parts of it but in fact it is not, because your brain already does it for you all the time. For instance, read the following:

Aoccdrnig to rsaeerch, it deos not mttaer in waht oredr the ltteers in a wrod are, the olny iprmoatnt tihng is taht the frist and lsat ltteer are in the rghit pclae. The rset can be in a toatl mses and you can sitll raed it wouthit porbelm. Tihs is bcuseae the huamn mnid deos not raed ervey ltteer by istlef, but the wrod as a wlohe.

There! Did you get the message? Recognition of language is about appreciating the whole just as it is with visual imagery. Our brain records things to make sense for us, even if they are jumbled or out of order, and often even when bits are missing. You will have been doing this unconsciously for almost all of your life.

You will not have to make a conscious effort when you are looking something up in a book and scanning down the page to miss out the introductory words and the connecting words. Although they may prove important at times, you do not initially need to register all the words such as 'the', 'and', 'but' etc. If you register initially on the 'nouns' (such as 'duty of care') and the verbs (the active words such as 'breaching the duty') then you are simplifying and speeding up your reading. Concentrating on words that have specific importance will allow you to spot the relevant and move straight to it. Remember, this does not mean that you will miss anything important. Once you have located the key words you can always move back as well as forward. When you have the context of what is written, you may begin to read in more depth.

So trhee you are i'nst taht azanmig!

Being good at scan reading will also make you much more competent at highlighting (dealt with in section 3.4). The importance of skilled highlighting is that when you go back to documents that you have already highlighted, you do not have to read the whole thing all over again and find out what was really important to you. You can go straight to it because it is highlighted. Being good at highlighting makes you a much more effective note-taker.

3.4 Highlighting

3.4.1 Identifying key points in primary and secondary source materials

Students often tend to read a chapter of a book or an article, or a judgment in a law report from start to finish. So it appears from our experience that students are not always fully aware of how to focus their reading, or how to scan through to capture the most significant points of information.

This is confirmed when we look at what students choose to highlight from books or articles or judgments. This is often pretty much everything, producing a page full of yellow highlight. It is shown up even more in a one-to-one tutorial when we ask the student to list the critical points that he or she has discovered from their reading. The consequence is that teachers have to coax the points out of the students by giving clues as to what might have been gathered from what a particular judge said in a particular part of a judgment. Students then have to spend some time looking through their extensive highlighting to try to find what the tutor is suggesting and the tutorial becomes more like a lecture in style.

With law, possibly even more than in other subjects, you need to develop these arts because you have lots of information to assimilate, often quite complex information, and only fairly limited time in which to do it. Besides this, if you go on to professional practice, the skill will be even more important, particularly if you choose to join the Bar. It is not unusual for barristers to have to get to know the brief on the day of the case itself and in court they may need to refer to documents and find what they need very quickly in order to react effectively to what is going on.

Scan reading is one obvious way of reducing the time spent reading. As we have said, this is when you focus on key words in the source. In a law report on a negligence case, for instance, you may want to find everything you can about the issue of remoteness of damage. Scanning the page and quickly identifying every time that the judge uses the words 'remoteness of damage' and, because the test for awarding damages is to only allow damage that is 'reasonably foreseeable', you could look for these words too. This is then a quick way of concentrating on the issue that you are most concerned with.

It is also important to develop the skill of reading the information and breaking it down into the basic points that you understand. You can then apply this process to your coursework and, just as importantly, the revision skills that you will find in Chapter 11 when you need to translate your knowledge and understanding into the tenser environment of the examination.

ACTIVITY

Extracting information from a law report adapted for a case book

You may be asked by your tutors to use case books as a quicker way of gaining familiarity with case judgments than going to the law reports themselves. Case books do not usually give all of the judgment. The author has selected wisely the parts that he or she feels tell the reader most about the principles that emerge from the case and that also use these edited extracts to identify the difficulties that can arise from a particular case. As a result you will often find some critical commentary which should prove useful.

Using adapted extracts from judgments, or indeed sections from articles or books, is one way of helping students to gain the required skills before practising on the real thing. Below is an adapted case extract taken from the judgment in *Church* [1966] 1 QB 59, an important case on involuntary manslaughter in criminal law.

The judgment has already been reduced to make the exercise more manageable. In learning what the case has to say about unlawful act manslaughter you can break it down still further into critical points. When you have mastered the skill of reading and highlighting the important points you can do the same with law reports themselves, by trying to build up the skill of taking what is important. This is identified below.

To show how the process should work in your own reading various parts of the judgment have been highlighted. The amount of highlighting should be a pointer for you when you are doing so yourself – because there is a lot more in this little extract than you would usually expect to make. In addition to the highlights, a simpler version of the point made, or some other commentary is included in the right hand box. Underneath the extract a list of bulleted points is included of the type that you could make as notes and feed into coursework or into key cards for revision (see Chapter 11).

CONTINUED ▶

R v Church (1966) 1 QB 59

Facts

Church was mocked about his impotence by his female victim. He knocked her unconscious and, not being able to revive her, he panicked thinking she was dead, and threw her into a river where she drowned. He was acquitted of murder but convicted of manslaughter. He appealed unsuccessfully on the direction of the trial judge on the requirements of manslaughter.

Significant fact is that he thought she was dead when he threw her in the river.

Judgment

EDMUND-DAVIES LJ:

Two passages in the summing up are here material. They are these: (1) 'If by an unlawful act of violence done deliberately to the person of another, that other is killed, the killing is manslaughter even though the accused never intended death or grievous bodily harm to result. If this woman was alive, as she was, when he threw her into the river, what he did was the deliberate act of throwing a living body into the river. That is an unlawful killing and it does not matter whether he believed she was dead or not, and that is my direction to you,' and (2) 'I would suggest to you, though it is of course for you to approach your task as you think fit, that a convenient way of approaching it would be to say: What do we think about this defence that he honestly believed the woman to be dead? If you think that it is true, why then, as I have told you, your proper verdict would be one of manslaughter, not murder.' Such a direction is not lacking in authority . . . Nevertheless, in the judgment of this court it was misdirection. It amounted to telling the jury that, whenever any unlawful act is committed in relation to a human being which resulted in death there must be, at least, a conviction for manslaughter. This might at one time have been regarded as good law . . . it appears to this court that the passage of years has achieved a transformation in this branch of the law and, even in relation to manslaughter, a degree of *mens rea* has become recognised as essential. To define it is a difficult task, and in *Andrews v DPP* Lord Atkin spoke of the 'element of "unlawfulness" which is the elusive factor'. Stressing that we are here leaving entirely out of account those ingredients of homicide which might justify a verdict of manslaughter on the grounds of (a) criminal negligence, or (b)

Trial judge has said that manslaughter is based on unlawful act – and no need for intent to kill or cause serious harm.

Trial judge said that if accused believed woman was dead then must be manslaughter not murder.

Appeal judge says that the above was a misdirection – because trial judge is suggesting that whenever an unlawful act results in death it must be a manslaughter. Appeal judge suggests that there must be some mens rea.

CONTINUED ▶

provocation, or (c) diminished responsibility, the conclusion of this court is that an unlawful act causing the death of another cannot, simply because it is an unlawful act, render a manslaughter verdict inevitable. For such a verdict inexorably to follow, the unlawful act must be such as all sober and reasonable people would inevitably recognise must subject the other person to, at least, the risk of some harm resulting therefrom, albeit not serious harm. If such be the test, as we judge it to be, then it follows that in our view it was a misdirection to tell the jury simpliciter that it mattered nothing for manslaughter whether or not the appellant believed Mrs Nott to be dead when he threw her in the river . . . in the circumstances, such a misdirection does not, in our judgment, involve that the conviction for manslaughter must or should be quashed.	*Appeal judge says that an unlawful act on its own is not sufficient.* *The act also has to be dangerous – judged against the standards of a 'sober and reasonable man'.* *Trial judge's direction was a misdirection – but no need for conviction to be quashed.*

Figure 3.4   Extract adapted from the judgment in R v Church *[1966] 1 QB 59*

So, having gone through the exercise above, highlighting the appropriate parts of the judgment, and making your own brief commentary on what the judge is saying, you can then reduce it still further into a set of small notes. You may find that using bullet points is a good way of remembering what you need to. One of the reasons for this is that in later testing yourself you are likely to remember the number of bullets that you have to remember for the case in question.

KEY FACTS

Key points from *Church*:

The extract from the judgment above seems to be seven critical points:

- Unlawful act manslaughter does not depend on the existence of an intention to kill or to cause serious harm.
- It does depend on a death resulting from the defendant's unlawful act.
- But the act on its own is insufficient for a conviction for manslaughter.
- There must be also the *mens rea* for the unlawful act.
- The act must be dangerous.
- What is dangerous is what would be what all sober and reasonable people would recognise would put the victim at risk of harm.
- This harm need not be serious harm.

ACTIVITY

Read the following very brief example of a judgment and, in the same way as in the example in Figure 3.4 above, highlight what you think is important in the extract, make brief explanatory notes in the right-hand margin, then add your own brief Key Facts chart. (A suggested answer can be found in the Appendix at page 304.)

Hyde v Wrench

Rolls Court [1840] 3 Beav 334; Jur 1106; 49 ER 132

June 6. The defendant wrote to the plaintiff offering to sell his farm for £1,000. The plaintiff's agent immediately called on the defendant and made an offer of £950, which the defendant wished to have a few days to consider.

June 27. The defendant wrote to say that he would not accept this offer.

June 29. The plaintiff wrote accepting the offer of June 6.

The plaintiff bought an action for specific performance.

The defendant filed a general demurrer.

THE MASTER OF THE ROLLS (LORD LANGDALE): Under the circumstances stated in this bill, I think there exists no valid binding contract between the parties for the purchase of the property. The defendant offered to sell it for £1,000, and if that had at once been unconditionally accepted, there would undoubtedly have been a perfect binding contract; instead of that, the plaintiff made an offer of his own, to purchase the property for £950, and he thereby rejected the offer previously made by the defendant. I think that it was not afterwards competent for him to revive the proposal of the defendant, by tendering an acceptance of it; and that, therefore, there exists no obligation of any sort between the parties; the demurrer must be allowed.

Once you have mastered the art of paraphrasing judgments or even articles and books in this way you will then be able to make much more effective use of your time. You will then end up with a much clearer understanding than if you try to associate with the pages and pages of writing that you have read in total.

When you look at what has been done in the highlighting exercise above, it really only reflects the points made in section 3.3 on scan reading. The one feeds into the other.

3.5 Making notes from reading

Not everybody makes notes in the same way. There are any number of different ways of putting down information. Note taking is a very personal process and the most important thing about your notes is that they should mean something to you, so that you are able to use them easily and effectively, and that they make perfect sense to you.

Many of the hints on structuring your notes and different styles of note taking in Chapter 2 are useful to you here, but of course making notes from your reading is slightly different:

*   because you have more time to do it
*   because you are not following the directions of your teachers
*   because you are taking notes from an entirely different source
*   because you are able to determine the structure of your notes and in what order you make them, rather than having it dictated for you.

In any case what you have to do at some point is to make a version of your notes that includes both the basis of your lectures and the extra information that you find from other sources. This is why it is so important to understand how to produce a good structure to your notes that makes sense to you. This is obviously vital to when you are preparing for your exams, because if you do not have a set of notes that you clearly understand, or if you have to move between a variety of different pieces of paper for the same point or the same area, then you are likely to miss important details and your revision will be less effective.

You do have certain aids already for creating a good structure for your notes if you think about it carefully:

*   If your lecturer has indicated headings or sub-headings or any natural breaks in a topic area during your lectures then you can take this as a reasonable breakdown of the subject area and use them yourself.
*   Your teacher may have given you handouts. These will almost certainly be broken down by heading and sub-heading and at the very least by different paragraphs. Again this is a useful indication of how the topic area breaks down and how you might structure your own notes.

- If you are taking notes from textbooks these will almost certainly have some headings and possibly sub-headings which again can feed into your own structure and the contents list (that we have already looked at) is another hint on how to structure notes.

- Even law reports, if you look at the letters down the side next to paragraphs, can give you some idea of structure.

There are also many other practical points about taking notes that you can follow to make your notes a more effective aid:

- Scan the material first. This allows you to build up an awareness of the material. It presents you with the big picture so you can appreciate what is important in the text. It will provide you with more effective notes and it will take less time.

- Try to make your notes clear but also try hard to be concise when taking notes. If you merely copy down everything from a book you will have a lot of irrelevant detail and what you have will be no different and no shorter (or indeed longer) than that section of the book.

- You can and should make good use of headings and sub-headings. This will give a structure not only to your notes but also to your learning as well as to your revision for exams. You have many sources, as indicated above, from which to work out how to divide up your notes by section. (You can test your ability to section off your notes under headings by choosing an area that you are currently studying. Divide the topic into what you think are the most the important headings and then look in a textbook and see how your headings and even sub-headings compare.)

- You can also make very effective use of bullet points. While you may want a lot of detail in your notes, they are for your later use when writing coursework assignments or revising for exams, so they do not need to be written like a book.

- Your notes are also very personal. So there is no reason why you should not make extensive use of abbreviations as long as you use them consistently and you do not forget what they are. There are some very obvious ones like D = defendant, C = claimant. Your teachers may in any case inform you of recognised abbreviations such as CA = Court of Appeal and HL = House of Lords. If you are lucky they may even allow you to use these recognised abbreviations in exams to save writing time.

- Because you are studying law your teachers will always want you to give authority for the points that you make in coursework assignments or in exams. So you should make sure that you do this in your notes too and use cases or statutory sources in your notes. (If you wanted your notes to flow from principle to principle and not be cluttered with the facts of every case you could have a separate set of notes containing case facts listed in some methodical order.)

- One other thing that you need to remember is that essay questions in coursework and examinations will require you to make critical comments. You need to include such comment from books and articles in your notes. You also might want to extract particular quotes in your notes or even copy down useful statistical information. With so many different features in your notes (basic information, key principles, cases, sections of Acts, as well as key comment or quotes) it may also be useful to have a set of key symbols. By doing this, when reading subsequently you can head straight to the particular feature you require. An alternative is to colour code.

- When you are reading from lots of different sources it is also useful to leave spaces so that you can add in other information from the different sources later.

- Visual stimuli are particularly useful learning aids. So if you are good at drawing diagrams add them or if you find pictures or diagrams in things that you read you might choose to photocopy them and cut and paste them into your notes.

3.6 Making use of your notes

It is important to remember that your notes can, and probably should, be the most central core of your learning. They represent the information that you have gathered from all of the different sources available to you: from your lessons, from the textbooks, from articles, from judgments or statutes, and from other sources that supplement and add extra detail to your class notes.

If your notes are effective they can not only be used to help with the overall development of your understanding. They can also be very useful when you are preparing coursework assignments and indeed when you want to make reduced notes or revision aids during your revision preparation for the exams (see Chapter 11).

There is one very important point that applies both to the notes that you have taken in your lectures and those that you have made in your reading, whether from paper sources like textbooks or from electronic sources. You should always read through your notes soon after you have made them to ensure you understand them. It is one thing developing the art of taking good notes but notes are only good if they make sense to you. Finding out that you do not understand your notes when you are in the middle of revision is probably worse than taking no notes at all because then you have little time left to do anything about it and you will probably panic.

For your notes to be of use to you remember that they must:

- be complete
- be up to date
- be organised and in order
- be compact but also comprehensive
- make use of all of your sources (lecture notes and from reading).

By doing this you can gain maximum value from them.

Your notes are vital to you in various respects:

- First, your lecture notes are one of the best guides that you have for making notes from other sources.

- Second, notes made from reading are the best way of clarifying, illuminating and expanding the notes that you take in lectures.

- Your completed notes are the basis of your coursework answers or the guide to other sources that you will use at that time.

- They also form the basis for whatever type of revision aids you devise in preparation for exams.

3.7 Keeping references

As we have said, it is important that your notes are organised and in order. This is vital at times of writing coursework assignments or revising for exams, so you can move methodically through the information without having to spend hours reading to find the bit that you want.

As you read to supplement your notes or for research you may come across and identify cases or even articles from journals that you think are worth referring to and include a reference to them in your notes.

You may find that you save a lot of time by highlighting passages from books or law reports that you have copied, instead of making notes from all the directed sources. You may feel that it is sufficient to return to these when needed rather than laboriously rewriting them in your notes.

In either case you need to be able to refer to these sources again and not waste time looking for them.

TIP

Make a habit at all times of providing a reference to all materials used when making your notes. Then if you want to go back and look at a particular case in a law report at some stage, you will be able to because you will have the full citation in your notes by the side of the case name or in the margin.

If you have collected materials such as articles, photocopies of pages from large textbooks in the library, or from specific law reports make sure that you create files of these with some form of code to identify where they are kept and insert a reference to your code in your notes so that once again you can easily go back to them and find them quickly.

3.8 Making sense of difficult material

Law texts are full of technical terms and difficult concepts. When you read material, you may fail to understand the issues you are reading about. If this is the case, try to adopt the following methods:

- **Summary or chapter overviews** – Many texts have introductory overviews or summaries. Read these to provide a context to the material. These sections are normally guides to the information that is presented.

- **Read critically** – By reading set material passively you will gain a poor understanding. Try to read the material actively. Make annotations next to areas on misunderstanding; try to link the subject matter to tutorial or coursework tasks in order to give it a context. Question the validity of the viewpoints. Make a note of the technical terms you do not understand and then look them up in a legal thesaurus.

- **Read the whole passage** – Do not give up if you find the material difficult. Many texts are not written in terms of ease of understanding. There may be greater explanation on issues that are causing you concern later on in the reading material.

- **Break the material into manageable chunks** – Look at the section headings. Read one section at a time and review it. Make a note of its key themes. Repeat this for the rest of the text.

- **Seek support** – Focus on the issues you do understand and then make a list of the issues that you do not. Seek tutor or peer support – they may be able to explain the issues in a way you will understand.

chapter 4 EXPLAINING PRIMARY SOURCES AND SECONDARY SOURCES ▪

AIMS AND OBJECTIVES

After reading this chapter you should be able to:

- Understand the difference between primary sources and secondary sources

- Understand the methods of citation for bills, statutes, statutory instruments and case law

- Understand the relevance of legal encyclopaedias, journal articles and textbooks

- Understand the basic sources of the law in England and Wales

- Use citations to research law

- Use legal encyclopaedias, journal articles and textbooks to research law

- Understand the difference between official and non-official sources of legislation

- Understand the range and importance of secondary sources of legal information

During the course of your legal studies you will be expected to use primary sources and secondary sources in your coursework. This chapter aims to explain what is meant by these terms and to give you an idea of when you should consult a primary source and when to consult a secondary one. The text of this chapter is correct at the time of writing, November 2007.

What are primary sources?

Primary sources fall into two categories: legislation and case law. What defines these as primary sources is the fact that they contain the actual text of the law – ie the text of an Act of Parliament or the judgment of the court. You may find reading primary sources heavy going at first as the language used can be very legalistic, but you should persevere as there is no real substitute for reading the primary source. A case summary or an article about an Act may present a particular point of view, but only by reading the primary sources can you get the full picture and begin to form your own opinions.

What are secondary sources?

Secondary sources provide background information to supplement the primary sources and include journal articles, legal encyclopaedias and textbooks. In conjunction with primary sources, secondary sources can help you become better informed about a topic.

4.1 Legislation

Legislation is defined as 'the whole or any part of a country's written law' (Martin, 2003). In the United Kingdom the term is most commonly used to mean law which is made by, or on behalf of, Parliament (as opposed to case law, which is made by judges). Legislation comes in two different kinds – **primary legislation** and **secondary legislation**.

4.2 Primary legislation

Primary legislation is the name applied to Acts of Parliament or Statutes.

NOTE

The terms 'Act of Parliament' and 'Statute' are interchangeable and refer to the same thing, so don't panic if one lecturer tells you to read an Act and another one tells you to read a Statute.

Acts of Parliament can be divided into two categories – Public General Acts and Local and Personal Acts.

Type of Act	Characteristics	Example
Public General Acts	• Cover matters of public policy • Apply to the whole country	• Human Rights Act 1998
Local and Personal Acts	• Limited application • Only apply to either a specific area, a specific individual or estate	• Nottingham City Council Act 2003 • Valerie Mary Hill and Alan Monk (Marriage Enabling) Act 1985

Figure 4.1 Types of Acts of Parliament

4.2.1 How to refer to primary legislation

Acts of Parliament can be referred to in a number of ways (see Figure 4.2 below):

- by short title
- by long title
- by official citation (year and chapter number).

An Act to amend the Charities Act 1960 and make other provision with respect to charities; to regulate fund-raising activities carried on in connection with charities and other institutions; to make fresh provision with respect to public charitable collections; and for connected purposes.

Figure 4.2 *Ways of referring to Acts of Parliament*

4.2.2 Official Citations

The Official Citation for Acts of Parliament is made up of the year (in which the Act received Royal Assent) and the Chapter number (a running number throughout each calendar year). Chapter can also be abbreviated to c, cap or chap.

1992 Chapter 41	1992 c. 41	1992 cap. 41	1992 chap. 41
All refer to The Charities Act, which was the 41st Act to receive Royal Assent in 1992.			

Figure 4.3 *Citations for The Charities Act*

> **NOTE**
>
> Public General Acts are cited using cardinal numerals (eg 1, 2, 3) and Local and Personal Acts are cited using roman numerals (eg i, ii, iii)
>
> 1994 Chapter 13 – Intelligence Services Act
>
> 1994 Chapter xiii – London Docklands Development Corporation Act

4.2.3 Regnal years

The Regnal year refers to the number of the year of the sovereign's reign (eg whether it is the first, second or third year of the sovereign's reign) and was used in Official Citations until 1963.

Colonial Courts of Admiralty Act
53 & 54 Vict c. 27
This was the 27th Act to be passed during the Parliamentary Session which commenced in the 53rd year of Queen Victoria's reign (1889) and ended in the 54th year of her reign (1890).

■ *Figure 4.4 Regnal years*

4.2.4 The difference between official sources and non-official sources

There are two official sources of primary legislation. The first is a series of annual volumes called Public General Acts and General Synod Measures, published by the Office of Public Sector Information (OPSI), formerly Her Majesty's Stationery Office (HMSO). This official source was first published in 1831, although from 1831 until 1870 the series was known as Public General Statutes.

OPSI also publish Public General Acts individually as they receive Royal Assent and their website – www.opsi.gov.uk – contains the full text of many Public General Acts which, at the time of writing, are available from 1988 onwards.

> **NOTE**
>
> Note The Public General Acts version of an Act contains the text as it was on the date on which it received Royal Assent. It does not include any subsequent changes to the legislation and can therefore be referred to as the original (or historical) version of an Act.

The second is the Statute Law Database (SLD), which is the official revised edition of the primary legislation of the United Kingdom made available online – www.statutelaw.gov.uk – and is produced by the Ministry of Justice. 'Revised' means that the text available on the Statute Law Database contains details of any amendments or repeals after the date of Royal Assent and so it provides an up-to-date, current version of an Act of Parliament.

Non-official sources of Acts of Parliament are those produced by commercial publishers. In order to encourage people to buy them, the commercial publishers add value to their products in a number of ways, such as including amendments to legislation or extensive notes. Figure 4.5 below lists the main non-official sources of Acts of Parliament and outlines the extra features of each.

Title	Publisher	Format	Features	Updated or historical text
Halsbury's Statutes of England and Wales	LexisNexis	Print and online	Annotations to the text – includes details of amendments and repeals.	Updated
Current Law Statutes	Sweet & Maxwell	Print	Reference service covering public and private legislation. Notes are provided for all Acts with major Acts receiving more detailed comment. Includes references to Hansard debates.	Historical
Westlaw	Sweet & Maxwell	Online	Annotations to the text – includes details of amendments and repeals.	Updated

Figure 4.5 The main non-official sources of Acts of Parliament

4.2.5 Finding older Statutes

If you are looking for the original text of an Act from before 1831 (the date when the Public General Acts series began to be published) then you could consult either of the following two series:

Statutes of the Realm

Statutes of the Realm covers Statutes from 1235 until 1713. Private Acts from before 1539 are also included. You can find the Act you want by consulting either the alphabetical, chronological or subject indexes.

Statutes at Large

The *Statutes at Large* series contains reprints of Statutes from the thirteenth century through to the eighteenth and nineteenth centuries.

4.2.6 Historical versions versus updated versions of an Act

Ultimately, the decision as to which version of an Act you should consult comes down to you and will depend very much on your essay question or coursework topic. For much of your studies, you will need to refer to legislation currently in force and so you should use updated versions of Acts of Parliament. However, there will be occasions when you need to look at the original text of an Act, perhaps to compare it to how it is in force currently, and then you will need to consult historical sources.

4.3 Secondary legislation

Secondary legislation is the term used to describe Statutory Instruments (also known by the abbreviation SIs). The term Statutory Instrument came into usage in 1946. Before this date, secondary legislation was known by the name Statutory Rules and Orders.

NOTE

Secondary legislation may also be referred to as subordinate legislation.

Whereas an Act of Parliament tends to give a broad outline of the law in a particular area, it is the Statutory Instruments which provide the detail. Statutory Instruments are drawn up under powers delegated by specific Acts of Parliament and a single Act can give rise to many individual Statutory Instruments. The actual drafting of Statutory Instruments can be done by individuals or bodies, to whom Parliament has delegated the authority.

NOTE

There are many more Statutory Instruments published each year than there are Acts. In 2006, 55 Acts of Parliament received Royal Assent and 3,511 Statutory Instruments were made.

> **TIP** A handy hint for spotting Statutory Instruments is that they often contain one of these words in their title: Rules, Regulations or Order.

Statutory Instruments can also be divided into two categories – local and general. Local Statutory Instruments apply only to a specific area of the country. General Statutory Instruments cover matters of public policy and can be broken down further into the following three types:

C – Commencement Orders, which bring an Act or part of an Act into force

L – Statutory Instruments relating to fees or procedures in England & Wales

S – Statutory Instruments applying to Scotland only

4.3.1 How to refer to Statutory Instruments

The Official Citation for Statutory Instruments is by year (the year in which the Statutory Instrument was made) and then a running number (allocated to all Statutory Instruments in a year), eg 2003, No. 118 or 2003/118.

> **NOTE**
>
> The year always comes before the Statutory Instrument number, so:
>
> - 1996/1997 refers to The Motor Vehicles (Driving Licences) (Amendment) (No. 4) Regulations 1996, (Statutory Instrument Number 1997 for the year 1996).
>
> - 1997/1996 refers to The Wireless Telegraphy (Short Range Devices) (Exemption) (Amendment) Regulations 1997, (Statutory Instrument Number 1996 for the year 1997).

Statutory Instruments can also be referred to by their short title, eg:

The Intercountry Adoption (Hague Convention) Regulations 2003

The County Court (Forms) (Amendment No. 2) Rules 1997

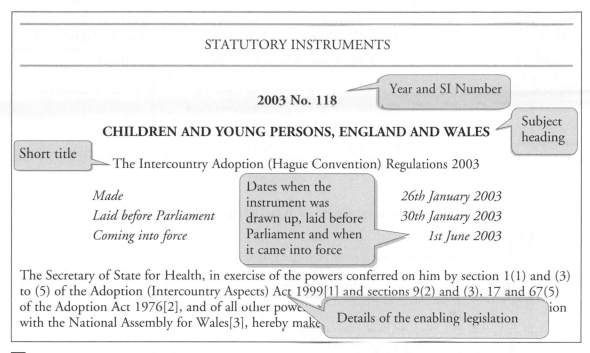

Figure 4.6 An example of a Statutory Instrument

4.3.2 The difference between official sources and non-official sources

The official source for Statutory Instruments is an annual printed series published by OPSI, formerly HMSO, known simply as Statutory Instruments. This series reprints only those Statutory Instruments still in force at the end of the calendar year in which they were made. OPSI also publishes Statutory Instruments individually, shortly after they come into force and the OPSI website – www.opsi.gov.uk – contains the full text of Statutory Instruments from the beginning of 1987 onwards (at the time of writing).

NOTE

The OPSI version of a Statutory Instrument contains the text as it was on the date on which the Statutory Instrument came into force. It does not include any subsequent amendments and so can be referred to as the original (historical) source.

The Statute Law Database – www.statutelaw.gov.uk – contains the text of Statutory Instruments from 1st January 1991 onwards, in their original (historical) text, ie not in an updated form.

The main non-official sources for Statutory Instruments are outlined in Figure 4.7 overleaf.

Title	Publisher	Format	Features	Updated or historical text
Halsbury's Statutory Instruments	LexisNexis	Print and online	Full text online. In print, full text of some SIs, summaries of many more.	Updated
Westlaw	Sweet & Maxwell	Online	Full text	Updated

Figure 4.7 Non-official sources for Statutory Instruments

4.3.3 Historical versions versus updated versions of a Statutory Instrument

As with Acts of Parliament, whether you choose the original text or the updated text of a Statutory Instrument will depend on the nature of your coursework topic. Use updated sources when you need to quote current law and historical sources when you need to quote the original text.

4.4 Parliamentary Bills

4.4.1 What is a Bill?

Bills are draft versions of proposed legislation. Although not actually legislation, they are still important and you may often be required to read a Bill or track its progress through Parliament.

NOTE

All Acts of Parliament began life as Bills, but not all Bills end up as Acts.

4.4.2 The different types of Bill

The three main types of Bills are Public, Private and Hybrid. Figure 4.8 below outlines these:

Type		Introduced by	On gaining Royal Assent, becomes
Public – relating to matters of public policy	Government Bill	Government Ministers	Public General Act
	Private Members' Bill	Private Members of Parliament (eg an MP or a peer)	
Private – relating to individuals, companies or local authorities		Outside bodies (eg local authorities or companies)	Local or Personal Act

CONTINUED ▸

Type	Introduced by	On gaining Royal Assent, becomes
Hybrid – has characteristics of both a public and a private Bill	Government ministers or private MPs	Public General Act

Figure 4.8 Different types of Bill

4.4.3 How Bills are structured

Figure 4.9 shows the structure of a Bill.

Food Labelling Bill — Short title

CONTENTS

1. Interpretation
2. Labelling: countries of origin
3. Labelling: production standards
4. Method of marking or labelling
5. Consequential amendment
6. Short title, commencement and extent

A

BILL

TO — Long title

Make further provision for relevant information about food, including information about the country of origin, contents and standards of production of that food, to be made available to consumers by labelling, marking or in other ways; and for connected purposes.

Be it enacted by the Queen's most Excellent Majesty, by and with the advice and — Enacting formula
Lords Spiritual and Temporal, and Commons, in this present Parliament assembl[ed]
authority of the same, as follows:

1   Interpretation

In this Act, unless the context otherwise requires—   Clauses

'food' is to be interpreted in accordance with section 1 of the Food Sa[fety Act 1990] (c. 16),

Figure 4.9 The structure of a Bill

63

4.4.4 How Bills are cited

Each Public Bill is given a serial number. This number will change if a Bill is reprinted at any stage. Public Bills should be cited as follows:

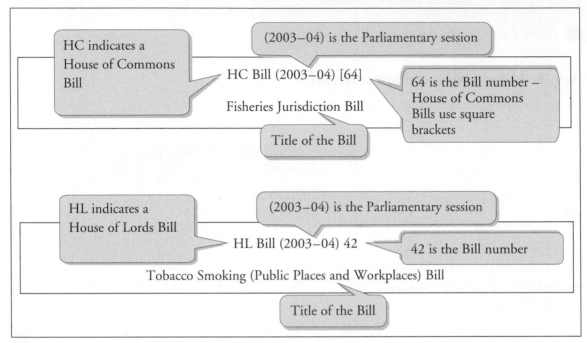

HC indicates a House of Commons Bill

(2003–04) is the Parliamentary session

HC Bill (2003–04) [64]

64 is the Bill number – House of Commons Bills use square brackets

Fisheries Jurisdiction Bill

Title of the Bill

HL indicates a House of Lords Bill

(2003–04) is the Parliamentary session

HL Bill (2003–04) 42

42 is the Bill number

Tobacco Smoking (Public Places and Workplaces) Bill

Title of the Bill

Figure 4.10 How Bills are cited

4.5 Case law

4.5.1 What is case law?

Case law is based on published reports of decisions and judgments of the courts on points of law.

4.5.2 What is a law report?

The published reports are known collectively as law reports. There are lots of different series of law reports, each with its own title and referred to by its own legal abbreviation. Most law reports are available in print and many are also available in electronic format.

4.5.3 The difference between a law report and a transcript

Law reports are published by commercial publishers who will add extra features such as catchwords, headnotes and subject indexing, to make the law report easier to trace and use. They will make decisions about which cases to include in their series, based on their own particular criteria (see section 4.5.5).

Law reports series can be divided into three categories in terms of the types of cases they include. Figure 4.11 gives you an idea of the types of law reports series available:

Type	Coverage	Examples	Citation
General series	Major cases from all subject areas	Weekly Law Reports	WLR
		All England Law Reports	All ER
Subject specific series	Major cases relevant to their subject coverage	Housing Law Reports	HLR
		Medical Law Reports	Med LR
Historical series	Reprints of historical cases, usually from before 1865	English Reports	ER
		Revised Reports	RR

Figure 4.11 Types of law reports series available

Transcripts will contain all the legal argument and reasoning, but they won't contain any of the added extras that come with a published law report. The advent of the internet has meant that it has become much easier to track down case transcripts, but there will still be many which do not appear on any websites or databases. Individual transcripts may be available by contacting the relevant court, but there is likely to be a cost involved in getting hold of them in this way.

4.5.4 Catchwords and headnotes

Figure 4.12 below illustrates the catchwords and headnote within a law report.

[2003] 4 All ER 78

Batchelor v Marlow and another

[2001] EWCA Civ 1051

Court of Appeal, Civil Division

Henry, Tuckey and Kay LJJ

28 June 2001

> The Catchwords summarise the main legal aspects of the case

Easement – Right to park cars – Claimant owning land which could accommodate parking for no more than six cars – Judge holding that defendants had right to park six cars on land during working hours – Whether right capable of existing as easement.

The defendants, who ran a garage business, parked cars on land [...] Jo more than six cars could be parked on the land. In proceedings be[...] asserted that they had an easement to park and store cars on[...] ey had acquired an exclusive prescriptive right to park six cars on the la[...] pm Monday to Friday in connection with their business. In so holdi[...] such a right was capable of subsisting as an easement since, being limite[...] tter of degree, amount to such exclusion of the claimant as to preclude[...] e claimant appealed.

> The Headnote summarises the facts of the case and the points of law. It also contains the Court's decision, after the word **Held**.

Held – The right found to exist by the judge was not capable of being an easement . . .

■ *Figure 4.12 Catchwords and headnote within a law report*

4.5.5 How cases get reported

You might think that every case heard in court gets reported in a law reports series, but that is not so. In fact, only a small percentage of the cases heard each year actually make it into a law reports series.

So what selection criteria do publishers use when deciding which cases should be included in their law reports series? In general cases should fall into one of the following categories:

* cases that make new law because they deal with a new situation

* cases that make new law because they extend the application of new principles

- cases that give a modern judicial restatement of existing principles

- cases that clarify conflicting decisions of lower courts

- cases that interpret legislation which is likely to have wide application

- cases that clarify an important point of practice or procedure.

NOTE

In general, reported cases have been heard in the High Court, the Court of Appeal or the House of Lords. This is because cases have to be of some significance in order to be referred on to the senior courts. Cases heard in the lower courts, eg local magistrates' courts, rarely get reported in law reports series.

Also you should note that *legal interest* is not the same as *media interest*. Cases which receive a lot of media coverage will not automatically be reported in law reports series. Murder cases, for example, often get a lot of coverage on television and in the newspapers, but are not often reported in law reports, as they rarely meet the criteria listed above.

You might also think that each case is only reported in one law reports series, but again this isn't true. The same case can be reported in a number of different law reports series and the version you use will depend on the law reports available to you and the hierarchy of law reporting (see section 4.5.6 below).

4.5.6 Knowing which version of a case to choose

If a case has been reported in five or six different law reports, does it matter which one you choose? The answer is yes, it does matter, as within the legal profession some law reports take precedence over others. Barristers will follow this hierarchy in court and you should also follow it in your coursework or moot trials. Figure 4.13 will explain the hierarchy:

	Title	Citation	Publisher	Comments
1	The Law Reports (*includes the Appeal Cases, the Chancery Division, the Family Division and the King's/Queen's Bench Division*)	AC Ch Fam KB/QB	Incorporated Council of Law Reporting for England and Wales	The most authoritative series available. The only reports that are checked by the judges and counsels involved before publication. Can take some time to appear in print.
2	Weekly Law Reports	WLR	Incorporated Council of Law Reporting for England and Wales	These appear more quickly than the above series. Many of the cases in the Weekly Law Reports will eventually appear in The Law Reports.
3	All England Law Reports	All ER	LexisNexis	A general series, covering cases on all subjects.
4	Individual law reports series	If your case has not been reported in any of the above three series, then you can cite whichever individual law report series you choose.		

Figure 4.13 Hierarchy of law reports

You should follow the hierarchy at all times, particularly for a moot or a piece of coursework.

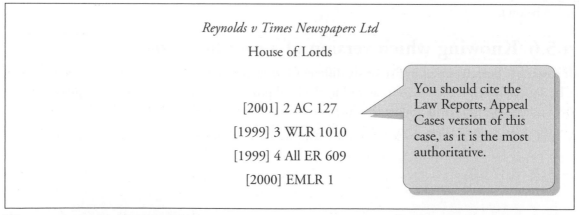

Figure 4.14 Applying the hierarchy

ACTIVITY

For each of the three cases below, say which law reports version you would cite in your essay. If you're feeling adventurous, you can also identify what each of the abbreviations stand for (see section 4.5.12 below).

Grobbelaar v News Group Newspapers Ltd
House of Lords
[2002] 4 All ER 732
[2002] 1 WLR 3024
[2003] EMLR 1

Rees v Darlington Memorial Hospital Trust
House of Lords
[2004] 1 FLR 234
[2003] 3 WLR 1091
[2004] 1 AC 309

MCC Proceeds Inc v Lehman
Court of Appeal
[1998] 4 All ER 675
[1998] 2 BCLC 659
(1998) 142 SJLB 40

You will find the answers in the Appendix on page 305.

4.5.7 'The Law Reports'

You might have noticed from some of the examples above, that there appears to be a series of law reports called *The Law Reports*. We know this sounds confusing but here is the explanation. The Incorporated Council of Law Reporting for England and Wales publish a series known as *The Law Reports*, illustrated in Figure 4.15. This series is the most authoritative version of a law report as it is the only series where the text of the report is checked before publication by the judges and counsel involved in the case.

4.6.1 Legal encyclopaedias

Legal encyclopaedias give definitions of the law and often focus on a particular subject area, such as environmental law or health and safety law. They can be an excellent starting point for research as they will refer you to relevant legislation and case law.

Halsbury's Laws of England and Wales

Halsbury's Laws is an exception to other legal encyclopaedias in that it does not simply focus on one specific subject area. Instead it aims to provide a 'restatement of the whole of the laws of England and Wales'. It is produced by LexisNexis Butterworths and is available in hard copy (some 58 volumes) or online – check in your own library to see if you have access to the print version, electronic version or both. Section 5.5.1 provides more information on how to use *Halsbury's Laws*.

Subject specific legal encyclopaedias

There are a number of legal encyclopaedias available covering a variety of different subject areas. These may be available in hard copy, usually in a loose-leaf format, or electronically. The loose-leaf approach means that old pages can be removed and new pages inserted as the law changes, ensuring that the information is as up to date as possible. The advantages of these encyclopaedias are that they bring together all the relevant materials on a particular subject and they are regularly updated.

Woodfall's *Law of Landlord and Tenant*, published by Sweet & Maxwell, is an example of a legal encyclopaedia. In hard copy, this is available in a multi-volume loose-leaf format. Woodfall's *Law of Landlord and Tenant* is also available electronically via the Westlaw database. In the electronic version, the text is updated online, so again you can be confident that the information is current and accurate.

Check your library's catalogue, browse the shelves or speak to your librarian to find out what legal encyclopaedias you have access to.

4.6.2 Journal articles

Journal articles are an excellent secondary source of legal information and you should get into the habit of reading them. Section 5.5.3 will discuss in detail how to locate relevant journal articles, but in this section you will learn about legal journals themselves.

Legal journals can be roughly divided into two categories – professional titles and academic titles. Professional titles are those journals which are primarily aimed at practising lawyers, while academic titles are those aimed at scholars and people studying and researching the law. Figure 4.23 opposite outlines some of the main differences between the two types of journal:

Type	Primary audience	Some examples	Defining characteristics
Professional	Practising solicitors or barristers	*Law Society's Gazette; The Lawyer*	Short articles; newsy approach
Academic	Scholars, academics, researchers, students	*Modern Law Review; Cambridge Law Journal*	Lengthier, in-depth articles; bibliographies and references

Figure 4.23 Differences between professional and academic journals

One specific advantage that journal articles have is that they take a lot less time to be published than books, which makes them a particularly good source for current topics. If you are looking for opinions on a recent case or you want background information about a Bill currently before Parliament, it is unlikely that there will be a book on your topic but quite likely that journal articles will have been written on it.

4.6.3 Textbooks

Textbooks are another very useful secondary source of information. The reading lists you are given by your tutors will recommend titles to you and you should use these as your starting point. If any items on your reading list are identified as essential purchases then you should buy a copy. After all, if a particular book is going to be used every week in tutorials, then it makes sense to have your own copy. But never forget that the library will have many more books on a subject than just those titles on your reading list and that by reading widely on a particular topic you will be better informed and more able to form your own opinion on a subject.

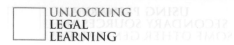

Current Law Statutes

Current Law Statutes is arranged by year, often with three or four volumes produced each year. The Acts are printed in chapter number order but there is also an alphabetical index for each year which you can use if you only know the Act's title. Each year of *Current Law Statutes* contains a numerical table of Statutory Instruments for that year, an alphabetical table of Statutes from 1700 onwards and a subject/title index to Acts passed within that year.

Public General Acts

These annual volumes are produced by the Office of Public Sector Information (OPSI), formerly Her Majesty's Stationery Office (HMSO), and contain the year's Acts in chapter number order. There is also an alphabetical index to Acts for each year.

Statutes at Large

This is a multi-volume printed work containing Acts from 1225–1865. The volumes are in chronological order and within each volume the Statutes are in chapter number order. Each volume also has an alphabetical list of Acts covered. *Statutes at Large* uses regnal years for its dates – see section 4.2.3.

Loose-leaf encyclopaedias

Loose-leaf encyclopaedias are another useful source for the amended text of Acts. Find out if there is a loose-leaf encyclopaedia covering the subject area you are interested in – you could do this by checking the library catalogue, by browsing the library shelves at the relevant class number or by asking your Law Librarian. As well as the updated text, loose-leaf encyclopaedias often provide additional annotations and commentary related to the subject.

Textbooks

Lots of textbooks also reprint whole or significant sections of Acts. 'Cases and Materials' books (eg *Cases and Materials on the English Legal System* by Michael Zander, or *Cases and Materials on Criminal Law* by Janet Dine and James Gobert) provide just that – key cases and legislation related to a particular subject.

Many legal publishers also produce their own books of Statutes in different subject areas, (eg *Blackstone's Statutes on Intellectual Property* edited by Andrew Christie and Stephen Gare), which bring together the main pieces of legislation on each topic.

Electronic sources

LexisNexis Butterworths

LexisNexis Butterworths is a subscription-based database provided by LexisNexis. The legislation section provides electronic access to the amended text of Statutes. You can search by Act name or subject, or alternatively you can browse an alphabetical list of Acts. Most amendments are incorporated into the main body of the text but you should always click on the 'Stop Press' icon, if displayed, as this is where very recent amendments will be listed before being amalgamated into the main text.

The OPSI website (www.opsi.gov.uk/acts.htm)

This freely available website contains the original (historical) text of Acts from 1988 onwards. Acts are grouped by year and can then be viewed in alphabetical or chapter number order. You can search the site at a basic or advanced level.

Westlaw

Westlaw is a subscription-based database produced by Sweet & Maxwell. The legislation section within *Westlaw* contains amended, full text Statutes. You can search it at a basic or advanced level, using any combination of title, section number or keyword, or you can browse an alphabetical list of Acts to find the one you want. The advanced search option allows you to search historic law, eg if you want to know what the text of an Act was on any given date.

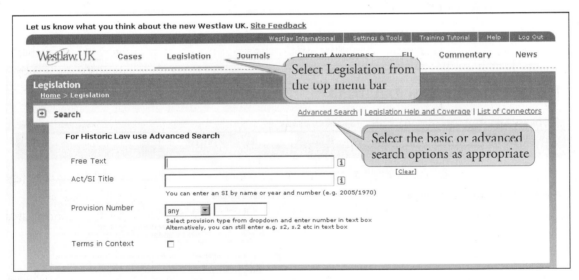

Figure 5.1 UK Legislation information on Westlaw

Lawtel

Lawtel is a subscription-based database produced by Sweet & Maxwell. To access Acts on *Lawtel* you should select the Statutory Law option. You can search by title or keyword. The text provided on *Lawtel* is the original (historic) version of the legislation, taken from the OPSI website.

JustCite

JustCite is a subscription-based database produced by Justis Publishing Ltd. *JustCite* will not provide you with the full text of an Act, but will instead point you in the direction of other databases and sources which contain the full text. It is up to you to find out which of these sources you have access to within your own institution. You can search *JustCite* using the title or official citation of an Act.

BAILII British & Irish Legal Information Institute (www.bailii.org)

BAILII is a freely available website which provides full text UK Statutes from the 1200s onwards. The text is taken from both the Statute Law Database and the OPSI website, so it can offer the original and updated versions.

Statute Law Database (SLD) (www.statutelaw.gov.uk)

The UK *Statute Law Database* (SLD) is the official revised edition of the primary legislation of the United Kingdom made available online. You can search by legislation title, legislation number or keyword. Extensive help is available within the database.

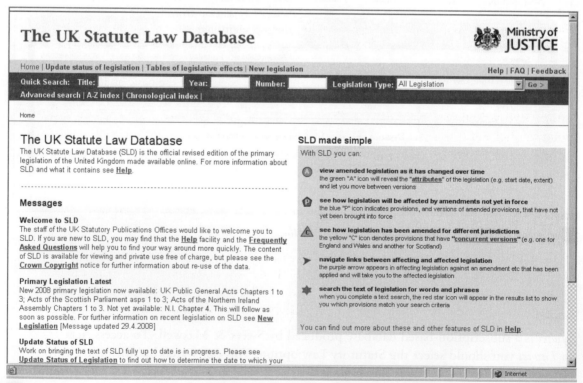

Figure 5.2 The Statute Law Database

ACTIVITY

Using any of the sources available to you (printed or electronic), answer the following questions:

- What is the chapter number of the Access to Justice Act 1999?
- What is the title of the Act with the official citation 1995 Chapter 50?
- On what date did the Education Act 2002 receive Royal Assent?

5.1.2 Checking if an Act is still in force

Legislation is constantly evolving and changing. Whole Acts or individual sections of an Act may be repealed, other sections may be amended and new sections may be inserted into an Act. If you need to quote current law, for example in a moot court case, then you must make sure that you use up to date legislation. The following sources will all provide the current status of primary legislation.

Printed sources

Halsbury's Statutes of England and Wales

This service provides the amended text of primary legislation currently in force in England and Wales. It keeps itself up to date through a combination of reissued main volumes, *Current Service Binders*, an annual *Cumulative Supplement* and a monthly *Noter-Up Service*. Where changes to the original Act occur, references to the amending or repealing legislation are included.

Is it in Force?

Is it in Force? is published by LexisNexis Butterworths and is a guide to the commencement dates of Acts in England and Wales passed since 1960. It is published twice a year, so each new volume includes recent statutes, as well as any recent amendments to the other Acts that *Is it in Force?* covers.

NOTE

Don't fall into the trap of automatically thinking that if an Act doesn't appear in *Is it in Force?* then it can't be in force. Remember that *Is it in Force?* tells you the current status of Acts from **1960 onwards only.** There are lots of Acts from before this date which are still in force but which won't be covered by *Is it in Force?* because of its specific date range.

Current Law Legislation Citator

The *Current Law Legislation Citator* is a member of Sweet & Maxwell's Current Law family of publications. In print, it will provide the current status of an Act of Parliament. Acts are listed in chronological order. It also gives details of commencement orders, Statutory Instruments made under the Act and gives references to cases where the Act was judicially considered. Figure 5.3 below provides an example of the citator's layout. Updates to the latest version of the citator can be found in the *Current Law Statutes* loose-leaf service binder.

Statute Citator	
12. Example Act 1993.	– Chapter number, name of Act and year
Royal Assent, May 5, 1993	– Date of Royal Assent
Commencement Orders SI 94/1234 SI 95/78	– Commencement orders bringing provisions into force
s.1, enabling, SI 94/1234; SI 95/78	– Statutory Instruments made under the powers of s.1 of the Act
s.2, see *R. v Brown* [1995] Crim.L.R: 43	– Case judicially considering s.2
s.3, amended: 1996 c.3 s.2	– s.3 amended by Act (s.2 of chapter 3 of 1996) and two SIs
s.3, enabling: SI 93/82; SI 96/70	
s.4, repealed: 1996 c.3. Sch. 4	– s.4 repealed by Schedule 4 of chapter 3 of 1996
s.4A added: SI 94/42	– s.4A added by SI Number 42 of 1994
Sch. 8, C. 1994 c. 1 s. 89	– Schedule 8 consolidated by s.89 of chapter 1 of 1994

Figure 5.3 Current Law Legislation Citator

Halsbury's Statutes Citator

This is an annual citator which is published as part of the *Halsbury's Statutes of England and Wales* series. Part 1 is a comprehensive alphabetical list of over 7,600 statutes which have been published in *Halsbury's Statutes*. Part 2 records any changes to the statutes included in the alphabetical list.

Loose-leaf encyclopaedias

Because of the ease with which these sources can be updated, they can usually be relied on for an up-to-date version of an Act. Check any loose-leaf encyclopaedias in your library related to your topic.

Electronic sources

LexisNexis Butterworths

LexisNexis Butterworths provides the amended text of primary legislation of general application in England and Wales. It is updated daily and so is an excellent source for the current text of an Act. Where changes to the original Act occur, references to the amending or repealing legislation are included – see Figure 5.4 opposite.

Within the legislation section, you can also access an electronic version of *Is it in Force?* Like the printed version, this will provide the current status of Acts passed since 1960. For Acts from before this date, you should use the main legislation section of *LexisNexis Butterworths*.

You can also access an online version of the *Halsbury's Statutes Citator*, which allows you to search the electronic version by keyword or browse a chronological list of Statutes.

Figure 5.4 *UK legislation information on LexisNexis Butterworths*

Westlaw

The legislation basic search screen only searches legislation currently in force and includes references to any amending or repealing legislation – see Figure 5.5 overleaf.

Lawtel

Lawtel's Statutory Law database has coverage from 1984 onwards. For each Act it provides a Statutory Status Table, which lists the current status of each section of the Act, with references to any amending or repealing legislation – see Figure 5.6 on page 88.

JustCite

JustCite provides a current status report for primary legislation and gives references to any amending or repealing legislation – see Figure 5.7 on page 89. Although JustCite will not provide the full text, it will refer you to other sources where the full text is available, so you should check which of these sources your institution subscribes to.

Statute Law Database (SLD) (www.statutelaw.gov.uk)

The Statute Law Database provides the current text of Acts of Parliament from the 1200s onwards, with details of annotations and amendments. See Figure 5.8 on page 89.

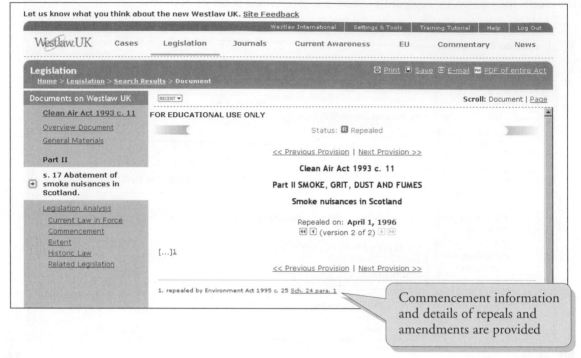

Figure 5.5 *UK legislation information on Westlaw*

Figure 5.6 *Statutory Law database from Lawtel*

Figure 5.7 JustCite

Figure 5.8 UK legislation information on The Statute Law Database

ACTIVITY

1. How many Acts of Parliament received Royal Assent in 2005 and 2006?
   Tip: Use the OPSI website www.opsi.gov.uk/acts.htm

2. What is the title of Section 13 of the Human Rights Act 1998? Which source did
   you use to find out?

Check your answers with those in the Appendix on page 306.

5.2 Secondary legislation

5.2.1 Finding Statutory Instruments

Printed sources

OPSI Statutory Instruments

OPSI has been publishing these volumes annually since 1949. They contain all those Statutory
Instruments made during the year which are still in force at the end of the same year. The text
provided is as it was on the date when the Statutory Instrument came into force, so it will not
include any amendments or repeals. Statutory Instruments are listed in numerical order and each
volume contains a subject index. The Statute Law Database also provides the original text of
Statutory Instruments.

Statutory Rules and Orders and Statutory Instruments Revised to December 1948

This series consists of 25 volumes arranged in broad subject order, giving the text of all general
Statutory Instruments, Rules and Orders in force on 31st December 1948.

Halsbury's Statutory Instruments

Halsbury's Statutory Instruments is a multi-volume work arranged in broad subject areas, listing all
general Statutory Instruments currently in force in England and Wales. Some are included in full text
with annotations, others are summarised, but the majority are simply listed. *Halsbury's Statutory
Instruments* is kept up to date through a combination of reissued main volumes and a regular
updating service.

Current Law Monthly Digest/Current Law Year Book

The Current Law series will provide a brief summary of many Statutory Instruments. The *Current
Law Monthly Digest* contains an alphabetical table of Statutory Instruments. The *Current Law Year
Book* has an alphabetical table and a numerical table of Statutory Instruments.

Halsbury's Laws of England and Wales Monthly Review

Halsbury's Laws of England and Wales Monthly Review provides brief summaries of many Statutory Instruments together with an alphabetical Table of Statutory Instruments. At the end of the year, this information is cumulated into the *Halsbury's Laws Annual Abridgment.*

Loose-leaf encyclopaedias

These bring together different types of legal material on a particular topic and will include relevant Statutory Instruments. They are especially useful because they are regularly updated and many of them also include annotations and commentary related to the subject.

Textbooks

Textbooks can be a useful way to locate Statutory Instruments on a particular topic. Even if they don't reprint the Statutory Instrument in full, 'cases and materials' books may give summaries of the key pieces of secondary legislation.

Electronic sources

LexisNexis Butterworths

The legislation section of *LexisNexis Butterworths* contains the updated text of Statutory Instruments currently in force. You can search by keyword, title or SI number or you can browse a chronological list.

Westlaw

The legislation section within *Westlaw* contains amended full text Statutory Instruments and can be searched at a basic or advanced level, by title or keyword. You can also browse an alphabetical or a chronological list of Statutory Instruments to find the one you want.

The OPSI website (www.opsi.gov.uk/stat.htm)

This freely available website contains the original (historical) text of Statutory Instruments from 1987 onwards. Statutory Instruments are grouped first by year and then in number order. You can search the site at a basic or advanced level.

The Statute Law Database (www.statutelaw.gov.uk)

This freely available website contains the original text of Statutory Instruments.

Lawtel

To access Statutory Instruments via *Lawtel*, select the Statutory Instruments option. You can search by title or keyword. *Lawtel* will provide links, where available, to the original (historical) full text version on the OPSI website: coverage goes back to 1984.

JustCite

JustCite will not provide you with the full text of a Statutory Instrument, but will instead point you in the direction of other databases and sources which contain the full text. It is up to you to find out which of these sources you have access to within your institution. Within *JustCite* you should select the 'Legislation' section as this also covers Statutory Instruments. You can search *JustCite* using the title or Statutory Instrument number.

BAILII (www.bailii.org)

BAILII provides full text UK Statutory Instruments from 2002 onwards. The text is taken from the OPSI website, so should be used as an historical source. You can search by title or keyword.

5.2.2 Checking if a Statutory Instrument is still in force

The following list details printed and electronic sources which will tell you the current status of a Statutory Instrument.

Printed sources

Halsbury's Statutory Instruments

Use the main volumes in conjunction with the loose-leaf service binder to get the up to date status of Statutory Instruments. Alternatively, you could check the *Halsbury's Statutory Instrument Citator*, which is an annual citator published as part of the *Halsbury's Statutory Instruments* series. It provides a guide to the current status of Statutory Instruments and is quick and easy to use.

Current Law Legislation Citator

The printed *Current Law Legislation Citator* (part of the Current Law family) provides the current status of a Statutory Instrument and also gives details of any cases where the Statutory Instrument has been judicially considered. Statutory Instruments are listed in chronological order. See Figure 5.9 below for an example of the citator's layout.

Updates to the latest volume of the citator can be found in the *Current Law Statutes* loose-leaf service binder.

SI Citator	
1234 Example Regulations 1993.	– Number, name and year of SI
Reg. 2, amended: SI 94/65 Art. 2	– reg. 2 amended by article 2 of SI number 65 of 1994
Reg. 3, revoked: 1994 c. 23 Sch. 15	– reg. 3 revoked by Schedule 15 of chapter 23 of 1994
Reg. 4. see *R. v. Smith* [1994] C.O.D. 54	– Case judicially considering reg. 4
Reg. 5, C. 1996 c.7 Sch. 4	– reg. 5 consolidated by Schedule 4 of chapter 7 of 1996

Figure 5.9 Current Law Legislation Citator – *Statutory Instruments*

Loose-leaf encyclopaedias

The ease with which these sources can be updated makes them an excellent source for the current status of Statutory Instruments. Check in your library for any loose-leaf encyclopaedias related to your topic.

Electronic sources

LexisNexis Butterworths

The legislation section is updated daily and contains the full amended text of UK Statutory Instruments – see Figure 5.10 below.

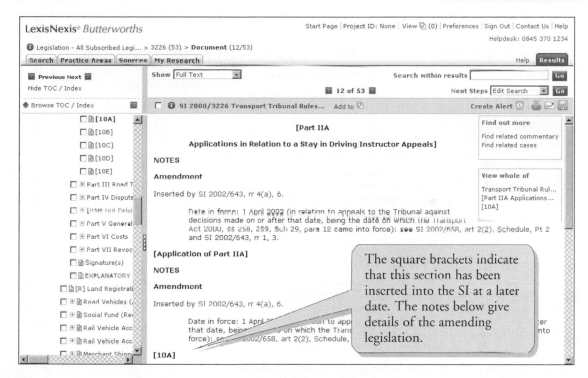

■ *Figure 5.10 LexisNexis Butterworths – Statutory Instruments*

You can access an online version of the *Halsbury's Statutory Instruments Citator*. You can search by keyword, or you can browse a chronological list of Statutory Instruments.

Westlaw

The basic legislation search screen only searches legislation currently in force and includes references to any amending or repealing legislation – see Figure 5.11 overleaf.

UNLOCKING
LEGAL
LEARNING

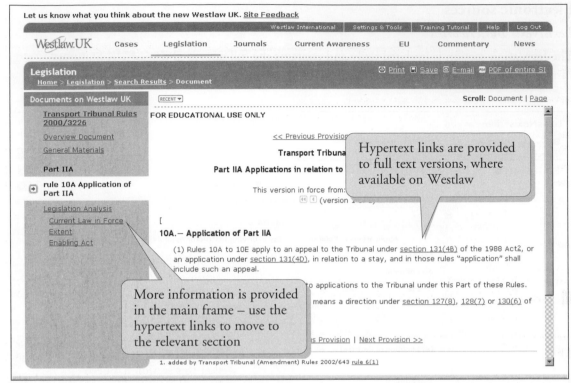

Let us know what you think about the new Westlaw UK. Site Feedback

Westlaw International | Settings & Tools | Training Tutorial | Help | Log Out

Westlaw.UK   Cases   Legislation   Journals   Current Awareness   EU   Commentary   News

Legislation   Print   Save   E-mail   PDF of entire SI
Home > Legislation > Search Results > Document

Documents on Westlaw UK   RECENT ▼   Scroll: Document | Page

Transport Tribunal Rules 2000/3226

Overview Document

General Materials

Part IIA

⊙ rule 10A Application of Part IIA

Legislation Analysis
   Current Law in Force
   Extent
   Enabling Act

FOR EDUCATIONAL USE ONLY

<< Previous Provision

Transport Tribuna

Part IIA Applications in relation to

This version in force from:

(version

[

10A.— Application of Part IIA

(1) Rules 10A to 10E apply to an appeal to the Tribunal under section 131(4B) of the 1988 Act2, or an application under section 131(4D), in relation to a stay, and in those rules "application" shall include such an appeal.

to applications to the Tribunal under this Part of these Rules.

means a direction under section 127(8), 128(7) or 130(6) of

s Provision | Next Provision >>

1. added by Transport Tribunal (Amendment) Rules 2002/643 rule 6(1)

> *Hypertext links are provided to full text versions, where available on Westlaw*

> *More information is provided in the main frame – use the hypertext links to move to the relevant section*

Figure 5.11 UK Statutory Instruments on Westlaw

Lawtel

Lawtel's Statutory Instruments index gives the current status of Statutory Instruments from 1984 onwards and provides references and links to any amending or repealing legislation – see Figure 5.12 opposite.

JustCite

JustCite will tell you the current status of a Statutory Instrument. Select the 'Legislation' option as this covers both primary and secondary legislation – see Figure 5.13 opposite. *JustCite* will not provide the full text of a Statutory Instrument, but will direct you to other electronic resources where the full text is available. Check within your library to see which of these sources you can access.

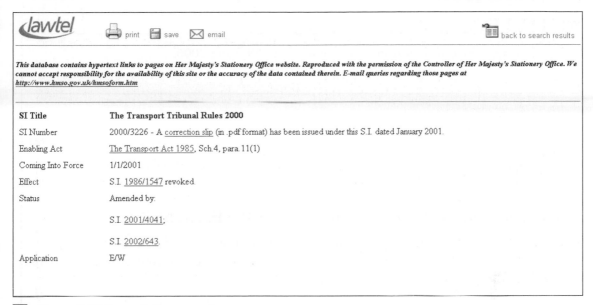

Figure 5.12 Lawtel's Statutory Instruments

Figure 5.13 JustCite's Statutory Instruments

ACTIVITY

> How many Statutory Instruments were made in 2005 and 2006?
> *Tip: Use the OPSI website www.opsi.gov.uk/stat.htm*

The answers are in the Appendix on page 306.

5.3 Parliamentary Bills

5.3.1 Finding out about Bills before Parliament

There are many different sources you can use to find the text of Bills and to track their progress before Parliament. This list contains some of the major ones, so check in your own library to find out which of these sources/databases you can access.

Printed sources

Current Law Monthly Digest

The *Current Law Monthly Digest* is an excellent current awareness tool. It contains a 'Progress of Bills' section for Bills before Parliament during the current parliamentary session. See Figure 5.14 for an example.

PROGRESS OF BILLS

The following Bills are those of the 2003–04 session. This statement is complete to **May 10, 2004**. Government Bills are in bold. *Lords* or *Commons* denotes the House in which the bill originated (Stages and dates in italics are provisional only.)

Bill	Parliamentary Progress
Age-Related Payments (*Commons*).	Commons, first reading, April 22, 2004. (*Second reading, May 12, 2004*).
Air Traffic Emissions Reduction (*Lords*).	Lords, passed. Commons first reading, No date. (*Second reading, no date*).
Armed Forces (Pensions and Compensation) (*Commons*).	Commons, Remaining Stages, May 6, 2004.
Arms Trade (*Commons*).	Commons, first reading, May 5, 2004. (*Second reading, July 16, 2004*).
Assisted Dying for the Terminally Ill (*Lords*).	Lords, Second reading, March 10, 2004. (*Committee, July 7, 2004*).
Asylum and Immigration (Treatment of Claimants, etc) (*Commons*).	Commons, passed. Lords, Committee Stage, April 26, 27 & 28 & May 4, 2004. (*Report Stage, May 18, 2004*).
Balance Charitable Foundation for Unclaimed Assets (Allocation) (*Commons*).	Commons, first reading, May 6, 2004. (*Second reading, June 18, 2004*).
Cardiac Risk in the Young (Screening) (*Commons*).	Commons, Bill withdrawn.
Carers (Equal Opportunities) (*Commons*).	Commons, Committee, March 10, 2004. (*Report Stage, May 14, 2004*).
Child Trust Funds (*Commons*).	Commons, passed. Lords, third reading May 4, 2004.
Children (*Lords*).	Lords, Committee Stage, May 4 & 6, 2004. (*Committee, May 20, 2004*).
Christmas Day (Trading) (*Commons*).	Commons, Second reading, March 26, 2004. (*Committee, No date*).
Civil Contingencies (*Commons*).	Commons, Committee, January 27 & 29 & February 3, 5 & 10, 2004. (*Report Stage, no date*).
Civil Partnership (*Lords*).	Lords, second reading, April 22, 2004. (*Committee, May 10, 12, & 17, 2004*).
Civil Service (*Commons*).	Commons, first reading, January 12, 2004. (*Second reading, May 14, 2004*).
Civil Service (No 2) (*Lords*).	Lords, Committee, March 26, 2004. (*Report Stage, May 13, 2004*).
Companies (Audit, Investigations and Community Enterprise) (*Lords*).	Lords, passed. Motion for approval, March 22, 2004. (*Report Stage, No date*).
Constitution for the European Union (Referendum) (*Commons*).	Commons, first reading, January 7, 2004. (*Second reading, June 18, 2004*).
Constitutional Reform (*Lords*).	Lords, Committee, April 1, 20, 22, 27 & 29, 2004.
Corporate Killing (*Commons*).	Commons, first reading, March 30, 2004. (*Second reading, May 21, 2004*).
Criminal Justice (Justifiable Conduct) (*Commons*).	Commons, first reading, January 12, 2004. (*Second reading, May 14, 2004*).
Crown Employment (Nationality) (*Commons*).	Commons, first reading, January 20, 2004. (*Second reading, May 14, 2004*).
Dolphins and other Cetaceans Protection (*Commons*).	Commons, first reading, March 31, 2004. (*Second reading, October 15, 2004*).
Domestic Energy Efficiency (*Commons*).	Commons, first reading, May 4, 2004. (*Second reading, July 16, 2004*).

Figure 5.14 Progress of Bills from Current Law Monthly Digest

Halsbury's Laws of England and Wales Monthly Review

Another current awareness service, this records the progress of Bills through Parliament in its Parliament section. It also includes summaries of new Bills.

PARLIAMENT

04/1535   Bills in Progress

The following is a list of Public Bills for England and Wales before Parliament this session. The list shows the state of progress as at 26 June 2004. Private Members' Bills are marked ★ and are not included until read a second time. A brief summary of each new Bill appears below.

Title of Bill	*Stage*
Age-related Payments	Passed the Commons, Lords, first reading, 9.6.2004
★Air Traffic Emissions Reduction (see REVIEW para 04/575)	Lords, third reading, 29.3.2004
★Assisted Dying for the Terminally Ill (see REVIEW para 04/870)	Lords, second reading, 10.3.2004
Armed Forces (Pensions and Compensation)	Passed the Commons, Lords, second reading, 10.6.2004

Figure 5.15 Bills in Progress from Halsbury's Laws of England Monthly Review

The Stationery Office Daily List – www.tsoshop.co.uk

This publication contains information about the progress of Bills before Parliament. *The Stationery Office Daily List* is available in print (often cumulated into a weekly publication) and is also available via The Stationery Office's online bookshop.

Electronic sources

LexisNexis Butterworths

Within the legislation section of *LexisNexis Butterworths*, is a subsection called Bill Tracker. You can search for a Bill here and the database will tell you which stages it has cleared so far, with the dates.

Lawtel

The *Lawtel* database has a section on parliamentary Bills which lists the progress of Bills so far. A useful feature of *Lawtel* is that it provides links to the UK Parliament website, so you can link straight to the text of the Bill or to discussions at the various committee stages.

UK Parliament website – www.parliament.uk/business/bills_and_legislation.cfm

The UK Parliament website has a page dedicated to Bills before parliament, covering Bills of all types. From this page, you can link to the Bill Index database (bills.parliament.uk/AC.asp) which lists all the various stages reached by a Bill so far and provides links to *Hansard* debates and other relevant reports and documents.

The House of Commons Weekly Information Bulletin – www.parliament.the-stationery-office.co.uk/pa/cm/cmwib.htm

The Weekly Information Bulletin covers the recent and forthcoming business of the House of Commons, plus some coverage of the House of Lords. You can use this site not only to check what has happened to a Bill but also to find out when the next reading is likely to take place.

5.4 Case law

In Chapter 4 we looked at how case law is made and how a case citation is constructed. Now let's move on to look at how to locate a law report for a particular case, or how to find out which law reports series have reported the case you want.

There are both printed and electronic sources which you can use to look up case citations and we will look at both kinds. It is important that you know about both kinds of sources, because even if you prefer to use electronic sources wherever possible, there may be times when your favourite database is unavailable and you need to refer to printed sources instead.

When you are searching for cases, you need to consider what information you have about the case you are looking for (do you know the names of the parties involved or do you just know what the case was about?), as this could affect the resource you use to locate it, particularly when using printed sources.

The next section will suggest some of the major sources for locating case law and highlight any particular strengths or weaknesses. Remember to check within your own library to see which printed sources it stocks and which electronic databases you are able to access.

5.4.1 Finding cases by name

If you know the names of both parties involved in the case (eg *Donoghue v Stevenson*) then you should consult one of the following sources.

Printed sources

Current Law Case Citator

The *Current Law Case Citator* series is published by Sweet & Maxwell and is best described as an alphabetical index of cases by appellant.

The *Current Law Case Citator* is available as a series of volumes which date from 1947 onwards. If you know the date of your case, as well as the party names, then you simply need to select the index containing that date and look up the case. When you don't know the year in which your case was reported then you will need to check all the citators starting with 1947, until you find it.

NOTE

The appellant is the first of the two parties and may sometimes also be referred to as the plaintiff. In the case of *Donoghue v Stevenson*, Donoghue is the appellant. The second party, Stevenson, is known as the defendant.

☐ ☐ ☐

Figure 5.16 below gives you an example of a *Current Law Case Citator* reference.

Crest Homes Plc *v.* Marks [1987] A.C. 829; [1987] 3 W.L.R. 293; [1987] 2 All E.R. 1074;
  [1988] R.P.C. 21; (1987) 84 L.S.G. 2362; (1987) 137 N.L.J. 662; (1987) 131 S.J.
  1003, HL; affirming [1987] 3 W.L.R. 48; [1987] F.S.R. 305; (1987) 84 L.S.G. 2048;
  (1987) 137 N.L.J. 318, CA . . . . *Digested,* 87/**2885**:
                    Applied, 88/2837, 91/2858, 93/3212, 93/4265, 96/5659, 98/471, 01/554:
                                Considered; 88/2833, 92/3475, 93/3211, 96/762:
                        Distinguished, 96/689; 00/309: *Followed,* 97/465, 99/321

■ *Figure 5.16 A* Current Law Case Citator *reference*

Let's use the *Crest Homes v Marks* case from Figure 5.16 as an example. As you'll remember from our earlier look at case law, it is common for cases to be reported in more than one series. *Crest Homes Plc v Marks* is a good example of this as it has been reported in the *Law Reports Appeal Cases*, the *Weekly Law Reports*, the *Solicitors Journal*, the *All England Law Reports* and more besides.

Your Law Library should stock at least one of these series, so check your own library catalogue to find out which ones are available to you. If your library stocks more than one of the series, then remember the hierarchy of cases as described in 4.5.6 in the previous chapter. In the *Crest Homes* example, the *Law Reports Appeal Cases* version ([1987] AC 829) is the most authoritative report.

Strengths	The printed *Current Law Case Citators* are very quick and easy to use. A table of abbreviations is included at the beginning of each volume.
Weaknesses	As it lists cases in order of appellant, you need to know this name to be able to use it. If you only know the defendant's name then you will need to consult one of the electronic sources.

Current Law Monthly Digest

The *Current Law Monthly Digest* is another member of the Sweet & Maxwell Current Law family. As its name suggests, it provides a monthly summary of legal happenings and is a very useful tool to use to keep yourself up to date with current events. If you are looking for a recent case (ie within the last year) then you will need to check the *Current Law Monthly Digest*. It will provide the same information as the *Current Law Case Citator* and eventually the cases will be cumulated into the *Current Law Case Citator*.

Malekshad v. Howard de Walden Estates Ltd (No.1)   [2002] UKHL 49. [2003] 1 A.C. 1013, [2003] 1 C.L. 375 . . . . **Mar** 413
MALEWSKI v. EALING LBC   [2003] EWHC 763, 89 Con. L.R. 1 . . . . **May** 409
Malik v. Bank of Credit and Commerce International SA (In Liquidation)   [1998] A.C. 20, [1997] C.L.Y. 2192 . . . . **Feb** 181, 311
MALLIA v. ISLINGTON LBC   [Ex rel.] . . . . **Jan** 40
Malloch v. Aberdeen Corp (No.1)   [1971] 1 W.L.R. 1578, [1971] C.L.Y. 12835 . . . . **Feb** 60
MALLONE v. BPB INDUSTRIES PLC see MALLONE v. BPB INDUSTRIES LTD
MALLUSK COLD STORAGE LTD v. DEPARTMENT OF FINANCE AND PERSONNEL; sub nom. ANGLO BEEF PROCESSORS LTD
    v. DEPARTMENT OF FINANCE AND PERSONNEL   [2003] R.A. 370 . . . . **Apr** 388
MAN NUTZFAHRZEUGE AG v. ERNST & YOUNG   [2003] EWHC 2245, [2004] P.N.L.R. 19 . . . . **May** 53
Mannai Investment Co Ltd v. Eagle Star Life Assurance Co Ltd [1997] A.C. 749, [1997] C.L.Y. 3256 . . . . **Apr** 311
Mannai Investment Co Ltd v. Eagle Star Life Assurance Co Ltd   [1997] A.C. 749, [1997] C.L.Y. 3256 . . . . **Feb** 339; **Mar** 292
MANX ELECTRICITY AUTHORITY v. JP MORGAN CHASE BANK   [2003] B.L.R. 477 . . . . **May** 87
MAPAH v. SECRETARY OF STATE FOR THE HOME DEPARTMENT see R. (ON THE APPLICATION OF MAPAH) v. SECRETARY
    OF STATE FOR THE HOME DEPARTMENT
MARCIC v. THAMES WATER UTILITIES LTD   [2003] UKHL 66, [2003] 3 W.L.R. 1603 . . . . **Mar** 364
MARIE BRIZARD ET ROGER INTERNATIONAL SA v. WILLIAM GRANT & SONS LTD (NO.2); MARIE BRIZZARD ET ROGER
    INTERNATIONAL SA, PETITIONER (NO.2) see MARIE BRIZZARD ET ROGER INTERNATIONAL SA v. WILLIAM GRANT & SONS
    LTD (NO.2)
Markass Car Hire Ltd v. Cyprus (51591/99)   (Unreported, November 6, 2002) . . . . **May** 118
MARKEM CORP v. ZIPHER LTD (NO.1)   [2004] R.P.C. 10 . . . . **May** 335
MARKEM CORP v. ZIPHER LTD (NO.2)   [2004] R.P.C. 11 . . . . **May** 52
Marley v. Mutual Security Merchant Bank & Trust Co Ltd   [1991] 3 All E.R. 198, [1991] C.L.Y. 1730 . . . . **Feb** 522
Marsden's Estate, Re   (1889) L.R. 40 Ch. D. 475 . . . . **Mar** 44
MARSH v. SOFAER   [2003] EWHC 3334 . . . . **Apr** 317
Marshall (Inspector of Taxes) v. Kerr   [1995] 1 A.C. 148, [1994] C.L.Y. 359 . . . . **Feb** 382
Marshall v. NM Financial Management Ltd   [1997] 1 W.L.R. 1527 . . . . **Feb** 182
MARSHALL v. RENNOCKS   [Ex rel.] . . . . **May** 402
MARTIN (ANTHONY EDWARD), RE; MARTIN (ANTHONY EDWARD), RE; R. (ON THE APPLICATION OF MARTIN) v. PAROLE
    BOARD see R. (ON THE APPLICATION OF MARTIN) v. SECRETARY OF STATE FOR THE HOME DEPARTMENT
MARTIN v. MCINNES see MARTIN v. MCGUINESS
MARTIN v. N (A CHILD)   2004 S.L.T. 249 . . . . **Apr** 562
MARTIN v. SOUTH BANK UNIVERSITY (C4/01)   [2004] 1 C.M.L.R. 15   . . . . **May** 191
MARTIN v. UNITED KINGDOM (63608/00)   The Times, February 26, 2004 . . . . **Apr** 251
MARTYN ROSE LTD v. AKG GROUP LTD see WAKE+WALKER v. AKG GROUP LTD
MARUBENI HONG KONG AND SOUTH CHINA LTD v. MINISTRY OF FINANCE OF MONGOLIA see MARUBENI HONG KONG AND
    SOUTH CHINA LTD v. MONGOLIA (JURISDICTION)
Maryland Estates Ltd v. Joseph   [1999] 1 W.L.R. 83, [1998] C.L.Y. 3634 . . . . **Apr** 312
MASON v. TOTALFINAELF UK LTD   [2003] EWHC 1604, [2003] 3 E.G.L.R. 91 . . . . **May** 365
Massey v. Boulden   [2002] EWCA Civ 1634, [2003] 1 W.L.R. 1792, [2003] 1 C.L. 477 . . . . **May** 480
MATHER SEAL/FRESH GROUND FOR OPPOSITION (T131/01)   [2003] E.P.O.R. 50 . . . . **Mar** 302
MATTILA v. COUNCIL OF THE EUROPEAN UNION (C353/01 P)   [2004] 1 C.M.L.R. 32 . . . . **Apr** 150
MAUD v. CASTLE POINT BC see R. (ON THE APPLICATION OF MAUD) v. CASTLE POINT BC
Max.Mobil Telekommunikation Service GmbH v. Commission of the European Communities (T54/99)   [2002] E.C.R. II-313,
    [2002] C.L.Y. 1540 . . . . **Feb** 67
Mayne v. Ministry of Agriculture, Fisheries and Food   [2001] E.H.L.R. 5, [2000] C.L.Y. 2338 . . . . **Feb** 208
MCAULEY v. MULHOLLAND see MCAULEY v. BROWN
MCAULEY, PETITIONER see MCAULEY v. HIGHLAND COUNCIL
McCall's Entertainments (Ayr) Ltd v. South Ayrshire Council (No.1)   1998 S.L.T. 1403, [1999] C.L.Y. 6324 . . . . . . **Feb** 638
McCann v. United Kingdom (A/324)   [1996] 21 E.H.R.R. 97, [1995] C.L.Y. 2665 . . . . **Apr** 5
McCathey v. Patriotic Investment Society Ltd (In Liquidation)   1910 1 S.L.T. 121 . . . . **Apr** 544
McColl v. Listing Officer   [2001] EWHC Admin 712, [2001] R.A. 342, [2002] C.L.Y. 3156 . . . . **Jan** 262
McCONDICHIE v. MAINS MEDICAL CENTRE   2004 Rep. L.R. 4 . . . . **May** 760
McConnell v. McConnell   1997 Fam. L.R. 108 . . . . **Mar** 583
MCCORMACK v. DPP see R. (ON THE APPLICATION OF MCCORMACK) v. DPP
McCORMACK v. TOPHAM [Ex rel.] . . . . **Jan** 291
MCDONALD v. PROCURATOR FISCAL, ELGIN see MCDONALD v. DICKSON
McDONNELL v. CONGREGATION OF CHRISTIAN BROTHERS TRUSTEES (FORMERLY IRISH CHRISTIAN BROTHERS)   [2003]
    UKHL 63, [2003] 3 W.L.R. 1627 . . . . **Feb** 45
MCDOUGALL v. SPEIRS see MCDOUGALL v. SPIERS
McDyer v. Celtic Football & Athletic Co Ltd (No.1)   2000 S.C. 379, [2000] C.L.Y. 6599 . . . . **Feb** 658
McFarlane v. Tayside Health Board   [2000] 2 A.C. 59, [2000] C.L.Y. 6162 . . . . **Mar** 132
McGhee v. National Coal Board   [1973] 1 W.L.R. 1, [1972] C.L.Y. 2356 . . . . **May** 404
McGINTY v. CORNWELL PARKER PLC   [Ex rel.] . . . . **Mar** 395
McGlennon v. Chief Constable of Cumbria   [2002] I.C.R. 1156, [2002] C.L.Y. 1415 . . . . **Jan** 316

For full case references see the *Current Law Case Citator*

Figure 5.17 Current Law Monthly Digest *from Sweet & Maxwell*

Strengths	Excellent printed source for recent cases.
Weaknesses	Cases are listed by appellant, so you won't be able to use it if you only know the name of the defendant.

Indexes to individual law reports series

Many law reports series produce their own indexes to the cases that they contain. An alphabetical table of cases covered will tell you where to find a full version of your case.

Strengths	Quick and easy to use.
Weaknesses	Only cover cases reported in that particular law reports series, so you may need to consult more than one index. In alphabetical order by appellant, so you need to know the names of both parties involved.

Halsbury's Laws of England and Wales

Halsbury's Laws of England and Wales has a Consolidated Table of Cases volume which refers to cases mentioned in the main volumes of *Halsbury's Laws*. Although the main volumes will not provide the full text of these cases, they should provide you with citations so you can track down a full version using another source.

Strengths	Also covers Commonwealth cases and older cases.
Weaknesses	Cases are listed by appellant, so you won't be able to use it if you only know the name of the defendant.

Electronic sources

Westlaw

To locate cases on *Westlaw*, select the Cases tab from the menu at the top of the screen. The basic search facility allows you to search by term, by party name or by citation (see Figure 5.18). The advanced search facility offers a more structured search screen which allows you to search using any combination of subject, legislation cited, case cited, court or date (see Figure 5.19). Alternatively, you can browse lists of case analysis documents, law reports and transcripts.

Your search results will be presented to you in brief, with a link to the Case Analysis document (an overview of the case and its history) and, where available on *Westlaw*, a link to the full text law report. See Figure 5.20.

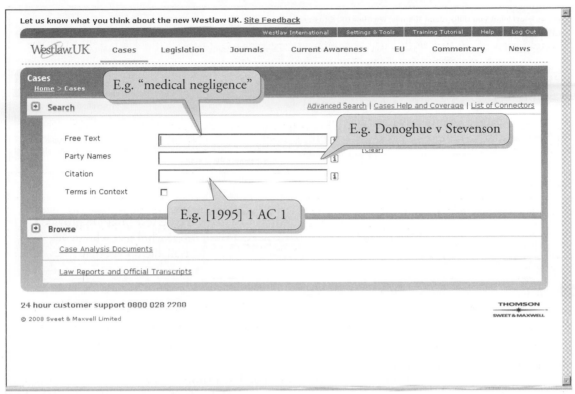

Figure 5.18 *Basic case searching on Westlaw*

Figure 5.19 *Advanced case searching on Westlaw*

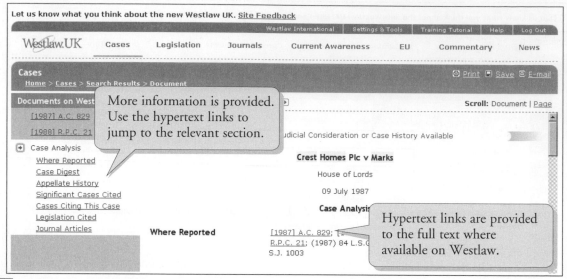

Figure 5.20 *Case analysis result from Westlaw*

Strengths	You don't need to know both parties involved, so if you only know the defendant you can still find your case. The history of the case is all presented on the same screen. You may be able to access the database from off campus. If the case is available on Westlaw in full text, you will be given a link to take you straight to it.
Weaknesses	Will be subject to 'normal' network/internet problems, so there may be times when access is unavailable.

JustCite

JustCite acts as a traditional case citator, providing citations and judicial history information and in addition, it also tells you which electronic services offer the full text. You can then choose a database that you have access to and view the full text. See Figure 5.21.

Figure 5.21 Case search on JustCite

Strengths	You can search by either party name, appellant or defendant. You may be able to access the database from off campus.
Weaknesses	Doesn't provide the full text. Will be subject to 'normal' network/internet problems so there may be times when access is unavailable.

Lawtel

Lawtel is made up of a number of different sections, one of which is Case Law. In the Case Law section, you can search by party name, court, judge or citation – see Figure 5.22 overleaf.

Strengths	You can search by either party name, appellant or defendant. Lawtel provides extensive summaries of cases and in many instances it also provides a link to the case transcript. You may be able to access the database from off campus.
Weaknesses	Can seem complicated to use at first, but definitely worth perserving with.

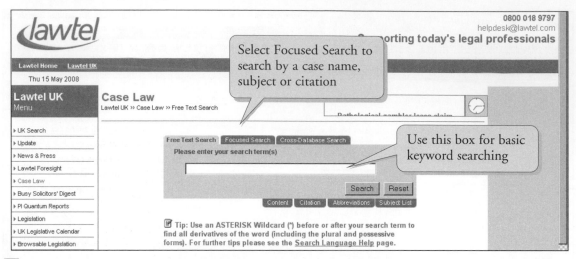

Figure 5.22 Case Law section on Lawtel

LexisNexis Butterworths

The Cases section within *LexisNexis Butterworths* contains case history documents and full text law reports and transcripts. You can search by any combination of keyword, headnote and catchwords, party name, citation, court or judge. Alternatively you can browse individual law reports series. See Figure 5.23.

Strengths	Can be searched by either party name, keyword or citation. Some links to full text are available. May be accessed from off campus.
Weaknesses	When entering a case name, the database does not recognise the 'v' between the parties so you need to type 'and' instead, eg Donoghue and Stevenson.

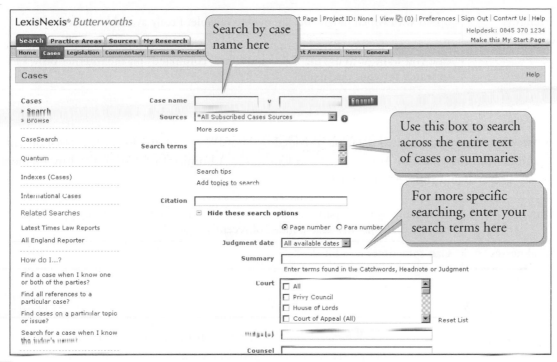

Figure 5.23 Case search options on LexisNexis Butterworths

BAILII (British & Irish Legal Information Institute) www.bailii.org

BAILII is a freely available website which contains case transcripts from courts in England and
Wales and the United Kingdom. The idea behind the website is to bring together legal information
in the public domain and make it available in one place. *BAILII* is based on a similar site which has
been running successfully in Australia for some time (AUSTLII, www.austlii.edu.au – the
Australasian Legal Information Institute).

Strengths	Unrestricted access. Search by either party name, keyword or neutral citation.
Weaknesses	Not comprehensive in coverage so not every case will be available. There can be delays in cases being added to the BAILII database so recent cases may not appear until sometime after the judgment has been given.

The House of Lords website (www.publications.parliament.uk/pa/ld/ldjudgmt.htm)

The House of Lords was quick to see the potential of the Internet and has been making its
judgments available online since November 1996. It aims to have the judgments available online
within two hours of their being delivered in the House of Lords, so you can often access the
judgment on the same day. The text of the judgment is a word for word account of what was said
in the House. On the website, the most recent judgments are displayed first, with the remaining
decisions listed in chronological order by year and then alphabetically.

Strengths	Speed with which judgments are made available. Freely available service.
Weaknesses	Poor search facility. Better options are either to scroll through the page to find the case you want or to use the 'Edit' and 'Find' commands on the internet browser to search for your case name.

Casetrack

Casetrack is a subscription-based database provided by WordWave International. *Casetrack* provides transcripts from the Court of Appeal, the High Court, the Administrative Court, the Employment Appeals Tribunal and the VAT Tribunal.

Strengths	Searchable by either party name, keyword or neutral citation. Off campus access may be available. Browsable index of recent judgments.
Weaknesses	Can sometimes be a bit slow.

ACTIVITY

Look up the case '*Whiston v Whiston*, Court of Appeal, Civil Division, 23 March 1995'. What is this case about? Which database or printed source did you use to find out?

The answers are in the Appendix on page 306.

5.4.2 Finding cases by subject

You may not always be lucky enough to have the name of the case you are looking for but instead you may be looking for any cases to do with a particular subject. This section will recommend printed and electronic sources that can be used to find cases in this way. Where a source has already been described in detail in the previous section, the description will not be repeated.

Printed sources

The Digest

Published by LexisNexis Butterworths, *The Digest* contains summaries of over 500,000 cases, as well as citations to direct you to a full text version. *The Digest* is a multi-volume work arranged in subject order, which comes with an extensive subject index to help you find what you're looking for – see Figure 5.24 opposite. There is a *Consolidated Table of Cases*, so you can also use this source to find cases by name. The series is kept up to date by means of reissued main volumes – see Figure 5.25 on page 110 – and a *Cumulative Supplement*.

ANNEXATION
> *See* SEIZURE
> effect of
>> conquered country
>>> articles of pace inviolable **8(2)** *Comwlth* 1563
>> conquered state
>>> contractual liabilities of, to individuals **8(2)** *Comwlth* 1565–1567
>>> financial liabilities of **8(2)** *Comwlth* 1564
> proclamation, necessity for **8(2)** *Comwlth* 1560, 1561

ANNOTATED EDITION
> literary work **13** *Coprt* 654

ANNOYANCE 36(2) *Nuis* 728, 739

ANNOYANCE, COVENANT RESTRAINING
> advertisement across shop front **31(2)** *L&T* 7812
> conversion of dwelling-house into flats **31(2)** *L&T* 7816
> dog show **31(2)** *L&T* 7811
> hospital **31(2)** *L&T* 7809, 7810
> inconvenience **31(2)** *L&T* 7813
> interference with reasonable enjoyment of adjoining premises **31(2)** *L&T* 7808
> interference with reasonable peace of mind **31(2)** *L&T* 7806, 7807
> letting wall to bill-posting company **31(2)** *L&T* 7814
> use of blind for business **31(2)** *L&T* 7813

ANNUAL ALLOWANCE
> car for private and business purposes **28(1)** *Inc T* 998; **28(2)** *Inc T* 2489
> industrial buildings, whether dwelling-houses qualify **28(2)** *Inc T* 3673

Figure 5.24 Subject index from The Digest

Strengths	Detailed subject index. Covers not only English cases but also cases from Scotland, Ireland, Canada, Australia, New Zealand, the Commonwealth and the EC. Its coverage goes back to medieval times so it is also a useful source for historical cases.
Weaknesses	Only a summary is provided so once you have identified a case you will need to consult another source to find the full text.

6 Provision of recreational facilities

LAW See Halsbury's Laws (4th edn) vol 5 para 544–547

STATUTE See RECREATIONAL CHARITIES ACT, 1958 (c 17); 5 Halsbury's Statutes (4th edn) 689

7 Other cases

CROSS REFERENCES See no 2664 ante (bell-ringing to celebrate the Restoration); nos 2694 et seq ante (publication of books)

2916 Reduction of National Debt – Charitable use

Ashton v Langdale (Lord) (1851) 4 De G & Sm 402; 20 LJ Ch 234; 17 LTOS 175; 15 Jur 868; 64 ER 888

ANNOTATIONS **Expld** Thornton v Kempson (1854) Kay 592 **Apprvd & Folld** Alexander v Brame (1861) 30 Beav 153 **Consd** Imperial Mercantile Credit Assocn v Newry & Armagh Ry (1868) 16 WR 1070; Attree v Hawe (1878) 9 Ch D 337; Jervis v Lawrence (1882) 22 Ch D 202 **Dbtd** Re Christmas, Martin v Lacon (1885) 30 Ch D 544

2917 Chancellor of Exchequer – Benefit of country – Valid

Nightingale v Goulbourn (1848) 2 Ph 594; [1843–60] All ER Rep 420; 17 LJ Ch 296; 11 LTOS 169; 12 Jur 317; 41 ER 1072, LC

ANNOTATIONS **Consd** Whicker v Hume (1858) 7 HL Cas 124; Re Tetley, National Provincial & Union Bank of England v Tetley [1923] 1 Ch 258 **Apld** Re Smith, Public Trustee v Smith [1932] 1 Ch 153

2918 Lifeboat – Good as to personalty

Johnston v Swann (1818) 3 Madd 457; 56 ER 573

ANNOTATIONS **Consd** Giblett v Hobson (1834) 5 Sim 651; Ellis v Selby (1836) 1 My & Cr 286 **Apld** Hartshorne v Nicholson (1858) 26 Beav 58 **Expld** Re Holburne, Coates v Mackillop (1885) 53 LT 212 **Dbtd** Re Piercy, Whitwham v Piercy [1898] 1 Ch 565

Figure 5.25 The Digest

Halsbury's Laws of England and Wales

Within its footnotes on a particular subject, *Halsbury's Laws of England and Wales* often refers to relevant cases, with citations to full text versions. *Halsbury's Laws* has a detailed subject index which will help you locate cases on any topic – see Figures 5.26 opposite and 5.27 on page 112.

BANKRUPT – *continued*
 distress for rent – *continued*
   loss of right, **3(2)**, 686
   persons able to distrain, **3(2)**, 693
   preferential debts, charge for, **3(2)**, 690
   restrictions, **3(2)**, 687; **13**, 729
   right of, **3(2)**, 686
   sheriff, claim against, **3(2)**, 689
 documents. *See* books and records *above*
 duties towards trustee, **3(2)**, 345
 dwelling house–
   meaning, **3(2)**, 401n[1]
   application for possession, **3(2)**, 651
   disclaimer of, **3(2)**, 482
   rights of occupation, **3(2)**, 650
   spouse's matrimonial home rights, **3(2)**, 648
 equity of redemption, **32**, 515
 estate of. *See* BANKRUPT'S ESTATE
 examination–
   private. *See* PRIVATE EXAMINATION (BANK-
     RUPTCY)
   public. *See* PUBLIC EXAMINATION (BANK-
     RUPTCY)
 executor, as, **17(2)**, 20
 false statement by, **3(2)**, 716
 falsification of books etc, **3(2)**, 714
 family: meaning, **3(2)**, 216n[8]
 farmer, **3(2)**, 416
 fraudulent dealing with property obtained on credit,
   3(2), 719, 720
 fraudulent disposal of property, **3(2)**, 717
 gambling by, **3(2)**, 723
 gift by, **20(1)**, 14, 62
 gift to or from spouse, passing of, **3(2)**, 427
 goodwill of business–
   passing to trustee, **3(2)**, 424
   sale by trustee, **3(2)**, 458
 income payments order. *See* INCOME PAYMENTS
   ORDER
 insolvency practitioner prohibition, **3(2)**, 701
 insurable interest, **25**, 609
 intellectual property, passing to trustee, **3(2)**, 425

Figure 5.26 Subject index from Halsbury's Laws

Strengths	Detailed subject index. Regularly updated, so can be used to find recent cases. Also useful for tracking down older pre-1865 cases.
Weaknesses	Provides a citation rather than the full text so you will still need to go elsewhere to find the full text.

717. Fraudulent disposal of property. The bankrupt is guilty of an offence if:

(1) he makes or causes[1] to be made, or has in the period of five years ending with the commencement of the bankruptcy[2] made or caused to be made, any gift or transfer of, or any charge on, his property[3]; or

(2) he conceals or removes, or has at any time before commencement of the bankruptcy concealed or removed, any part of his property after, or within two months before, the date on which a judgment or order for the payment of money has been obtained against him, being a judgment or order which was not satisfied before the commencement of the bankruptcy[4].

A person who commits such an offence is liable on conviction on indictment to imprisonment for a term not exceeding two years or a fine, or to both, or on summary conviction to imprisonment for a term not exceeding six months or a fine not exceeding the statutory maximum, or to both[5].

A person is not, however, guilty of such an offence if he proves that, at the time of the conduct constituting the offence, he had no intent to defraud[6] or to conceal the state of his affairs[7].

1   For the meaning of 'cause' see para 713 note 4 ante.
2   As to the commencement of bankruptcy see para 213 ante.
3   For the meaning of references to property comprised in the bankrupt's estate see para 708 note 2 ante. For these purposes, the reference to making a transfer of or charge on any property includes causing or conniving at the levying of any execution against that property: Insolvency Act 1986 s 357(2). 'Conniving' imports knowledge together with acquiescence in the facts constituting the offence. Suspicion may, however, be enough, although mere negligence is not: *Rogers v Rogers* (1830) 3 Hag Ecc 57.
4   Insolvency Act 1986 s 357(1), (3).
5   Ibid ss 350(6), 357(1), (3), 430, Sch 10. For the meaning of 'the statutory maximum' see para 4 ante.
6   See para 708 note 6 ante.
7   Insolvency Act 1986 ss 352, 357(1), (3).

Figure 5.27 Footnotes from Halsbury's Laws

Indexes to individual law reports series

Many individual law reports series produce their own subject indexes. Simply look up the subject you're interested in and you'll be referred to relevant cases that have been published within that particular series.

Strengths	Quick and easy to use.
Weaknesses	Only covers cases reported in a particular law reports series, so you may not always find what you are looking for. If you don't get any results then this does not necessarily mean that there aren't any cases on your subject, but just that there aren't any cases on it reported in that particular series – so try another one.

Textbooks

Don't overlook textbooks as a means of tracking down cases on a particular subject. A textbook on land law, for example, is going to refer to key cases which illustrate specific areas of land law. A textbook is unlikely to reprint the whole case, normally just summarising the main points or including a key paragraph or two, but you should find the case name and citation to enable you to locate a full text version.

Strengths	The author of the textbook has done much of the hard work for you.
Weaknesses	You'll still need to go elsewhere to find the full text of the law report.

Current Law Monthly Digest

The *Current Law Monthly Digest* has a subject index to recent cases. A summary is provided and, where possible, a citation.

Strengths	Good source for locating recent cases.
Weaknesses	Summary only, so you'll need another source to find the full text.

Electronic sources

Westlaw

Strengths	Comprehensive database of case summaries. Westlaw allows you to search by keyword, subject or phrase. Links to the full text, where available within Westlaw, are provided. Off campus access may be available.
Weaknesses	Not all cases will be available in full text within the Westlaw database, so you may have to consult other sources.

LexisNexis Butterworths

Strengths	Search by keyword or phrase. Full text links may be available to other sections of the database. Off-campus access may be available.
Weaknesses	Not all cases will be available in full text within LexisNexis Butterworths, so you may have to consult other sources.

Lawtel

Strengths	Search by keyword or phrase. Extensive summary with citations. Links to transcripts provided where available.
Weaknesses	You will need to consult another source to access a law report of the case, rather than just the transcript.

JustCite

Strengths	Search by keyword or phrase. Indicates where a full text version is available electronically.
Weaknesses	You will need to consult another source to access the full text.

BAILII

Strengths	Transcripts are available.
Weaknesses	The search engine is not as sophisticated as those on subscription-based databases. You can search for a phrase, but you can't specify where that phrase appears, eg in the subject field.

Casetrack

Strengths	Subject, keyword and phrase searching is permitted. You can search for more than one keyword or phrase at a time.
Weaknesses	Will be subject to 'normal' network/internet problems, so there may be times when access is unavailable. Can sometimes be a bit slow.

5.4.3 Finding cases by legislation cited

Printed sources

Current Law Statute Citator

The *Current Law Statute Citator* will refer to cases brought under particular sections of an Act. When you look up the Act you are interested in, you will find relevant cases listed by section – see Figure 5.28 opposite.

Electronic sources

Westlaw

If you want to search for cases by legislation using Westlaw, you need to select cases from the menu at the top of the screen and then select the advanced search option. You can then enter your terms in the 'Legislation Title' search box. You can even add a particular provision in the 'Legislation Provision No.' box, if you want to make your search even more specific – see Figure 5.29 on page 116.

STATUTE CITATOR 1996–1999   **1994**

CAP.   CAP.

1994—cont.   *1994—cont.*

26. Trade Marks Act 1994—*cont.*

s.1—*cont.*

see *BACH and BACH FLOWER REMEDIES Trade Marks* (1999) 96(42) L. S. G. 42 (CA), Morritt, L.J., see *Philips Electronics NV v Remington Consumer Products Ltd* [1998] R.P.C. 283 (Pat Ct), Jacob, J.; see *Swizzels Matlow Ltd's Trade Mark Application, Re* [1998] R.P.C. 244 (TMR), RA Jones

s.3, see *AD2000 Trade Mark, Re* [1997] R.P.C. 168 C, Geoffrey Hobbs Q.C.; see *BACH and BACH FLOWER REMEDIES Trade Marks* [1999] R.P.C 1 (Ch D), Neuberger, J.; see *BACH and BACH FLOWER REMEDIES Trade Marks* (1999) 96(42) L.S.G. 42 (CA), Morritt, L.J.; see *Dualit Ltd's Trade Mark Application (No.2023846)* Times, July 19, 1999 (Ch D), Lloyd, J.; see *FROOT LOOPS Trade Mark, Re* [1998] R.P.C. 240, Simon Thorley Q.C.; see *Philips Electronics NV v Remington Consumer Products Ltd* [1998] R.P.C. 283 (Pat Ct), Jacob, J.; see *POST-PERFECT Trade Mark, Re* [1998] R.P.C. 255, Geoffrey Hobbs Q.C.; see *Procter & Gamble's Trade Mark Application* [1999] E.T.M.R. 375 (CA), Robert Walker, L.J.; see *Swizzels Matlow Ltd's Trade Mark Application, Re* [1998] R.P.C. 244 (TMR), RA Jones; see *Waterford Wedgwood Plc v David Nagli Ltd* [1998] F.S.R. 92 (Ch D), Sir Richard Scott V.C.

s.4, See *AUTOMOTIVE NETWORK EXCHANGE Trade Mark* [1998] R.P.C. 885 C, Geoffrey Hobbs, Q.C.

s.5, see *AUDI-MED Trade Mark* [1999] E.T.M.R. 1010 (TMR), Allan James; see *Oasis Stores Ltd's Trade Mark Application* [1998] R.P.C. 631 (TMR), Allan James; see *POSTPERFECT Trade Mark, Re* [1998] R.P.C. 255, Geoffrey Hobbs Q.C.

s.6, amended: SI 1999/1899 Reg.13

s.9, see *Beautimatic International Ltd v Mitchell International Pharmaceuticals Ltd* [1999] E.T.M.R. 912 (Ch D), Neuberger, J.

s.9, applied: SI 1996/714 Art.4

s.10, see *AUTOMOTIVE NETWORK EXCHANGE Trade Mark* [1998] R.P.C. 885 C, Geoffrey Hobbs, Q.C.; see *Avnet Inc v Isoact Ltd* [1998] F.S.R. 16 (Ch D), Jacob, J.; see *Barclays Bank Plc v RBS Advanta* [1996] R.P.C. 307 (Ch D), Laddie, J.; see *Beautimatic International Ltd v Mitchell International Pharmaceuticals Ltd* [1999] E.T.M.R. 912 (Ch D), Neuberger, J.; see *British Sugar Plc v James Robertson and Sons* [1996] R.P.C. 281 (Ch D), Jacob, J.; see *British Telecommunications Plc v One in a Million Ltd* [1999] 1 W.L.R. 903 (CA), Aldous, L.J.; see *Cable & Wireless Plc v British Telecommunications Plc* [1998] F.S.R. 383 (Ch D), Jacob, J.; see *Emaco Ltd v Dyson Appliances Ltd* [1999] E.T.M.R. 903 (Ch D), Jonathan Parker, J.; see *European Ltd v Economist Newspapers Ltd* [1998] F.S.R. 283 (CA), Millett, L.J.; see *Marks & Spencer Plc v One in a Million Ltd* Times, July 29, 1998 (CA), Aldous, L.J.; see *Vodafone Group Plc v Orange Personal Communications Services Ltd* [1997] F.S.R. 34 (Ch D), Jacob, J.; see *Waterford Wedgwood Plc v David Nagli Ltd* [1998] F.S.R. 92 (Ch D), Sir Richard Scott V.C.

s.10, applied: SI 1996/714 Art.4

26. Trade Marks Act 1994—*cont.*

s.11, see *Allied Domecq Spirits and Wine Ltd v Murray McDavid Ltd* 1998 S.C. 354 (OH), Lord MacFadyen; see *Bravado Merchandising Services Ltd v Mainstream Publishing (Edinburgh) Ltd* [1996] F.S.R. 205 (OH), Lord McCluskey; see *NAD Electronics Inc v NAD Computer Systems Ltd* [1997] F.S.R. 380 (Ch D), Ferris, J.; see *Scandecor Development AB v Scandecor Marketing Ltd* [1998] F.S.R. 500 (Ch D), Lloyd, J.

s.11, applied: SI 1996/714 Art.4

s.12, see *Microsoft Corp v Computer Future Distribution Ltd* [1998] I.T.C.L.R. 88 (Ch D), Rimer, J.

s.12, applied: SI 1996/714 Art.4

s.14, applied: SI 1996/714 Art.4

s.15, applied: SI 1996/714 Art.4

s.16, applied: SI 1996/714 Art.4, SI 1999/929 r.3.5.2

s.17, applied: SI 1996/714 Art.4

s.18, amended: SI 1996/729 Art.2, Sch para.2

s.18, applied: SI 1996/714 Art.4

s.19, amended: SI 1996/729 Art.2, Sch para.3

s.19, applied: SI 1996/714 Art.4, SI 1999/929 r.3.5.2, r.3.5.3

s.19, enabling: SI 1999/929

s.20, applied: SI 1996/714 Art.4

s.20, repealed: SI 1996/729 Art.2, Sch para.4

s.21, see *Prince Plc v Prince Sports Group Inc* [1998] F.S.R 21 (Ch D), Neuberger, J.

s.21, applied: SI 1996/714 Art.4, SI 1996/1908 Reg.4

s.22, applied: SI 1996/714 Art.5

s.23, applied: SI 1996/714 Art.5

s.24, applied: SI 1996/714 Art.5

s.28, applied: SI 1996/714 Art.7

s.29, applied: SI 1996/714 Art.7

s.30, ammended: SI 1996/714 Art.6

s.30, applied: SI 1996/714 Art.7

s.31, amended: SI 1996/714 Art.6

s.31, applied: SI 1996/714 Art.7

s.32, amended: SI 1996/714 Art.3

s.33, amended: SI 1996/714 Art.3

s.34, amended: SI 1996/714 Art.3

s.34, enabling: SI 1998/925

s.35, applied: SI 1996/714 Art.8

s.37, see *AUDI-MED Trade Mark* [1999] E.T.M.R. 1010 (TMR), Allan James; see *POSTPERFECT Trade Mark, Re* [1998] R.P.C. 255, Geoffrey Hobbs Q.C.

s.37, applied: SI 1996/714 Art.20

s.38, see *AUDI-MED Trade Mark* [1999] E.T.M.R. 1010 (TMR), Allan James

s.38, applied: SI 1996/714 Art.20

s.38, enabling: SI 1998/925

s.39, applied: SI 1996/714 Art.8

s.41, see *Interlego AG's Trade Mark Applications, Re* [1998] R.P.C. 69 (Ch D), Neuberger, J.

s.41, enabling: SI 1998/925

s.43, applied: SI 1996/1908 Reg.3

s.43, enabling: SI 1998/925

s.45, applied: SI 1996/1908 Reg.3

s.46, see *United Biscuits (UK) Ltd v Asda Stores Ltd* (1997) R.P.C. 513 (Ch D), Robert Walker, J.

s.46, applied: SI 1996/714 Art.13, SI 1996/1908 Reg.3

s.47, see *DUCATI Trade Mark* [1998] R.P.C. 227 (TMR), SJ Probert

■ *Figure 5.28* Current Law Statute Citator

2837. Discovery – use of documents – Anton Piller order – committal proceedings
[Civil Evidence Act 1968 (c.64), s.14]
S.14 of the 1968 Act does not extend to proceeding for committal for contempt of court.
G. sued two companies for wrongful dismissal, arrears of salary and an account of profits. She obtained a Mareva injunction, and later an Anton Piller order covering documents which might be used in proceedings for committal for contempt of the Mareva injunction. Th... *The reference to our original case* ...obtained subject to a requirement that leave be obtained befo...
Held, on G... of the Civil Evidence Act di...not apply to proce... *The name of the case which has applied the decision from Crest Homes v Marks* ...0) 15 Ch.D. 435 and *Crest Homes v Marks* [198... ...ing M.R. in *Comet Products U.K. v Hawkex Plas*... ...971] C.L.Y. 9083 applied).
GARVIN v. DOMUS PUBLISHING [1988] 3 W.L.R. 344, Walton, J.

Figure 5.33 Excerpt from the Current Law Year Book 1988

Put simply, **applied** means that the court has applied the principle of law of an earlier case (*Crest Homes v Marks*) in a subsequent case (*Garvin v Domus Publishing*).

NOTE

In the example in Figure 5.33 above, the annotating case is *Garvin v Domus Publishing* and the annotated case is *Crest Homes v Marks*.

5.5 Using secondary sources

5.5.1 Using *Halsbury's Laws of England* in print

Halsbury's Laws of England is a loose-leaf legal encyclopaedia that aims to provide a 'restatement of the whole of the laws of England and Wales'. It is available in print and online versions and how you search it depends on which version you are using.

The main volumes of *Halsbury's Laws* are arranged alphabetically by broad subject areas such as agriculture, animals or children and young persons. The legal definitions are provided in numbered paragraphs and every statement is backed up with a footnote which provides the authority for that statement, such as a Statute, Statutory Instrument or law report.

131. Offences. Any person who knowingly contravenes any prohibition or fails to comply with any duty or requirement imposed by or under the provisions relating to travel restrictions[1] is guilty of an offence and liable on summary conviction to imprisonment for a term not exceeding three months or a fine not exceeding level 4 on the standard scale, or to both[2].

1 ie the provisions contained in the Prevention of Terrorism (Temporary Provisions) Act 1989 s 16(1), Sch 5: see paras 121–130 ante.
2 Ibid Sch 5 para 11. For the meaning of 'the standard scale' see para 808 post.

F. TERRORIST INVESTIGATIONS

132. Search for material other than excluded or special procedure material. On an application made by a constable, a justice of the peace may issue a warrant if satisfied that a terrorist investigation[1] is being carried out and that there are reasonable grounds for believing:

(1) that there is material on premises[2] specified in the application which is likely to be of substantial value, whether by itself or together with other material, to the investigation;

(2) that the material does not consist of or include items subject to legal privilege[3], excluded material[4] or special procedure material[5]; and

(3) that any of the specified conditions are fulfilled[6].

The specified conditions are:

(a) that it is not practicable to communicate with any person entitled to grant entry to the premises;

(b) that it is practicable to communicate with such a person but it is not practicable to communicate with any person entitled to grant access to the material;

(c) that entry to the premises will not be granted unless a warrant is produced;

(d) that the purpose of a search may be frustrated or seriously prejudiced unless a constable arriving at the premises can secure immediate entry to them[7].

A warrant so issued authorises a constable to enter the premises specified and to search the premises and any person found there and to seize and retain anything found there or on any such person, other than items subject to legal privilege, if he has reasonable grounds for believing:

(i) that it is likely to be of substantial value, whether by itself or together with other material, to the investigation; and

(ii) that it is necessary to seize it in order to prevent it being concealed, lost, damaged, altered or destroyed[8].

1 'Terrorist investigation' means any investigation to which the Prevention of Terrorism (Temporary Provisions) Act 1989 s 17(1) applies: s 17(1), Sch 7 para 1.

For the purposes of s 17, 'terrorist investigation' means (1) an investigation into (a) the commission, preparation or instigation of acts of terrorism to which s 14, applies (see para 118 ante); or (b) any other act which appears to have been done in furtherance of, or in connection with, such acts of terrorism, including any act which appears to constitute an offence under s 2 (see para 111 ante), s 9 (see para 115 ante), s 10 (see para 114 ante) or s 11 (see para 116 ante) or the Northern Ireland (Emergency Provisions) Act 1978 s 21; or (c) without prejudice to head (b) supra, the resources of a proscribed organisation within the meaning of the Prevention of Terrorism (Temporary Provisions) Act 1989 s 1 (see para 111 note 1 ante) or a proscribed organisation for the purposes of the Northern Ireland (Emergency Provisions) Act 1978 s 21 (see para 114 note 2 ante); and (2) an investigation into whether there are grounds justifying the making of an order under the Prevention of Terrorism (Temporary Provisions) Act 1989 s 1(2)(a) or the Northern Ireland (Emergency Provisions) Act 1978 s 21(4): Prevention of Terrorism (Temporary Provisions) Act 1989 s 17(1).

Figure 5.34 Excerpt from Halsbury's Laws of England

5.5.2 Using the online version of *Halsbury's Laws of England*

As well as the normal benefits that electronic access has over hard copy, such as 24-hour access and not physically having to be in the library, the online version of *Halsbury's Laws* has the added benefit of presenting all the relevant information on one screen. You can see at a glance which text is taken from the main volume and which comes from the *Cumulative Supplement* or *Noter-Up Service*, without having to juggle three separate volumes – see Figure 5.37 below. The numbering system for the online *Halsbury's Laws* is the same as for the printed version, so the same subject volume and paragraph numbers are used. This means that you can refer to a section of *Halsbury's Laws* in an essay by volume and paragraph number and your tutor will be able to find it using either the printed or electronic versions.

You can search the database by keyword or you can browse the individual subject volumes.

Figure 5.37 Halsbury's Laws *online*

ACTIVITY

> Using *Halsbury's Laws* (either in print or online via LexisNexis Butterworths), find out what the punishment is for possessing a live badger.

The answer is in the Appendix on page 307.

5.5.3 Finding journal articles

In Section 4.6.2 we looked at why journal articles are valuable, so now let's look at how to track them down. Most library catalogues will tell you which journals are in stock within the library but they are unlikely to tell you which articles have appeared in the individual issues. To find that level of information you need to consult an abstracting and indexing service or database.

Legal Journals Index

The *Legal Journals Index*, published by Sweet & Maxwell, is the most comprehensive index to UK law journals. It covers over 400 law journal titles and also incorporates the *European Legal Journals Index* to give more extensive coverage. It is available in print and also in electronic format via the *Westlaw* database.

> ## NOTE
>
> Finding a reference to a journal article by using an indexing service or database that your library subscribes to does not necessarily mean that your library will stock the relevant journal. These services are commercially produced and cover many relevant journals in their particular field, so they will tell you what has been written about a topic, regardless of whether those journals are available in your library. When you have identified relevant articles in this way you must then search your own library catalogue to see if your library holds the individual journals.

Using the printed version

The printed version of the *Legal Journals Index* has a subject index, author index, case index, legislation index and book review index. Information provided in the *Legal Journals Index* consists of the titles of relevant articles, the author(s), the bibliographic details (ie the year, volume, issue and page numbers) and a brief summary. It will not provide the full text of an article but it will direct you to where the full text is available.

Using the electronic version via Westlaw

The *Legal Journals Index* is also available through the *Westlaw* database and the electronic version has many advantages. It is quick and easy to use and can be searched at a basic or advanced level, but the major advantage that it has over the printed index is that it provides links to full text articles also on *Westlaw*. *Westlaw* contains a number of law journal titles in full text, so hypertext links are provided to these from the *Legal Journals Index* – see Figure 5.38 overleaf.

ACTIVITY

> Using the *Legal Journals Index* (either in print or online via *Westlaw*), find out how many articles have been written about the case 'Savage v Fairclough'.

Compare your answer with that in the Appendix on page 307.

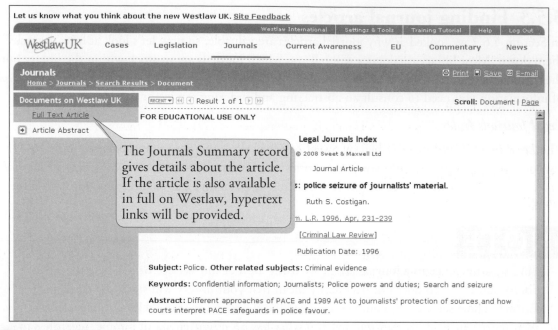

Let us know what you think about the new Westlaw UK. Site Feedback

Westlaw.UK   Cases   Legislation   Journals   Current Awareness   EU   Commentary   News

Westlaw International   Settings & Tools   Training Tutorial   Help   Log Out

Journals   Print Save E-mail
Home > Journals > Search Results > Document

Documents on Westlaw UK   RECENT ◄◄ ◄ Result 1 of 1 ► ►►   Scroll: Document | Page

Full Text Article   FOR EDUCATIONAL USE ONLY

Article Abstract

> The Journals Summary record gives details about the article. If the article is also available in full on Westlaw, hypertext links will be provided.

Legal Journals Index

© 2008 Sweet & Maxwell Ltd

Journal Article

s: police seizure of journalists' material.

Ruth S. Costigan.

m. L.R. 1996, Apr, 231-239

[Criminal Law Review]

Publication Date: 1996

Subject: Police. **Other related subjects:** Criminal evidence

Keywords: Confidential information; Journalists; Police powers and duties; Search and seizure

Abstract: Different approaches of PACE and 1989 Act to journalists' protection of sources and how courts interpret PACE safeguards in police favour.

Figure 5.38 The Legal Journals Index *on Westlaw*

Lawtel

The *Lawtel* database contains an Articles Index. This index is not as extensive as the *Legal Journals Index*, covering just some 75 titles at the time of writing, but it does have some points to recommend it. First, *Lawtel*'s Articles Index includes the legal sections of broadsheet newspapers, which can be useful for current topics or if you want to get a media perspective on a subject. Second, where an article summary refers to a case or piece of legislation, *Lawtel* provides hypertext links, where available, to other sections of the database so you can read more about the case or Statute mentioned.

Index to Legal Periodicals & Books

Published by HW Wilson, this is a particularly useful source for locating US and international law journal articles, while still covering a significant number of UK titles. The *Index to Legal Periodicals & Books* is available in both print and electronic formats and searching is by author, subject, case name or legislation. If you are able to access the electronic version of this index, then you can take advantage of the 200 law journal titles available on it in full text.

Current Law Monthly Digest

The *Current Law Monthly Digest* contains information about recently published articles, so can be useful for current research. Articles are indexed according to their subject.

Halsbury's Laws of England Monthly Review

Similar to the *Current Law Monthly Digest*, *Halsbury's Laws Monthly Review* contains details of very recently published UK articles.

Index to Periodical Articles Related to Law

Published by Glanville Publishers Inc, this index covers articles that are about legal topics, but which have appeared in non-law journals. If you have access to this index then you may find it a useful one to consult to get a wider perspective on a particular topic.

Index to Foreign Legal Periodicals

Published by The University of California Press, this service indexes articles from over 400 legal periodicals. Foreign is defined as not the UK, USA, Canada or Australia, so if you are researching the legal system in France or Germany then this would be a useful source to choose. It should be pointed out, however, that although the index is published in English, many of the articles referred to will be published in their original languages.

Current Law Index

Published by The Gale Group, the *Current Law Index* is another extensive index covering journals from the USA, UK, Ireland, Canada, New Zealand and Australia. In total, it indexes over 900 titles and is available in print and electronic formats. The printed version has a subject index, an author/title index, a Table of Cases and a Table of Statutes, while the electronic version will allow basic and more advanced searches to be constructed.

British Humanities Index (BHI)

The *British Humanities Index* covers the humanities subject fields in a very broad sense. It includes a number of UK law journals within its coverage, as well as the broadsheet newspapers. In its printed format, you can search by subject and by author. The *British Humanities Index* is also available electronically, which allows searching at a basic and more advanced level.

Applied Social Sciences Index & Abstracts (ASSIA)

ASSIA is similar to the *British Humanities Index* in that it covers the social sciences very broadly, including criminology and legal issues. *ASSIA* is an online database, which offers greater flexibility in searching than a printed index.

Other subject databases

As we've seen from the *British Humanities Index* and *ASSIA* examples above, a non-law index or database can have some legal content within it, so it is worth considering other non-law databases when researching particular subjects. As an example, business and management databases may also include articles on different aspects of business law, such as insolvency or directors' duties, so it would be wise to search these too. The best advice to offer here about non-law databases is to have a chat with your Law Librarian. Explain to them that you have a piece of work to do about environmental law or business law (or whatever it may be) and ask them if they can recommend any other resources (apart from the law ones) that you could use.

5.6 Some tips for effective library use

5.6.1 Getting the most out of your library

You may think that you know perfectly well how to use a library – you walk in, choose the book you need from the shelves and borrow it; what could be simpler? In an ideal world this would be the case, but unfortunately, in the real world it doesn't always work like that. Think about how many other students there are in your year, doing your course and how all of you are likely to be competing to get hold of the same library materials. Sadly, most libraries don't have book budgets large enough to enable them to buy a copy of each reading list item per student (not to mention the library shelf space that would be needed to shelve them all). But before you get too despondent and start thinking that there's obviously no point in even going to the library, read on, and you will discover some tips to help you get the most out of your library and your Law Librarian.

NOTE

No two libraries are the same, so you may find that some of the services mentioned are not available through your library. ☐ ☐ ☐

5.6.2 Visit the library as early as possible

This doesn't necessarily mean that you should be standing outside the library's door first thing in the morning, waiting for it to open (although that's not such a bad idea – you may find that your library is much quieter and less busy early in the morning). Instead, it refers to the fact that once you've been set a piece of coursework or other task, you should go to the library as soon as possible.

Lots of students will all want to look at the same books as you do, so it makes sense to get to the library and borrow them as soon as you can. Whatever you do, please don't commit the cardinal sin of leaving things until a few days (or hours!) before your deadline and expecting all the books you need to be right there on the library shelves. **They won't be** because the more organised students, who manage their time well, will have borrowed them weeks ago.

5.6.3 Make use of any reservations or booking facilities

Most libraries offer a reservation facility, so if someone else has beaten you to one of the key texts, you should make use of this service. In many instances, the person who has the book out on loan can be asked to return it at an earlier date, so you may find that you get access to the item sooner than you originally thought.

5.6.4 Use short loan collections

A short loan collection is a common feature within most academic libraries, although the length of the loan period may vary. Check within your own library to find out if you have such a collection and how it operates.

The items kept in the short loan collection are usually key texts on your reading lists and the shorter loan period means that more people have an opportunity to use them. Although not long enough to read the whole book, the loan period (whether it be an hour, a morning or a day), is usually long enough for you to make any necessary photocopies (abiding by the copyright guidance given out by your institution of course!) or to do the required preparatory reading before a lecture or a tutorial.

Some libraries offer a booking service for short loan material, so you may be able to order a particular item for a specific time when you know you'll be able to use it. Again, check within your own library to find out exactly what services they offer.

5.6.5 Consult other books with the same class number

There will be times when the key texts on your reading list are all out on loan and you haven't got time to wait for a reserved copy, so what should you do in these situations? A good tip is to look for other books with the same class number as the book you originally wanted to use. In library terms the class number represents the subject content of the book, which means that all books about criminal law should have the same class number, as should all books about family law or employment law. It doesn't matter which classification scheme your library uses (or even which version of the classification scheme), you will find that books about the same subject have the same class number.

If, for example, you need to read up on a particular aspect of company law before your next tutorial, you will find that topic covered in many more books than just those ones referred to on your reading list. OK, so you haven't read the chapter from the recommended textbook, but at least you have read something. Your lecturer is far more likely to be impressed by the fact that you've used your initiative than if you had just turned up to the tutorial saying, 'I haven't done any reading because the book on the reading list was out.' Remember – no reading you do is ever wasted.

5.6.6 Use your library staff

One of the greatest resources in any library is its staff (and I'm not just saying that because I'm a librarian). Think about it – they work in the building, they know about the loan procedures and the collections, they use the electronic databases and other material – so who better to answer your library questions?

Most academic library staff are friendly and helpful people who are used to working with students, so don't be afraid to approach them if you have any questions, however stupid you think you might appear. Chances are you won't be asking anything the library staff haven't been asked before. Also, the staff would much prefer that you leave the library satisfied, instead of wandering aimlessly around the shelves hoping to find what you need, getting gradually more frustrated before deciding that the library is hopeless and you'll never come back. As was said before, most academic library staff are friendly and helpful, but they're not psychic. If you need help, ask – and you should find that you receive it.

If you are lucky enough to have a dedicated Law Librarian (a professionally qualified librarian who specialises in the subject of law), then you would be well advised to get to know this person. The Law Librarian will have an in-depth knowledge of the law resources within your library. They can help you locate material, understand citations and references and can recommend sources to you for particular courseworks. A word of caution, however – Law Librarians are not lecturers and generally won't be able to pass comment on your work. Academic librarians are in the business of 'helping students to help themselves' by making students aware of the range of resources available and encouraging them to research more effectively and efficiently. When it comes to advice about whether or not the case you've selected accurately illustrates the point you're trying to make, then these questions are better directed at your tutors.

5.6.7 Take advantage of any training offered

If you have the opportunity to attend any training sessions run by the Law Librarian or other library staff, then you would be strongly advised to do so. Most Law Librarians offer training sessions not because they like the sound of their own voice, but because they want to help students get the most out of the library resources. As you've probably realised by now, law can be a confusing and challenging subject with lots of different resources (in print and electronic formats) to consult. Knowing which resource to choose is a skill in itself, as is knowing how to get to the information you're looking for when you've chosen your resource. Any library training sessions that will help you navigate your way through this vast array of information should be seized with both hands.

Library training sessions are often run on a voluntary rather than compulsory basis (that is to say they are not a timetabled lecture or tutorial slot) but this doesn't mean that they are any less valuable. By attending these sessions, you'll be investing in your future success and equipping yourself with the skills you need to become an independent learner.

chapter 6 UNDERSTANDING LEGAL SKILLS AND USING LEGAL REASONING ■

After reading this chapter you should be able to:

- Understand the basic rules of precedent
- Understand the basic rules of statutory interpretation
- Use legal reasoning
- Apply the rules of precedent to factual situations
- Apply the rules of statutory interpretation to factual situations

6.1 The process of deductive logic

Law depends completely on the process of deductive logic. When judges make decisions in cases they have to do so on the basis of legal reasoning. They cannot simply make their own minds up on what they want to decide, they must have a reason based on law. This can come from law found in statutes (Acts of Parliament) or it can come from a principle of law found in decided cases. This is the so-called *ratio decidendi* of a case, which simply means the reason for the decision.

Wherever the law comes from the process in court is the same:

- both sides introduce the facts on which the dispute hinges
- the lawyers then introduce the law that is appropriate to those particular facts
- the law is applied to the facts by the judge
- a decision is reached.

6.2 The use of precedent

6.2.1 A brief overview of the rules of precedent

As you will learn in your English Legal System course on your degree, the doctrine of precedent is one of the most important features of English law. This is because judges are not allowed to decide the law as they see fit but must base their decisions on existing law.

There are a few key areas that you need to remember about precedent:

- where the law comes from
- the nature of binding precedent
- other things that are influential on judges when deciding cases
- the hierarchy of the courts
- the ways of avoiding binding precedent.

You will learn about precedent in much more detail in your English Legal System course and from those textbooks recommended to you by your teachers. Below are some brief notes of the key areas to give you a general idea and for you to be able to complete the exercises in section 6.2.3.

Where the law comes from

Precedents to be followed in later cases come from principles of law that are found in existing cases.

- The part of the judgment where the law is found and that provides precedent for later judges to follow is called the *ratio decidendi*. This simply means the reason for the decision, the principle of law that decided the case. A *ratio* may simply extend or develop the previous law or it may be 'original', which means in effect that there was no previous law on the particular issue. It is of course possible to find more than one *ratio* in a case and, as you will find, it is not always easy to find the *ratio*.

- Judges will make other statements in a case, for instance saying what the law might be if the facts of the case were slightly different. These statements are referred to as *obiter dicta*. This simply means 'things said by the way', or in other words things that have no relevance to the outcome of the actual case. These can still be influential on later judges, particularly if they are made by high ranking judges such as those in the House of Lords.

Binding precedent

The doctrine of *stare decisis* (simply meaning stand by what has already been decided) is followed quite rigidly in English law. This means that whenever a judge is deciding a case if there is a principle of law from a previous case that applies to the facts of the present case then this principle should be followed in the present case.

In fact a binding precedent is a principle of law that must be followed by the court in a later case, if the facts in the case are analogous, even if the judges do not agree with the principle in it.

Binding precedent comes from only one place, the *ratio decidendi* of the past analogous case. It will only apply in the present case if the facts of this case are sufficiently similar to those in the case in which the precedent is found and also only if the precedent was made in a court capable of binding the court hearing the later case. Normally, this would be a court on a level with or higher up the hierarchy of courts, although the Human Rights Act 1998 has had an effect on when courts are bound by a higher court's decision made before the Act came into force on a decision made after that date.

Persuasive precedent

Persuasive precedent will not bind a future court so it does not have to be followed. However, the judges in a future case may well be influenced by the principle and wish to apply it in later cases. This will be the case particularly when in the present case there is no obvious binding precedent to follow.

Persuasive precedent can come from a variety of different sources, including:

- *Obiter dicta* from a decided case. For example the *obiter* comments in *Rondel v Worsley* [1969] 1 AC 191 were later applied by the court in *Saif Ali v Sidney Mitchell & Co* [1978] 3 WLR 849.

- Dissenting judgments (these are statements made by judges in an appeal case who disagree with the principles stated by the majority judges and want to state what they think the law should be). They may well be followed in the future if sufficiently senior judges make them. For example the House of Lords eventually followed Lord Denning's dissenting judgment from *Candler v Crane Christmas & Co* [1951] 2 KB 164 in *Hedley Byrne v Heller & Partners* [1964] AC 465.

- Minority judgments (these are additional comments made by the judges in a case who do not give the leading judgment).

- Judgments made in the Privy Council and in other Commonwealth courts, eg the definition of remoteness of damage for negligence from *The Wagon Mound (No 1)* [1961] AC 388 of foreseeable damage is now the standard test.

- The works of leading academics. For example the House of Lords in *Dunlop v Selfridge* [1915] AC 847 approved Sir Frederick Pollock's definition of consideration contained in his 'Principles of Contract' that '. . . *an act of forbearance or the promise thereof is the price for which the promise of the other is bought, and the promise thus given for value is enforceable* . . .'

The hierarchy of courts

- **The European Court of Justice** – EU law applies mostly to economic areas and does not affect every area of English law. However, if a case is affected by a point of EU law then from 1st January 1973 the European Court of Justice (ECJ) is the highest court. Decisions made in this court are binding on all courts in England & Wales, although not on itself.

- **The House of Lords** – This is the highest domestic court. Decisions made here bind all lower courts. Traditionally the court was bound by its own past decisions following *London Street Tramways v London County Council* [1898] AC 375. Now it can avoid its past decisions through using the 1966 *Practice Statement* [1966] 3 All ER 77.

- **The Court of Appeal** – The Court of Appeal is made up of two divisions: the Civil Division and the Criminal Division. Each division is bound to follow decisions of the House of Lords and the ECJ. The divisions also bind the respective civil and criminal courts below them. It is generally bound to follow its own past decisions except in certain circumstances.

- **The Divisional Courts** – The term Divisional Court is used when one of the three divisions of the High Court (Family, Chancery and Queen's Bench) acts as an appeal court or in a supervisory capacity. The Divisional Courts are bound by all courts above them, and bind all lower courts. They are generally bound by their own past decisions but with some flexibility similar to the Court of Appeal.

- **The High Court** – The High Court is bound by all higher courts and in turn binds lower courts. Judges are not bound by the decisions of other High Court judges but usually follow them.

- **The inferior courts** – The Crown Court, the County Court, and the magistrates' court are bound by the decisions of the higher courts. They do not themselves create any precedent. Technically, however, a point of law made by a judge in the Crown Court binds the magistrates' court.

Ways of avoiding precedent

There are a few limited ways that enable certain courts to avoid binding precedent:

- **overruling** – this is where one of the appeal courts finds in a later case that the precedent from the case was wrong

- **reversing** – this is where during the appeal in a case a higher court changes the decision from the court below

- **distinguishing** – this is available to all courts and is where the court finds that the material facts of the present case are essentially different from the precedent it is being asked to apply eg the principle in *Balfour v Balfour* [1919] 2 KB 571 was not applied in *Merritt v Merritt* [1970] 1 WLR 1211.

The House of Lords can also use the *Practice Statement* [1966] 3 All ER 77 to change its past decisions and can depart from a previous decision when 'it appears right to do so'.

This only applies in two situations:

- to avoid injustice in the present case, and

- to allow for the proper development of the law.

However, the House of Lords judges rarely do use it, even where they think that the law may lead to injustice, eg in *Jones v Secretary of State for Social Services* [1972] AC 944 they would not overrule the decision in *Re Dowling* [1967] 1 AC 725 even though they all felt this would lead to injustice and some felt the case had been wrongly decided:

- It was first used in *Conway v Rimmer* [1968] AC 910 but only on a technical point.

- The first major use was in *B R Board v Herrington* [1972] AC 877 overruling *Addie v Dumbreck* [1929] AC 358 on the duty of care owed to a trespasser.

- The first use in criminal law was *R v Shivpuri* [1986] 2 WLR 988, overruling *Anderton v Ryan* [1985] AC 567 on impossible attempts and this was only to correct their own error.

- In any case the *Practice Statement* itself identifies the need for certainty in the law, particularly in the case of contracts, tax arrangements and in the criminal law.

- The Court of Appeal is usually bound by its own past precedent but there are exceptions in *Young v Bristol Aeroplane Co* [1944] KB 718

  - where there are two conflicting past Court of Appeal decisions it may choose one and reject the other

  - where a Court of Appeal decision, though not overruled, is inconsistent with a later decision of the House of Lords, then it must follow the House of Lords decision

  - where a Court of Appeal decision was made *per incuriam* (or without reference to all the appropriate authorities) then it may ignore that decision.

- The Criminal Division of the Court of Appeal can also avoid its own decisions if the law has been 'misapplied or misunderstood' because of the possible loss of liberty as in *R v Taylor* [1950] 2 KB 368 and *R v Gould* [1968] 2 QB 65.

- More recent exceptions include the Court of Appeal being able to ignore House of Lords precedent when

  - a House of Lords decision has been overruled by the European Court of Justice or

  - a House of Lords decision is incompatible with the European Convention on Human Rights.

ACTIVITY

Now test your understanding of the basic elements of precedent above by answering the following questions:

1. What is the difference between the *ratio decidendi* of a case and *obiter dicta*?

2. What is the difference between 'binding' precedent and 'persuasive' precedent?

3. What is a dissenting judgment and what effect can it have on precedent?

4. Which court is higher in the hierarchy of courts the High Court or the Court of Appeal (Civil Division)?

5. Which courts do not create precedent?

6. Which courts are able to use the practice of 'distinguishing' in order to avoid past precedent?

7. When does the Practice Statement suggest that judges should be careful to avoid changing the law?

CONTINUED ▶

8. What are the three exceptions in *Young* when the Court of Appeal is able to avoid its own past precedent?

9. What precisely does *per incuriam* mean?

10. In what circumstances does the Court of Appeal (Criminal Division) have extra power to avoid its past precedent?

An alternative version of precedent in a diagram form similar to those that you will find in Chapter 11 is produced below.

Basic principles	Ways of avoiding precedent
Stare decisis (stand by decisions of past cases) is the basis of the doctrine of precedent. All courts are bound to follow decisions (*ratio decidendi*) made by courts above them in the hierarchy – this is **binding precedent**. Only the principles of law which are essential to the decision are the *ratio decidendi*. Statements of principles of law which are not relevant to the decision are *obiter dicta* and do not need to be followed. **Persuasive precedent** is when a court does not have to follow the principle but may do so. It comes from a variety of different sources: • *Obiter dicta* statements by a higher ranking court • a dissenting judgment • *ratios* from decisions by courts lower in the hierarchy • decisions by courts outside the English legal system.	**Distinguishing** If the material facts of the present case are sufficiently different from an earlier case, the case may be distinguishing so that the earlier decision is not followed: *Shepherd* (1987) and *Sharp* (1987). **Overruling** Where a court changes a past precedent of its own (eg House of Lords under the *Practice Statement*). **Reversing** Where a higher court changes the ruling of a lower court in the same case.

CONTINUED ▶

Court of Appeal	The House of Lords and the Practice Statement
Must follow decisions of the House of Lords **Exceptions** to this rule are where a House of Lords' decision • has been overruled by the European Court of Justice or • is incompatible with the European Convention on Human Rights. The Court of Appeal must follow its own past decisions. *Young's case* (1944). **Except** • where there are conflicting decisions, the Court of Appeal can choose which to follow • where a decision has been impliedly overruled by House of Lords, the Court of Appeal must follow the House of Lords' decision and not its own • where a decision has been made *per incuriam*. The Criminal Division of the Court of Appeal will also not follow where law has been misapplied or misunderstood. *Gould* (1968).	1966 *Practice Statement* gave the House of Lords power to depart from past decisions. The Statement said that former decisions would normally be treated as binding but the Lords could 'depart from a previous decision when it appears right to do so'. • 'to avoid injustice in the present case' or • 'to allow for proper development of the law'. But the Statement stressed the need for certainty, *especially in the criminal law*, and the danger of disturbing retrospectively the basis on which contracts, settlements of property and fiscal arrangements had been entered into. The first civil use was in *Herrington v BRB* (1972); and the first criminal use was in *Shivpuri* (1986).

Figure 6.1 Alternative version of precedent in diagram form

The basic rules on precedent and the ways that courts may avoid past precedents, as indicated above are reasonably straightforward. While precedent is often stated to be rigidly applied in the English legal system, this is in fact not always the case, a factor that can often prove confusing to students of substantive law areas. This is illustrated below in an article written for the *A-Level Law Review* (published by Philip Allan Updates) by one of the authors of this book, Chris Turner.

As law students you are taught that, while there are complex rules regarding when courts can avoid their own past precedent, one aspect of the doctrine of precedent is quite simple. A court in England and Wales is strictly bound to follow decisions of a court equal to it or higher than it in the hierarchy of courts, subject to those well defined exceptions.

Students are also taught that decisions of the Judicial Committee of the Privy Council, while it includes the most senior judges, can be persuasive only, because the Court is not strictly part of the hierarchy of courts.

The basic rule is very straightforward and even the exceptions are once you know them. However, once you begin to study [areas of substantive law] you will realise that the reality is not so straightforward.

CONTINUED ▶

In an important recent case, *R v Holley* [2005], the Privy Council, hearing an appeal from Jersey, decided that the House of Lords was wrong in *R v Smith (Morgan James)* [2000] on the issue of loss of self control in the defence of provocation in murder. *Smith* has been unpopular with both judges and academics. However, as we know *Holley* is at best persuasive. In fact the Privy Council had already decided in previous cases that, where a case in front of it was in effect bound by English law, then it should follow it. On this basis, the result of *Holley* should have been clear, the Privy Council should have followed *Smith*.

In an even more recent case, *R v James, R v Karimi* [2006], the Court of Appeal (Criminal Division) had to consider whether to apply *Smith* or whether it had in fact been overruled by the Privy Council in *Holley*. The Court of Appeal chose the latter view and held that, in very exceptional circumstances, a decision of the Privy Council can take precedence over a decision of the House of Lords. It justified this on the grounds that the Privy Council in *Holley* was made up of 9 of the 12 judges from the House of Lords and, as it was decided 6:3, the majority of the House of Lords wished the rule in *Smith* to be changed. What the Court of Appeal did in *James* and *Karimi* in effect was to overrule the precedent of a higher court.

It is not unusual for courts to overrule their previous decisions. In *Davis v Johnson* [1978] Lord Denning ignored two recently decided Court of Appeal cases on domestic violence. Nevertheless, he was severely criticised by the House of Lords for doing so. Without being subjected to the same criticisms but with equally important effect, the Court of Appeal in *Doughty v Turner Manufacturing* [1964] chose to ignore its own well established test on remoteness of damage in negligence from *Re Polemis and Furness, Withy & Co* [1921] and applied instead a different test established by the Privy Council in an Australian appeal, *The Wagon Mound (No 1)* [1961], which is now the established law.

Of greater significance is where a court ignores the precedent of a higher court. The Court of Appeal was again strongly criticised by the House of Lords in *Miliangos v George Frank Textiles Ltd* [1976] for applying its own precedent in *Schorsch Meier GmbH v Henning* [1975], in which it in effect overruled a House of Lords decision from *Re Havana Railways* [1961] on the ground that the reason for the rule had gone so the rule should go too. The House of Lords reminded the Court of Appeal that only the House itself could overrule its past decisions.

In *Great Peace Shipping Ltd v Tsavliris Salvage (International) Ltd* [2002] the Court of Appeal held that equity did not apply to common mistake in contract law and that in effect its previous decision in *Solle v Butcher* [1950] was wrong. It is interesting to analyse this decision applying the rule in *Young v Bristol Aeroplane*. The Court of Appeal can avoid its own past precedents:

CONTINUED ▸

- Where the case (here it would be *Solle v Butcher*) is inconsistent with a later decision of the House of Lords – here there is no later House of Lords decision which is inconsistent.
- Where there are two conflicting decisions of the Court of Appeal – this could not apply in *Great Peace* since the two main decisions, *Solle v Butcher* and *Magee v Pennine Insurance Co Ltd* [1969], were consistent.
- Where the decision was decided *per incuriam* (without reference to relevant statute or case law) – in *Solle v Butcher* there was no appropriate law that had not been referred to.

Applying the rule in *Young*, the Court of Appeal in *Great Peace* had no justification for overruling its previous precedent.

All judges can also avoid past precedent by distinguishing where the material facts of the two cases are sufficiently different. Distinguishing has been criticised because judges may split hairs and suggest illogical distinctions just to avoid law they do not like. In *Williams v Roffey Brothers & Nichols* [1990] the House of Lords distinguished from *Stilk v Myrick* [1809]. In that case the court had decided that a person could not use something that they were already bound to do under an existing contract as consideration for an entirely new arrangement. In *Chappell v Nestle Co* [1960] the court explained that consideration must be something real, tangible and of (economic) value. In *Williams* the claimant was trying to enforce a second agreement where he would gain more money merely for doing what he was already bound to do under his existing contract. As the other party would suffer financially if the contract was not performed, the House of Lords decided that there was consideration in the 'extra benefit' gained by that party. It is possible to see the economic benefit here but it could never be seen as either real or tangible. So in essence the court was bending the rules to reach the decision that it wanted.

Sometimes judges even just make up the law. The House of Lords in *Shaw v DPP* [1962] created the offence of 'conspiring to corrupt public morality', even though there was no precedent for it and no statutory offence. It was heavily criticised but justified its decision, arguing that judges are the moral guardians of the public. Nevertheless, it promised not to do it again. However, in *Knuller v DPP* [1973] it declared that there was a crime of 'outraging public decency', which was later accepted and applied by the Court of Appeal in *R v Gibson* [1991].

Adapted from *Precedent. A-Level Law Review,* Volume 2, Number 1, pp 10–12

6.2.2 Understanding how precedent works

In your first year at law school, if you have not already studied law at A-Level, you will usually undertake a course in the English legal system. In this course you will inevitably be taught about the doctrine of precedent.

The doctrine sometimes seems complex and certainly you will come across many aspects of it that seem to be contradictory once you start looking at what judges have said or done in decided cases. Despite this, the basic operation of the doctrine makes perfect sense if you have a practical understanding of what is going on and how the various peculiar phrases that you come across apply.

The brief extract below is taken from a fairly simple case in Contract Law that you may also study in the first year of your course. It is taken from a case-book so it has already been reduced in size.

The purpose of using the extract is to show you the different aspects of the judgment and how a principle of law, a precedent, develops from the case. The extract from the judgment is in the left hand box, a simple commentary identifying the key aspects of the judgment is in the right hand box and explanations of these are given below.

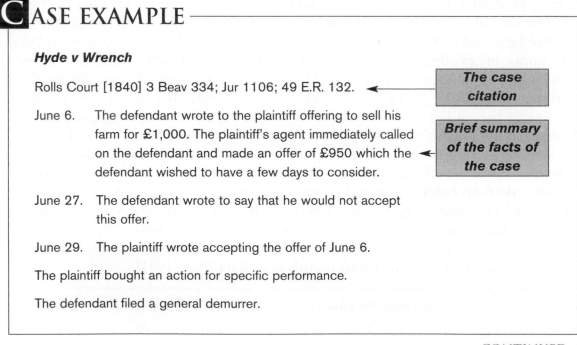

CASE EXAMPLE

Hyde v Wrench

Rolls Court [1840] 3 Beav 334; Jur 1106; 49 E.R. 132. ◀—— **The case citation**

June 6.   The defendant wrote to the plaintiff offering to sell his farm for £1,000. The plaintiff's agent immediately called on the defendant and made an offer of £950 which the ◀—— **Brief summary of the facts of the case** defendant wished to have a few days to consider.

June 27.   The defendant wrote to say that he would not accept this offer.

June 29.   The plaintiff wrote accepting the offer of June 6.

The plaintiff bought an action for specific performance.

The defendant filed a general demurrer.

CONTINUED ▸

THE MASTER OF THE ROLES (LORD LANGDALE): ← **The judgment**

Under the circumstances stated in this bill, I think there exists no valid binding contract between the parties for the purchase of the property. The defendant offered to sell it for £1,000, and *if that had ← at once been unconditionally accepted, there would undoubtedly have been a perfect binding contract*; instead of that, the plaintiff made an offer of his own, to purchase the property for £950, and *he thereby rejected the offer previously made by the defendant.* ← *I think that it was not afterwards competent for him to revive the proposal of the defendant, by tendering an acceptance of it; and that, therefore, there exists no obligation of any sort between the parties*; the demurrer must be allowed. ←

Brief statement of the existing law

The ratio decidendi *of the present case*

The decision

The citation

Your lecturers, and no doubt the law librarian, will tell you how important it is for you to learn the abbreviations for the various law reports so that you can find the cases for yourself once you have found the citation in the particular text book you are using. The crucial parts of the citation for finding the case are the names of the parties, the year and the abbreviation indicating the particular law report. In this extract it is 49 ER 132 that is important to you. This is an old report that came before the Incorporated Council for Law Reporting was created and therefore we would usually be looking in what are called the *English Reports*. An index is available to go with these.

Brief summary of facts

Professor Michael Zander defined the principle of law coming from a case (the *ratio decidendi*) as 'a proposition of law which decides the case, in the light or in the context of the material facts'. Therefore, the facts of each case are important because, when compared with the facts of previous cases, it can be seen whether the past precedent applies, or whether a new or modified principle has to be developed.

In our example here the facts can be briefly stated in bullet form:

*   one party made an offer to sell at a set price
*   the other party wanted to buy at a lower price
*   the party making the offer rejected the alternative price
*   the party to whom the offer had been made then tried to accept the offer at the original price by which time the other party had sold the farm
*   the party receiving the original offer then tried to sue for breach of contract.

These facts would have to be compared with the material facts of earlier cases to see whether or not a contract was actually formed.

Brief statement of existing law

Precedent is a process of applying past principles of law to existing cases. If the principles are appropriate because the facts fall within them then the answer is relatively straightforward, the past precedent must be applied and the case decided in this way. If the facts of the present case do not allow this then the difference between the cases must be established to see what the developed principle in the present case would be.

In our case above Lord Langdale states the past law very clearly in the first passage underlined. It can be stated simply by saying that if an offer is unconditionally accepted then a contract is formed.

The facts in the case above of course are slightly different. Hyde did not unconditionally accept the offer of the farm for £1,000. Instead he suggested that he wanted to pay only £950.

The *ratio decidendi* of the case

This is the principle of law, the precedent, to emerge from the case, and one which will bind future judges if the material facts are analogous.

In this instance the *ratio* provided by Lord Langdon has two key components:

- changing the terms of the offer is the same as rejecting the offer
- rejecting the offer means that it can no longer be open to the party to whom it was made, and so they can no longer accept it.

The decision

The decision in a case is only the result of the principle of law being applied to the facts in question.

Here the defendant in the case was asking for a 'demurrer'. This is an old-fashioned word, but what it basically means is that he was suggesting that the claimant, in effect, did not have any reason for bringing an action, that there was no legal substance to the claim that he was making.

In the circumstances, by applying the principle of law to the facts, Lord Langdale was agreeing with this argument in his decision.

6.2.3 Exercises using precedent and deductive reasoning

As in the example above both lawyers and the judges in a case must use both the existing precedents (the principles of law found in earlier cases) and the processes of deductive logic that they have been trained to adopt. They will do so in order to reach conclusions about how they should interpret the facts in front of them and apply the appropriate law.

To do this they will look back at the law reports as we have already seen and it is the responsibility of the lawyers to introduce into the case all of the appropriate cases that may influence the outcome of the current case. It is with the benefit of the law coming from these cases (the *rationes decidendi* – or legal principles) that deductive reasoning can be used, applying the appropriate law to the facts of the current case in order to reach a conclusion.

Below are a series of exercises on precedent. The exercises involve the judgments from five different completely fictitious cases reported upon in entirely fictitious law reports, the *Hodder Weekly Reports* (HWR). Following the judgment in each case is a series of questions. The expected solutions to the questions are given to you for the first set of questions together with some explanation for the answers. Using these and the information given in the later four judgments you should try to answer the questions that follow each case. The answers are given in the Appendix at the end of the book, except for the first exercise where the answers are reproduced to give you an idea of what is expected.

In answering the questions you should ignore any precedents of which you are aware and concentrate entirely on the law to be found in the judgments themselves. In fact the judgments concern areas of law that would ordinarily be found in the law of torts and more particularly negligence. However, you should treat the cases here as though the first judgment, *Berry v Branch*, is an original precedent and the first time that the particular issues have been considered and, therefore the first time that the legal principles arising have been stated. In the exercises then you should use only the law given to you in the various extracts to decide the answers to the questions that follow them.

ACTIVITY

Exercise 1

The judgment in *Berry v Branch*

Hodder Weekly Reports [2002] 2 HWR 1142

Berry v Branch

QUEEN'S BENCH DIVISION

Rough-Justice J

1 April. 1 May 2002

a *Civil liability – tree growing into neighbour's garden – leaves eaten by neighbour's dog – leaves poisonous – dog dies – whether owner of tree liable.*

b The defendant planted a yew tree in his garden which, over many years, grew across the fence between the defendant's garden and the claimant's. The claimant's dog ate

CONTINUED ▸

some of the leaves which fell into the claimant's garden and, as a result, died. The claimant claimed damages from the defendant for the loss of his dog.

c Held – civil liability attaches to any damage done by anything which a person throws off his property or allows to escape from his property.

Cases referred to in judgment

R v Woodstain [1992] 3 HWR 198

Action

d The claimant, Arnold Berry, brought an action against the defendant, Henry Branch, for agreed damages of £350 for the death of the claimant's dog, Ginger, which was agreed to have been caused by the dog's eating the leaves of a yew tree which grew in the defendant's garden and overlooked the claimant's garden. The facts are set out in the judgment.

Herbert Leafmould for the claimant

Alicia Twig for the defendant

1 May. The following judgment was delivered.   *Cur adv vult*

e ROUGH-JUSTICE J This is an action for damages arising out of the distressing and entirely unnecessary death of a noble specimen of man's best friend. The setting for this sad tragedy is Westiddling Avenue, one of Allwhiting's loveliest streets.

f The houses on Westiddling Avenue are substantial and all have very large gardens. Most of the properties are owned by professional people, including doctors, lawyers and accountants. In this case, however, the defendant is an American car salesman and the claimant is a university lecturer.

g At No 29, the defendant planted a yew tree in his back garden. The defendant was a wholly novice gardener – he had always lived in high-rise apartments in New York prior to moving to England. He chose the yew tree solely because he had seen wooden bowls made out of yew logs and thought that any tree which had such pretty wood must be a good one to have in his garden.

h Now it has always been well known in England that yew trees, apart from being lugubrious looking objects, reminiscent of old churchyards and quite unsuitable for suburban gardens, are poisonous in all their parts. That is, of course, why they are planted in churchyards – to keep cattle out.

i In the course of time this particular yew tree grew, as even yew trees will, albeit slowly, as is their nature. It grew so that it towered over the claimant's garden at No 27.

CONTINUED ▶

j The claimant was away, working abroad, for five years before the incident which this claim concerns. When he returned home he brought with him a very valuable pet golden retriever. He shipped the dog to England six months prior to his own return so that it would come out of quarantine only a few days after he arrived back in England.

k As a result of the excitement of seeing its master once again, this lovely animal, of which I have been shown numerous fetching photographs, was off its food for the first two days after it arrived home. It is a well known fact that when they have some gastric upset, dogs will often eat grass or leaves. When this hapless animal was turned out into the back garden for a run, it ate some of the leaves of the yew tree which had dropped into the claimant's garden. It was unfortunate that in his first few days at home, the claimant had given higher priority to other jobs than clearing away the accumulation of yew leaves and other debris which he found had built up during his absence.

The inevitable result of the dog consuming the yew leaves was that the poor dog died. The claimant naturally expects damages for his loss.

l Ms Twig, for the defendant, argues that the fault for the demise of the dog lies with the claimant who failed to keep his lawn clean of what he, as a botanist, must have known were poisonous leaves. Ms Twig says that the defendant cannot be held responsible for where the wind, willy-nilly, deposits the leaves which fall from his tree.

m Since our laws have not previously dealt with this point – there is neither a decided case nor a Statute to assist me – I am thrown back upon first principles. This is despite the Herculean efforts of Ms Twig to convince me that I should be guided by the case of *R v Woodstain* [1982] 3 Hod Cr Rep 198. [Hodder Criminal Reports] I am afraid that I am unable to see the relevance of this case, which first was heard in our criminal courts and second concerned the destruction of a common garden fence, despite Ms Twig nagging on about it for quite some time.

n It seems to me to be a matter of ordinary fairness that if someone embarks on any activity which is dangerous, then they should take the consequences. So, if someone plants a poisonous tree, they must be liable for the damage it does and this is true whether the damage occurs on the planter's property or off it.

o Is this situation not akin to one where a man throws acid into his neighbour's property or fires a shotgun over the fence? In such cases the neighbour is entirely innocent and should not suffer a loss. It is entirely obvious in such cases that the neighbour may well suffer damage and the miscreant takes the risk, not the neighbour. People who live cheek by jowl with each other in cramped suburbia must pay due regard to those who live next to them.

CONTINUED ▶

p Accordingly, I award damages of £350 to the claimant.

Solicitors: *Cherry, Lime, Walnut and Co.*, Allwhiting (for the claimant); *Roots and Roots*, Allwhiting (for the defendant)

Rafael Valentine-Collins Barrister

Having read *Berry v Branch* you now have an idea of how a law report looks and the various elements from which it is made up. Rough-Justice J is obviously a very interesting judge, with very particular attitudes. He clearly has very particular views about the facts of the case also. Before you look at the questions below look back at the judgment. Underline the key points that Rough-Justice J makes.

The answers to the questions are printed below, but before you look at the answers see if you can answer the questions without their guidance.

Questions on the judgment in Berry v Branch

1. When looking at the judgment of Rough-Justice J what legal propositions can you identify?

2. Legal principles can be both narrow (meaning that they will only apply in very few and specific factual circumstances) and broad (meaning that the principle could be used in lots of different factual circumstances). Try to place the legal principles that you have found in the case for question 1 in order, with the narrowest principle first moving to the broadest principle last.

3. Decide on which of these principles Rough-Justice J actually based his decision – (ie using the proper legal terminology, decide what you think what is the '*ratio decidendi*' of the case).

4. Looking back at the principles of law you have found, consider whether there are any *obiter dicta* statements in the judgment. (In other words does Rough-Justice J make any comments on what he thinks the law would have been if the facts had been different? Look for any statements that have no bearing on the outcome of the case itself but could be useful to judges in later cases.)

Answers to Exercise 1

You will have noticed that Rough-Justice J spends a good deal of his judgment setting out and commenting on the facts of the case. So it is only really in the last few paragraphs of his judgment that he discusses what he thinks are the legal issues.

1. In respect of question 1 you might have been able to discover the following 'legal principles' set out in Rough-Justice J's judgment:

CONTINUED ▶

- '. . . if someone embarks on any activity which is dangerous, then they should take the consequences.' (He states this in lines 1 and 2 of **n**.)

- '. . . if someone plants a poisonous tree, they must be liable for the damage it does and this is true whether the damage occurs on the planter's property or off it.' (He states this in lines 2, 3 and 4 of **n**.)

- In cases where acid is thrown into a neighbour's property or a shotgun is fired over a neighbour's fence, the neighbour, being innocent, should not suffer a loss; 'the miscreant takes the risk.' (This is a paraphrase of the statement that he makes in lines 1–4 of **o**.)

- 'People who live cheek by jowl with each other in cramped suburbia must pay due regard to those who live next to them.' (Finally he states this in lines 4–5 of **o**.)

2. The next question demanded that you should be able to set these in a particular order, so you needed to be think about the potential application of the principles to other factual situations. Rearranged in order, with the narrowest application first and the broadest last you should have arranged them as follows.

- '. . . if someone plants a poisonous tree, they must be liable for the damage it does and this is true whether the damage occurs on the planter's property or off it.' (*This is quite a narrow principle. It applies only to poisonous trees causing damage. It could of course be even narrower for example if it only applied to a particular type of tree or it could apply to damage done on only one property rather than both planter and neighbour.*)

- In cases where acid is thrown into a neighbour's property or a shotgun is fired over a neighbour's fence, the neighbour, being innocent, should not suffer a loss; and if he does, 'the miscreant takes the risk.' (*This principle is still quite narrow but unlike the one above it applies to two things, 'acid thrown into a neighbour's property' and 'a shotgun fired over a neighbour's fence'. So it is not as narrow as the first which only applies to one thing: 'poisonous trees that cause damage'.*)

- 'People who live cheek by jowl with each other in cramped suburbia must pay due regard to those who live next to them.' (*This of course is quite a broad principle as it applies in a general sense to neighbours living in suburbia who it is clear from Rough-Justice J's statement owe a duty to each other.*)

- '. . . if someone embarks on any activity which is dangerous, then they should take the consequences.' (*This, however, is clearly the broadest judgment of all with the widest application to different factual circumstances since it imposes liability on anyone who is responsible for a dangerous activity and presumably for any kind of damage caused by that activity.*)

CONTINUED ▶

3. You may well have found it difficult to highlight which of the principles set out above is the actual *ratio* of the case. You should not worry about this. It is a quite common difficulty when reading judgments. This is why the barrister writing the report identifies what he or she thinks the *ratio* is in the section headed **Held** in section **c** of the judgment, and this is checked with the judge. Nevertheless, on reading the judgment it is easy to say that Rough-Justice J did not actually indicate any preference for one legal principle over another or say precisely on what basis he decided the case. Clearly the facts of the case would also support any of the principles that have been laid out, except of course for the one that refers to acid and shotguns. We are able, therefore, to eliminate this principle and decide definitely that this is not the *ratio*. However, it would be for a future judge referring to the case to determine which of the remaining principles would be the *ratio*. If the facts of the future case were to match exactly this one then it is likely that the narrowest of the principles would be applied. The more the facts in the future case differed from *Berry v Branch*, then the wider of the principles coming from the case is likely to be applied by the future judge.

4. You may by now have worked this one out and it is really quite easy. *Obiter dicta* are statements of legal principle that concern circumstances that cannot be found in the case itself. In this case it is the statement about acid and shotguns in lines 1–4 of **o**.

   It is also true to say that, if you have a fairly clear idea what the *ratio* is then the other statements of principle must be *obiter*. In other words any statements of legal principle made by the judge which prove not to be decisive in the case will be *obiter*, ie if the case was decided on the narrowest principle (planting of poisonous trees), then the wider principles (responsibility for their dangerous acts), will be *obiter*. It is of course also possible for there to be more than one *ratio* in a case.

Whatever we take as being the *ratio* of the case, it is clear that *Berry v Branch* has developed original law, since we stated at the beginning that none of the issues involved had been discussed before. Once a decision was reached in *Berry v Branch* the next question inevitably would be for later judges to decide whether a new form of liability had entered into the law. If it had, it would be for judges in later cases to decide how wide ranging this liability was in respect of injuries to other persons or property.

Let us now imagine that the legal significance of the case was tested in a later case in the same year and in the same court, the case of *Bunny v Browning* [2002] 4 HWR 62 which again was heard in the Queen's Bench Division of the High Court. Once again you should read the report, remembering what you have discovered from the judgment in *Berry v Branch*, and now, applying the law from that case, answer the questions that follow. This time the answers are at the back of the book in the Appendix and you should try to answer the questions without referring to the answers, but of course check that you are right after you have completed Exercise 2.

ACTIVITY

Exercise 2

The judgment in *Bunny v Browning*

Hodder Weekly Reports [2002] 4 HWR 62

Bunny v Browning

QUEEN'S BENCH DIVISION

Jittery J

1 October. 1 November 2002

a *Civil liability – rabbit loose in garden – neighbour shoots air rifle pellet at target on fence – pellet penetrates target and goes through knothole hitting rabbit – rabbit dies – whether neighbour firing air rifle liable.*

b The defendant fired an air rifle from his back garden at a target on a fence. The pellet passed through the target and through a knothole in the fence into the claimant's garden killing the claimant's pet rabbit.

c Held – civil liability attaches to any damage done by anything which a person throws off his property or allows to escape from his property.

Cases referred to in judgment

Berry v Branch [2002] 2 HWR 1142

Action

d The claimant, Hermione Bunny, brought an action against the defendant, Bradley Browning, for agreed damages of £100 for the death of the claimant's rabbit, Floppy, which was agreed to have been caused by the rabbit having been shot by the defendant while it was in the claimant's garden. The facts are set out in the judgment.

Julian Bobtail for the claimant

Daphne Trigger for the defendant

1 November. The following judgment was delivered.   *Cur adv vult*

e **JITTERY J** The death of a loved one is at times distressing for the bereaved, even if that loved one is a mere pet – in this case a rabbit named Floppy. Floppy had indeed occupied a highly esteemed place in the Bunny household for more than four years since he was first purchased. He was in fact a constant companion of Mrs Hermione Bunny. It was Mrs Bunny's habit to turn Floppy out into her back garden for several hours each day so that he might graze in the grass there. While the rabbit was thus occupied one day in October of 2001, the 22nd to be precise, his life was brought to a

CONTINUED ▸

sudden and most untimely end when young Bradley Browning, who lived in the next house along the terrace, at No 87, shot him with an air rifle.

f Mr and Mrs. Browning and their two children had moved into No 87 only one month previously. Bradley was given the air rifle as a present on his 18th birthday, which was on that very day, 22nd October 2001. His immediate reaction on receiving the gift was to rush outside to try it out. He pinned a paper target on the fence which separated the gardens of the two houses and fired the gun at the target. Even without practice Bradley was a good shot. The pellet penetrated the target, and then, remarkably enough, it passed straight through a knothole in the fence behind the target and it struck poor Floppy a fatal blow.

g Mr Bobtail, who is acting as counsel for Mrs Bunny, has said that the claimant freely accepts Bradley Browning's assertion that he had no intention at all of causing harm to the poor deceased animal – and I am bound to agree on a study of the facts presented to this court that this is indeed the case. But, says Mr Bobtail, a mere absence of intention does not negate young Mr Browning's liability to compensate Mrs Bunny for her loss. He has urged upon me the views of the eminent jurist Rough-Justice J as he expounded them in the recent case *Berry v Branch*: '. . . if someone embarks on any activity which is dangerous, then they should take the consequences,' and also 'People who live cheek by jowl with each other in cramped suburbia must pay due regard to those who live next to them.' Mr Bobtail points out that firing a gun over the fence into a neighbour's garden is one of the situations which Rough-Justice J actually instanced as creating such a liability.

h Miss Trigger, counsel for the defendant, argues that *Berry v Branch* should be distinguished on the ground that the essential facts of the current case are too dissimilar from those in *Berry v Branch*. She argues that there is no inherent, natural hazard here as there was in the earlier case. Floppy's demise, though unfortunate, could never have been foreseen, she says; while in the case of the much loved pooch whose death brought about the action in *Berry v Branch*, his tragic end may have been unlikely, but given the proximity of the deadly yew tree to his owner's garden, and the natural proclivity of dogs to consume vegetation as a remedy for stomach-ache, it could be foreseen that eventually the dog might be poisoned. Nor, says Miss Trigger, can Mr Justice Rough-Justice's remarks regarding the mutual duty of care owed to each other by neighbours living in 'cramped suburbia' be regarded as binding me to decide this case in favour of the claimant. Given the spaciousness of the properties on Westiddling Avenue, Rough-Justice J's remarks concerning the duty of neighbours living in cramped suburbia must be considered to be no more than *obiter dicta*. In connection with the distinguished judge's comments regarding a general liability to others of those who undertake

CONTINUED ▶

dangerous activities, Miss Trigger argues that if such views were regarded to be the law of the land it would result in a revolutionary extension of legal responsibility. Miss Trigger asserts and I find myself bound to agree, that such a principle is not a part of the law. The day may come when it may be found to be, but, in my opinion, that time has not yet arrived.

i   Despite the fervour with which Miss Trigger has pressed me to treat this case as being without precedent, I feel that the decision in *Berry v Branch* leaves me little choice but to honour convention and to find in favour of the claimant. I do so willingly for I find Rough-Justice J's statement regarding the duties owed each other by city-dwellers to be highly persuasive. Life in Westiddling Avenue may be a wholly more spacious affair than that enjoyed by Mrs Bunny and the Browning family, but compared to country living they are both cut from the same cloth.

j   Therefore, I award damages in the amount of £100 to Mrs Bunny.

Solicitors: *Hare, Brer and Co.*, Bighampton (for the claimant); *Load and Lock*, Bighampton (for the defendant)

Rafael Valentine-Collins *Barrister*

Questions on the judgment in *Bunny v Browning*

1. Jittery J in his judgment indicates that he is bound by the decision of Rough-Justice J in *Berry v Branch*. Consider what you think Jittery J believes to be the *ratio decidendi* of *Berry v Branch*. (Remembering that it is only the *ratio decidendi* of a previous decision which can bind a judge in a later case.)

2. Consider whether in his judgment Jittery J has in fact widened the application of the principle from *Berry v Branch*.

3. Identify the *ratio decidendi* of *Bunny v Browning*.

4. Assuming that *Berry v Branch* is sufficiently analogous to *Bunny v Browning* to serve as a precedent in the case, consider whether it a persuasive precedent or a binding precedent.

The answers can be found in the Appendix on page 307.

Now let us imagine that these basic principles in the law continue to develop. So on the same day that *Bunny v Browning* is decided let us suppose that there is a contemporaneous case being heard by another judge in the QBD where again the judgment in *Berry v Branch* is being referred to and considered.

The issue was in effect settled when the case was appealed to the House of Lords. Their Lordships, in a unanimous opinion given in a brief judgment, declined to explore in any greater depth the leading speech of Highman LJ but upheld the ruling of the Court of Appeal in the case.

The final stage in our fictitious series of cases can now be seen in one final case heard the following year, again in the High Court. This decision, *Fly v Porker*, is outlined below.

Once again use your understanding of the cases so far, remembering that *Blaster v Burns* is a Court of Appeal decision and answer the questions that follow.

Again the answers are given in the Appendix on page 310.

ACTIVITY

Exercise 5

The judgment in *Fly v Porker*

Hodder Weekly Reports [2004] 1 HWR 77

Fly v Porker

HIGH COURT

CLEARLY J

1 April 1 May 2004

CLEARLY J This action for damages arises as a result of the most unfortunate destruction of one of the finest stretches of river for trout fishing in the countryside surrounding Bighampton. Mr Porker is a pig farmer and the effluent from his pig houses he stores in a large tank that is situated at the top of a hill near to the boundary between his own land and that of Mr Fly. As the result of a most unhappy sequence of events, and indeed without fault on the part of Mr Porker, the effluent container was breached with the result that 200,000 gallons of the effluent flowed down the hill and onto Mr Fly's land, eventually finding its way into the river which traversed his estate. The effect of the effluent on the trout in the stream was to say the least catastrophic. Virtually every one was killed and the stream itself was rendered quite worthless as an attraction for anglers, who up to the time of the unfortunate event had been prepared to pay hundreds of pounds for a day's fishing. Mr Fly now seeks compensation for the loss of his valuable enterprise.

The question which I am now called on to answer is whether or not there is any precedent that might guide me in reaching an appropriate decision. Counsel for the claimant, Miss Gill, in an eloquent and convincing speech, has asserted that I am bound

CONTINUED ▶

by the recent decision of the Court of Appeal in *Blaster v Burns* to decide in favour of her client, the claimant. She has drawn my attention to certain words in the judgment of Highman LJ in that case:

> 'even though the cause of the damage in this case was different from that in *Berry v Branch*, it is clear that such an undertaking, involving the mixture of highly and unstable and volatile chemicals, was inherently dangerous, even if Mr Blaster's knowledge of chemistry was insufficient for him to know this. And as Rough-Justice J stated in *Berry v Branch*: "if someone embarks on any activity which is dangerous, then they should take the consequences".'

Highman LJ then went on to say that this was especially so when one considers that Mr Blaster's experiments were, wholly foolishly, being conducted in the back garden of a house located in the middle of a congested inner city council estate. And he then agreed with the claimant's counsel that even if the experiments had been carried out in open country, Mr Blaster would have been liable for the damage they caused.

According to Miss Gill, this statement leaves me no choice but to find in favour of her client, especially as the Court of Appeal's decision in *Blaster v Burns* has been affirmed unanimously by the Judicial Committee of the House of Lords.

Mr Trotter, Mr Porker's eminent advocate, argues that *Blaster v Burns* provides no authority for a decision favouring the claimant. *Blaster v Burns* was a case concerning neighbours living in the close confines of a large city. In such situations it seems only sensible to impose a strict duty of care not to cause damage to your neighbours. And that is exactly what Highman LJ did. But, Mr Trotter says, since the facts of *Blaster v Burns* were wholly to do with life in the city I must treat Highman LJ's statement quoted above as an *obiter dictum*. He says I am not bound to follow. Nor should I be persuaded by the Lord Justice's *dictum* to open up such a huge new potential area of litigation as would arise if the law were considered to give people in any circumstances of living the right to hold their neighbours liable for any injury they suffer as a result of the neighbours' inattention or carelessness.

Now what is the balance that should be struck between these two arguments? An academic might be prepared to contend that the opinion expressed by Highman LJ as to the liability of Mr Blaster had this incident taken place in the country amounts to no more than *obiter dictum*. After all, it is true that nothing in *Blaster v Burns* had to do with activities outside the cramped circumstances of urban life. But I believe that to regard Highman LJ's opinion as having no more than persuasive authority is not only unrealistic,

CONTINUED ▶

given the unanimous support of the Judicial Committee of the House of Lords for the Court of Appeal's judgment in *Blaster v Burns*, but that it would also amount to discourtesy to a judge of a court of authority superior to this one. And I am not prepared to be discourteous to a jurist of the eminence and sagacity of Highman LJ.

Therefore I am willing to take it that it is now good law that if a person undertakes a dangerous activity, whether in the context of urban confines or in the countryside, he or she must bear responsibility for the consequences. But that is not to say that I also find for the claimant in this case. For what is required is a 'dangerous activity' and I do not believe that the storing of pig effluent is dangerous. It is not the same thing at all as, for example, the storage of explosives or volatile substances. Pig muck may be offensive but there is no necessary equivalence between offensiveness and danger. Danger requires that some inherent risk of injury to persons or to their property is present. Risk which arises merely out of an unfortunate combination of circumstances will not suffice.

Therefore I would reject this claim and find for the defendant.

Questions on the judgment in *Fly v Porker*

1. Identify the *ratio decidendi* of the case.

2. Is the law on responsibility of neighbours now settled and in what way could it be developed or changed?

3. Consider whether any of Clearly J's comments in the case amount to *obiter dicta*.

4. Consider in what way the case is a development from the decision in *Berry v Branch*.

Answers are provided in the Appendix on page 310.

If you managed to answer most of the question in the above exercise successfully than you should now have a pretty good understanding of the way in which the law develops through precedent. This will be useful to you not only in your English legal system course but in all areas of substantive law also.

6.3 The interpretation of statutes

6.3.1 The purpose of statutory interpretation

As we have already identified at the start of this chapter in any case before a judge he or she will be called on to reach a decision by applying the existing law to the facts of the case. This as we have said is because judges are prevented from making up the law as they go along. Parliament is the supreme law maker and statute law takes precedence over case law. The so-called 'declaratory theory of law' assumes that judges discover the law in a given factual situation from existing law.

Judges then, as we have seen, play an important role in developing and applying the law through the doctrine of precedent. They also though have a major role in relation to statute law also. This is because, whereas the common law is based on individual principles arising from specific factual circumstances, statute law is essentially theoretical. Parliament states what the law is, but not necessarily how to apply it in factual circumstances. Even where statutes state the law in fairly explicit terms the law still needs to be understood before it can be applied. Since drafters of Acts are likely to engage in some fairly technical legal language the whole process of interpretation comes into play where the law in a particular case comes from statute.

Lawyers will inevitably, in representing their clients, question the actual meanings of words. Judges in these circumstances are bound to decide what is meant in the Act and to give effect to what Parliament was trying to do in passing the Act. This is the process known as statutory interpretation.

You may think that the meanings of words should be straightforward and not need questioning. Sometimes this is the case. For instance if you were studying Occupiers' Liability in Tort this is a statutory area of negligence represented in the Occupiers' Liability Act 1957 (which covers problems suffered by lawful visitors caused by the state of the occupiers' premises) and the Occupiers' Liability Act 1984 (which does exactly the same but for visitors who are not classed as lawful – most importantly for trespassers). You would be surprised to find few cases on the tort other than those that existed before the Acts when the law was still part of the common law of negligence. There are probably two main reasons for this:

- The 1957 Act in particular is usually accepted as being a very straightforward and well drafted Act.
- The principles involved are already well established in the law of negligence and are generally well understood.

However, you will soon find out when you study criminal law that statutory interpretation can be very important and that the meaning of words are not necessarily at all straightforward when it comes to law. If you want a good example of this you will find it when you study the concepts of 'dishonesty' and 'appropriation' in the Theft Act 1968. If you want an even better example you will find it in the wording of the various non-fatal offences under the Offences Against the Person Act 1861.

Generally then you will find that there is no particular need for statutory interpretation unless the words in an Act or other instrument are in dispute. There are, however, many reasons why lawyers might dispute the meaning of words or why judges feel that they need to interpret statutory interpretation. Figure 6.2 overleaf is a table of just some of them.

Problem	Example
Bad drafting It may be as simple as the Parliamentary draftsmen getting the provisions in the Act wrong in some way	A classic example of this that you are likely to learn about fairly early in your law course either in English legal system or in contract law is the case of *Fisher v Bell* [1961] 1 QB 394 where the draftsman used a word usually given another meaning in law. As a result Parliament had to pass another Act.
Ambiguous words The word may have more than one meaning.	In *R v Allen* [1965] 2 QB 295 applying the meaning 'being validly married' to the words 'shall marry' would have made the offence of bigamy unworkable. 'Going through a marriage ceremony' was preferred.
Technical meanings and particular legal meanings Some words have specific technical meanings	*Royal College of Nursing v DHSS* [1982] AC 800 is a good example of this: the words 'registered medical practitioner' can only really be applied to a doctor. This was the difficulty identified by the Court of Appeal.
Social or technological developments Many things change over time and were not envisaged at the time of the legislation	*Royal College of Nursing v DHSS* [1982] AC 800 is also a good example of this. This involved interpreting the words 'registered medical practitioner' under the Abortion Act 1967. By the time of the case it was nurses rather than doctors who were carrying out the procedures.
Terms phrased too broadly	An example of this is *Brock v DPP, The Times*, 23 July 1993 where the words 'type of dog' were used and the problem was whether this referred only to breed or had a wider meaning.

■ *Figure 6.2 Some reasons for statutory interpretation*

6.3.2 A brief overview of the rules of statutory interpretation

There are two approaches

- **The literal approach** – where interpretation relies mainly on the words themselves in isolation.
- **The purposive approach** – a result of our membership of the EU, this approach is concerned with discovering and giving effect to the purpose for which the legislation was enacted regardless of what the technical meaning of the words may be.

There are three rules (which fit into different approaches above)

The literal rule

Judges using this rule give the words in dispute their 'plain, ordinary literal meaning', 'even though they lead to a manifest absurdity' (Lord Esher in *R v City of London Court* (1892))

The golden rule

This is a subsidiary of the literal rule.

In its narrow sense it is only used where using the literal rule might lead to an absurd result. In *Adler v George* [1964] 2 QB 7 it was an offence to be 'in the vicinity' of a prohibited place. The defendant was actually found in the prohibited place and the words 'in the vicinity of' were held to include 'in' otherwise the prosecution under the Official Secrets Act would have failed.

In its broad sense it is used to give a different meaning where the plain meaning would be unacceptable for policy reasons. So in *Re Sigsworth* [1935] Ch 89 the word 'issue' was held not to include a person who had killed his parent to prevent a son inheriting from the mother he had murdered.

The mischief rule (purposive approach in modern usage)

This originally derives from *Heydon's case* (1584) 3 Co Rep 7a which identified a four point procedure:

1. examine the common law prior to the Act
2. locate the mischief or defect in the common law
3. identify the remedy Parliament proposed to eliminate the mischief
4. give effect to that remedy.

So in *Corkery v Carpenter* [1951] 1 KB 102 the offence was for being drunk in charge of a 'carriage' but the court held that this included a bicycle because the mischief in the previous law was the absence of protection of road users from those who were drunk and therefore not in control of their actions.

There are also three language rules

- *Noscitur a sociis* – meaning a word is known by the company it keeps. So in *Beswick v Beswick* [1968] AC 58 the words 'other property' was held to refer only to interests in land otherwise known as real property, because that was what the whole statute was about.

- *Expressio unius est exclusio alterius* – meaning that the express mention of one thing impliedly excludes other things not included. So in *Tempest v Kilner* [1846] 3 CB 249 a list in a section of an Act included 'goods wares and merchandise' and so the section was held not to apply to stocks and shares which were not included in the list.

- *Ejusdem generis* – meaning of the same type. The rule applies where general words follow lists of specific words. The general words must then correspond to the specific words to fall within the scope of the provision. So in *Powell v Kempton Park Racecourse* [1899] AC 143 the list included 'house, office, room or other place used for betting' so the provision could not apply to an outdoor betting area as all the named places in the list were indoor.

The court makes certain presumptions

Judges presume certain things unless the contrary is demonstrated to their satisfaction. Examples include:

- that the common law is not changed by the statute unless it says so
- that in Acts defining crimes *mens rea* (or criminal intent) is required to prove the crime unless the Act identifies it as a strict liability crime
- that the crown will not be liable
- that the jurisdiction of the courts is not ousted.

There are certain other aids to interpretation: intrinsic (internal to the Act) and extrinsic (external to the Act)

Inside the Act

Long and short titles; margin notes; schedules; headings; preambles; interpretation sections.

Outside the Act

Commonly used aids include dictionaries; other similar statutes; and some academic works. More controversial aids are Royal Commission Reports; Law Commission Reports; *Travaux Preparatoires*; and most controversially *Hansard* (the reports on debate inside the Houses of Parliament) (but see now *Pepper v Hart* (1992) which has now validated the use of *Hansard* if certain conditions are met).

6.3.3 Understanding how statutory interpretation works

You now have a reasonable idea of why judges engage in statutory interpretation and of the basic rules and various rules and other aids that they use. You will in any case learn about these in much more detail in your English legal system course.

It is of course all very well to learn about all of these rules so that you can then write about them and the cases in which they appear in coursework or exams. However, if you are able to understand how to apply them, as the judges have to, you have a much more practical understanding not only of the process itself but also of the sorts of problems that the process throws up.

Below are a couple of exercises where you can put into effect your understanding of the process of statutory interpretation and think about using the rules and aids in the way that judges would have to in a case.

ACTIVITY

Exercise on statutory interpretation

Trouble at football grounds is something that is regularly in the news, and there has been a big push recently to end racist abuse by football fans. Let us imagine then the following fictitious situation leading to a fictitious EU Directive and a **fictitious** Act of Parliament.

The European Commission has been put under pressure by MEPs from a number of different EU member states to deal with unacceptable behaviour. This follows from disturbances at various football matches in European football grounds, in international matches, in European club competitions, and indeed more regularly at ordinary league matches. One thing that MEPs have complained about is abusive, partisan and hostile chants and singing by supporters.

As a result, the Commission has produced draft legislation, under both Community discrimination law and health and safety law, in the form of a Directive which was then passed by the Council following consultation with the European Parliament. The major provisions of this Directive, the Football (Prohibition of Provocative Verbalisation) Directive, are reproduced below. Member states are required to put in place the provisions within the Directive within the time specified. Also reproduced below are the major provisions from the UK's Act passed in response.

Read the extracts from the Directive and the Act, and apply the rules of statutory interpretation to the factual situations that follow. You are provided with the answers to the first two situations to give you an idea. You should then try to complete all of the others on your own. When you have finished, the answers are in the Appendix at the back of the book for you to check against. Try to complete the answers without referring to the answers in the Appendix to see if you really know how to apply the rules and aids.

Remember both pieces of legislation are entirely fictitious.

COUNCIL DIRECTIVE

Council Directive 2012/102 on the approximation of laws, regulations and administrative provisions of the Member States concerning the prohibition of racist and abusive verbal behaviour by football supporters in and in the immediate vicinity of football stadia.

The Council of the European Union, having regard to the Treaty establishing the European Community, having regard to the proposal from the Commission, in cooperation with the European Parliament, has adopted this Directive.

CONTINUED ▸

Preamble

Whereas the Council of Ministers considers racist, hostile and provocative verbal abuse by football supporters in and in the immediate vicinity of football grounds to be injurious to the general public, constituting, as it does, harassment of individual groups of people and having the potential for risk to health and safety through public disorder, that the practice of provocative verbalisation by racist, hostile or otherwise abusive singing, chanting or other provocative verbal behaviour by football supporters in and within a 2 kilometre radius of football grounds be prohibited in all Member States ...

Article 1

Scope

This Directive shall apply to all Member States

The date by which the Directive shall be implemented in all Member States is the 1st January 2015.

The extract above contains the major provisions of the Directive for your purposes. The UK Parliament, conscious of the past reputation of UK football fans and keen to be seen to be taking a lead, acted quickly, not by introducing regulations through delegated legislation, as would normally be the case, but by passing an Act, the Football Anthems Act 2012. The major provisions of the Act are reproduced below.

THE FOOTBALL ANTHEMS ACT 2012

An Act to prohibit racist, hostile, abusive and provocative singing and chanting at football matches

s 1(1) It shall be an offence for any person to engage in racist, hostile, abusive or otherwise provocative singing or chanting in association with football matches, whether within a football ground or in a public place within reasonable proximity of a football ground.

(2) A person committing an offence under this Act shall be liable upon conviction to a fine not exceeding five hundred pounds and a ban from attending football matches up to and including a lifetime ban.

s 2(1) In this Act 'public place' shall include any of the following to which the public has access:

CONTINUED ▶

(a) any public thoroughfare within reasonable proximity of a football ground or on the route to a football ground;

(b) any car park or coach park open to the public within reasonable proximity of a football ground or on the route to a football ground;

(c) any building licensed for the purposes of eating food or for the consumption of alcoholic beverages within reasonable proximity of a football ground or on the route to a football ground or other similar place;

(d) any clinic, surgery, hospital or other similar recognised health care facility within reasonable proximity of a football ground or on the route to a football ground where persons injured in connection with a football match may be treated.

s 2(2) In this Act 'thoroughfare' means any road, pavement, precinct or other similar place along, over or through which vehicles or pedestrians pass.

s 4 This Act shall not apply to private residential properties or business premises not open to the general public.

s 5 This Act shall come into effect on 1st August 2012.

You will see instantly that the UK Government has passed the Act within the time limit imposed by the EU. It is more questionable, if you think about it carefully, whether the UK Government has either fully or properly implemented the Directive. First, the Directive covers not only singing and chanting (as specified under the Act), but other forms of abusive verbal behaviour. Secondly, the Directive was limited to the football grounds themselves and the near vicinity, specifically within a 2 kilometre radius. The Act, on the other hand, refers to 'within reasonable proximity', a somewhat loose and ambiguous description. There is also no interpretation section to explain what 'within reasonable proximity' means.

Now that you have read through the extracts from the fictitious Directive and fictitious Act above, try to give answers to the situations below. Remember you are given the answers to the first two straight away so that you have a good idea of how to apply the rules.

All the scenarios that follow occur after the introduction of the Act in 2012.

Scenario 1

Alan, Barry and Chris have been convicted under the Act. They were stopped while walking on a footbridge over a main road about 100 metres from the Rovers stadium where

CONTINUED ▶

Rovers were due to play Albion. While Albion fans were walking on the pavement underneath the footbridge, Alan, Barry and Chris were singing 'We hate Albion, say, we hate Albion'. Alan, Barry and Chris wish to know whether there is any issue of interpretation of the Act that might allow them to appeal successfully.

Answer to Scenario 1

This is a nice straightforward one to start you off and you should be able to easily answer that Alan, Barry and Chris will have no chance of winning an appeal.

- They are all singing and at the very least the song is provocative to Albion fans – which satisfies s 1(1).

- They are in a public place according to s 2(1)(a) and the definition of thoroughfare in s 2(2) as a footbridge is a similar place to a pavement and pedestrians would commonly use it.

- If the literal rule was applied, Alan, Barry and Chris would be guilty because they satisfy the plain, ordinary, literal meaning of 'public place' and of 'thoroughfare' – there is therefore no need to apply the golden rule.

- If the mischief rule was used, then they would still be guilty because the mischief that was remedied by the Act was the lack of any common law prohibiting provocative and abusive football chants and singing.

- If the purposive approach was used, then they would also be guilty because the whole purpose of the Act was to put in place the provisions of Directive 2012/102, the purpose of which was to prohibit racist, hostile and provocative verbal abuse in and in the vicinity of football grounds because of potential discrimination and health and safety risks through public order disturbances.

- You might also spot that there is an intrinsic aid that even a literalist judge might use here which is s 2(2), an interpretation section.

Scenario 2

Dai, a Welshman, has recently received two convictions under the Act. Both arose following Dai's attendance at an international match between England and Wales. The first conviction relates to Dai singing along when the Welsh national anthem was being played over loudspeakers before the start of the game. The second relates to an incident after the game. Dai was injured in a scuffle with England fans and sang abusive anti-English songs in the ambulance on his way to hospital. Dai is appealing on the basis that neither incident falls within the scope of the Act.

CONTINUED ▶

Answer to Scenario 2

This one is a bit more difficult. There are clearly two problem areas that Dai is focusing on. First whether or not singing along to the Welsh national anthem can be classed as 'racist, hostile, abusive or otherwise provocative singing or chanting' for the purposes of s 1(1).

- Dai is inside the ground when he sings the national anthem so both these aspects of s 1(1) are satisfied.

- It would be hard to describe the singing of a national anthem as either hostile or abusive, but the whole point of a national anthem is a demonstration of patriotism and a recognition of different nationality which could therefore be construed as provocative to other nationalities and possibly even racist, if a literal interpretation was used.

- So there is possible ambiguity in the words and the narrow approach of the golden rule might be applied, although it is less certain what the result of this would be.

- For policy reasons the broad approach of the golden rule, the mischief rule or the purposive approach might all be used to determine that this was not the sort of behaviour that the Act intended to prohibit.

- However, there is also an intrinsic aid which complicates things, the title of the Act, since the word 'anthem' is actually used in the title. Of course football anthems are not the same as national anthems so it can be argued that the two, in any case, should be interpreted differently.

Second, whether an ambulance can be classed as *'any clinic, surgery, hospital or other similar recognised health care facility … where persons injured in connection with a football match may be treated'* for the purposes of s 2(1)(d):

- Dai is singing anti-English songs so this aspect of s 1(1) is satisfied whichever rule is used.

- An ambulance can possibly be classed as a 'health care facility' and obviously people injured in connection with a football match could receive some treatment in an ambulance on the way to hospital, so it is an interpretation of s 2(1)(d) that is needed under any rule of statutory interpretation.

- However, looking at the wording, the specific examples given are all buildings and even using the general words 'other similar recognised health care facility', if *ejusdem generis* was applied, the place would need to be a building so that under the literal rule the conviction would fail.

- 'Facility' might be seen as ambiguous and it is possible that the narrow approach of the golden rule could be used, in the way that it was in *Adler v George,* to uphold the conviction and policy reasons, as in *Sigsworth,* under the broad application of the rule, may also be a factor to achieve the same result.

CONTINUED ▸

- Both the mischief rule and the purposive rule, of course, could be used to uphold the conviction since the mischief was the lack of any prior common law prohibiting provocative and abusive football chants and singing, and the clear purpose of the subsection is to prevent health care professionals being subjected to such abusive behaviour and to avoid further trouble.

Now that you feel quite familiar with the application of the different rules and aids, look at the scenarios that follow and see if you can do the same. The answers to these scenarios are in the Appendix at the back of the book.

Scenario 3

Eric has been convicted under the Act. Eric lives in a house in the same street as the United football ground. On match days Eric regularly leans out of his open upstairs window and sings abusive songs to the away supporters. Eric is appealing.

Scenario 4

Freddie runs a portable fast food stand on a piece of waste land five kilometres from the Wanderers' football ground in the north of England. Coaches bringing away fans to the ground regularly pull up in a lay-by near to the wasteland for fans to buy refreshments. Freddie has been convicted after a fight occurred when Freddie told some fans from a London football club that he should not have to serve them because 'all cockneys are animals and you should get your food from the pet shop in town'. Freddie is appealing.

Scenario 5

Gregory, a Town fan, is appealing against his conviction for singing abusive songs about the number of foreign players in the City team. The song includes verses of racial and personal abuse to named members of the City team. He did this while he was on his way to a match at the City ground and was walking on the platform in an underground railway station which (at the surface) is only 200 metres away from the City ground.

Scenario 6

Henry and 17 members of his staff or members of their families have all been convicted under the Act. Henry manages a call centre, which is not open to the public and which is 100 metres from the Borough football ground. Many of the staff, including Henry, are Borough supporters and on match days Henry allows them to park in the company's car park. They were convicted following a recent match against Athletic when they chanted abusive anti-Athletic chants from the company car park at passing Athletic supporters. Henry believes that they should not have been convicted.

If you managed to apply the rules of statutory interpretation in the scenarios in the above exercise successfully then you should now have a pretty good understanding of the way in which judges interpret statutes and the problems they encounter. This will be useful to you not only in your English legal system course but in most areas of substantive law. Even in the law of torts, which is probably the area of law with the least statutory intervention, there are still some important Acts such as the Law Reform (Contributory Negligence) Act 1945 and the Occupiers' Liability Acts 1957 and 1984. Other areas such as criminal law are almost exclusively based on statute, so interpretation is very important.

A familiar instruction in an essay title would commence 'Critically evaluate . . .'. In this event, you would provide an objective assessment, structured clearly so the marker or examiner understands the progression of your argument, of the positive and negative points of the subject.

The most commonly used instructing word in law essays is 'discuss'. Many students, especially in the first year of their studies, find this a vague and misleading direction. They say 'Discuss *what*?' or 'Discuss *how*?' The answer to the first question is to discuss the key words – which are dealt with below. The second question is to remember that a discussion is a two-sided (it may be more) debate where one side holds one particular view and the other side(s) disagree(s). The debate is based on the presentation of arguments for and against each particular view. This is what you must present when you 'discuss' in an essay. The arguments used should be based on evidence (cases, Statutes or authors; see below).

The *key words* tell you what specifically to tackle on that topic – they answer the question asked by the student 'Discuss *what*?'

For example, underline the key words in the following three sample essay titles. You should be able to do this even if you are not studying the topic areas used as examples:

ACTIVITY

> Discuss whether the right to elect trial by jury is a fundamental constitutional right or an argument put forward by guilty offenders who think they will be acquitted.
>
> 'The decision of the courts to find that a duty of care exists between the claimant and defendant is a matter of policy not legal principle.' Discuss.
>
> 'Oblique, or indirect, intent is not based on intention at all. It is based on foresight and foresight is recklessness, not intent.' Discuss.

What you should be able to discern from this activity is that an essay that is just a general (even if accurate) discussion of when a defendant can elect trial by jury will not attain as high marks as an essay that contains the same information, but from the differing points of view that jury trial is and is not a constitutional right. Similarly, a student who merely submits an accurate essay which explains the cases where the judges have and have not found a duty of care to exist, will attain a lower mark than the student whose essay explains the same cases, but also includes an analysis of the policy reasons behind the decisions. A strong essay in the criminal law would use the leading cases on the topic of oblique (or indirect) intent and, for each case, would refer the reader back to the key words in the title and comment on whether the case was decided on the basis of intent or foresight alone. This technique is especially important where the title includes a quote. Good essays use the words of the quote in the essay as regularly as possible (do not be afraid of repetition of the key words – it helps the reader identify you are answering the question).

Subdivided questions

Some titles are broken into smaller components: For example (i), (ii) . . . or (a), (b) . . . The approach here is to answer each sub-question in turn *clearly identifying the two separate parts by a note in the margin.* Unless you are told to the contrary, it would be reasonable for you to assume each subdivision carries equal marks.

Even if not specifically subdivided, take a note of those titles which contain more than one issue. As you can see from the essay titles above, the criminal law essay requires a discussion of both recklessness and intent. The marker may not specifically allocate 50 per cent to each; but a discussion of both is obviously necessary.

Where there is an obvious subdivision by (i), (ii) etc or where there is more than one element to the question, answer in the order asked;

For example, using the ELS/M title above:

Discuss whether the right to elect trial by jury is – FIRST DISCUSS WHAT THE RIGHT TO TRIAL BY JURY IS, WHEN IT ARISES ETC:

a fundamental constitutional right – NOW CONSIDER THE VALIDITY OF THIS VIEW. WHAT EVIDENCE IS THERE IN SUPPORT OF THIS CONTENTION?

or an argument put forward by guilty offenders who think they will be acquitted. – THEN MOVE ON TO THE VALIDITY OF THIS ASSERTION. YOU WILL ALSO NEED TO PROVIDE A WELL REASONED CONCLUSION.

7.4 Time management

How long do you have from the date of receiving the title to the submission date? Between these two dates, how much time (realistically) can you spend on:

- research (hard and electronic copy; textbooks; journals)
- drafting (first and second at least)
- proof reading (at least once; preferably twice or more)
- re-drafting (often a couple of times)
- finalising the essay
- and handing it in (bearing in mind that your computer will crash, the printer will not work and the bus will break down on the way to hand it in)?

In planning the essay, you need to find time for all of these, *and* try to keep full attendance at lectures, full preparation for tutorials and you may have other courseworks to write as well. You may also have a job, a family and other commitments (not including excessive socialising; put it on hold until the coursework is done!). To achieve your full potential in this essay, you need to spend as much time as possible on it, but the term *as much as possible* does not mean you must exclude everything else that has to be done.

First, how much is this essay worth? It is not a good use of your time to spend 90 hours on an essay worth 10 per cent of one module from three or four in a year, but it might be for an essay worth 50 per cent of a module. Either way, it is certainly not worth missing lectures and tutorials on other key topics to do a coursework – you might miss a topic that comes up in the exam which could be worth far more! The best advice is to plan your time carefully, using a diary, including all stages of the essay writing process as well as the other commitments you may have. An example follows in Figure 7.3 based on a two-week hand-in date where the student plans to work at their studies from 9.00 am until 5.00 pm but has a part-time job on Saturday (opposite and overleaf).

Obviously, two hours' preparation for each tutorial may not be enough, and under normal circumstances, this student is likely to dedicate more time to this activity; but with careful time management, they will have been able to plan in advance for those weeks where courseworks have to be done to get ahead of themselves. You might also have noticed this student does not work in the evenings. In fact, they approach their studies as a normal full-time job; and it appears to be a very effective and efficient approach.

Some students work best under pressure; within tight deadlines. The student who uses the diary in Figure 7.3 does not, but prefers to work steadily and to include reflection in the drafting process. Either way is fine, but ask yourself whether a last-minute approach will get you the marks you need and/or you think you deserve. You need to answer that question for yourself, but do think about it. The most common discussion tutors have with students who are disappointed with their marks centres around when the essay was started and how much time was put into it. Most students concede; not early enough and not enough time.

7.5 Creating a structure

As with all the best novels, so too with essays: they have a beginning, a middle and an end.

From your essay writing experience so far, you will know that starting the essay is difficult – so do not start writing until you have an idea of what you want to say. If you just cannot seem to get the opening words right, plan the rest of the essay in full, then decide what the start, middle and conclusion should be.

TIP

One of the most common and useful beginnings to a law essay is to start with a definition of the subject area. This might be an explanation of the basic topic area – but do not be too basic; you must presume your reader is intelligent.

Week 1		Monday	Tuesday	Wednesday	Thursday	Friday	Saturday	Sunday
	9–10	Library – preparation for tutorial subject 1	Library – preparation for tutorial subject 2	Tutorial subject 3	Go to IT room to log on to Westlaw and see if there are any recent developments	Have a lie in until 10.00	Job	Work from home, typing up first draft. Aim for 1,000 words. Make sure case citations etc are added in footnotes. Back up draft to 2 disks
	10–11		Lecture subject 1	Library – preparation for tutorial 4				
	11–12	Tutorial subject 1	Tutorial subject 2	Tutorial subject 4	Lecture subject 2	Library – final stage of research including double check against assessment criteria		
	12–1	Lunch then library for research for coursework – look in textbooks and photocopy the leading cases to take notes tomorrow	Lunch then library for research for coursework – read the key cases; highlight important quotes. Make notes		Finish reading journals, texts and cases. Have lunch			
	1–2			Lunch then library for research for coursework – continue reading cases and also have a look for journals and other texts to expand bibliography	Plan a flow chart – the beginning, middle and end of the essay. Think about which cases and which articles' quotes work best. Roughly estimate word limit per paragraph to stay within 2,000 word limit	Lunch		Lunch
	2–3							Start tutorial preparation for next week
	3–4	Lecture subject 4	Coffee break then Library – preparation for tutorial subject 3 – tomorrow			Lecture subject 3		
	4–5	Library – preparation for tutorial subject 2 – tomorrow				Write up lecture notes from all 4 lectures this week		

Figure 7.3 Plan your time carefully using a diary – week 1

175

Never start an essay with the phrase 'In this essay I am going to . . .' The marker knows what you need to do – it is in the title; so do not talk about doing it; just do it! The earlier you can start explaining the law, the more marks you will attract and the more focused the answer will be. You may wish to start with a definition of the key terms in the title, but in the following title:

> 'The decision of the courts to find a duty of care exists between the claimant and defendant is a matter of policy not legal principle.' Discuss.

do not discuss the meaning of the terms defendant and claimant, but you may wish to explain your understanding of the terms legal principle and policy. Had the assessor wished to know such basic points, he would have asked for them; and the question is clearly focused on the principle/policy point in establishing a duty; not on the meanings of the terms defendant and claimant.

7.5.2 The main debate

The middle of the essay is the bulk of the answer and, on the whole, is where the marks will be awarded. At the planning stage, make sure the middle of your essay progresses logically through the statute or case law explaining the issues that arise in the question. Structure your answer so that each sentence is short and clear. As a rule of thumb, deal with only one issue per paragraph, but do deal with all of that issue within that paragraph – do not make the reader look around for the rest of the point.

In an essay, rather than a problem-style question, an analysis of the development of case law is often required (and it certainly is for the torts and criminal law examples used above); so be logical and deal with the cases in chronological order. Use the word count carefully; you are taking a law degree (of one form or another), so make sure your analysis is of the law, not the facts of the case. There is no hard and fast rule about reciting case facts in law essays, but generally, do not spend too long merely explaining facts. It is often a waste of valuable words to do so and if it does not further your argument, leave it out. Case facts may be helpful, particularly if you wish to use the facts to make a specific point with them. For example, a paragraph in the torts essay above might be:

> In *Alcock v CC of South Yorkshire* [1992] 1 AC 310, there was held to be no duty of care to the friends and relations of those who died in the Hillsborough disaster who watched the event on television. Whilst a live television transmission of a disaster could be regarded as equivalent to seeing the events in person, there are broadcasting regulations governing what may and may not be shown; and the suffering of recognisable individuals falls into the latter.

This explanation shows the student knows the facts of the case and they have used the facts to make a point. However, a paragraph that merely explains the facts of the famous case of *Donoghue v Stevenson* [1932] AC 562 is almost certainly wasting words.

As for the end of the essay, see the advice on how to conclude below.

7.6 Using the assessment criteria or learning outcomes

Before you start writing the essay, check your plan meets the assessment criteria or learning outcomes. Here are two examples of typical assessment criteria in undergraduate essays:

Example 1

When marking your coursework, particular regard will be had to the following matters:

- depth of understanding of key legal principles
- evidence of independent planning and research (including use of a range of information from both primary and secondary sources)
- ability to apply the law concisely and in good English to the facts
- knowledge and appropriate use of legal language
- critical analysis of relevant legal issues
- ability to construct logical, coherent and sustainable legal arguments.

Example 2

The student should be able to:

Substance

- demonstrate knowledge and understanding of the relevant legal principles
- demonstrate the ability to apply relevant case law to the question
- demonstrate research skills to locate paper or electronic versions of the principal cases and/or legislation
- construct logical, coherent and well-ordered legal arguments
- provide a conclusion indicating reasoned conclusions on the present state of the law.

Presentation

- present the essay as a neat word-processed or typescript document (min size 11 font) correctly spelt and punctuated and free from grammatical errors
- provide accurate citations in the proper form for all case references and proper references for all other sources cited or relied on
- provide a bibliography.

It is worth double checking that you understand what each means – if not, use your student handbook, or go to see your tutor.

7.7 Grammar, syntax and spelling

Grammar is a branch of language. It is an abstract system of rules which deals with such matters as not saying: 'they was'. Syntax is another branch of language. It deals with the arrangement of words in a sentence. It deals with such matter as not saying: 'Which is why Nottingham Forest lost'.

Why should we care about grammar so much? A good grasp of English is vital for students of law because the law is about words. Words convey and affect meaning. Words produce clearer and more persuasive communication. Well written answers have more authority. If none of these reasons satisfies you, the final point should: Good command of English maximises marks.

You may never have been taught grammar to a high level before; you may think it harsh that you can lose marks for not knowing the rules; but it is the same as not knowing a leading case on an issue. There is no excuse! Spell check can help with spelling BUT avoid American spellings because most programmes accept them and always *always* proof read.

AVOID	REPLACE WITH
Isn't	Is not
Don't	Do not
Can't	Cannot
Defendants	Unless you mean more than one defendant in the plural, you almost certainly mean defendant's (eg the defendant's right to trial by jury).
Judgement	Judgment
Lord Justice Auld	Auld LJ
It's when you mean *its*	If you are discussing a decision of a court: *its* decision. If you want to write *it is*, then write *it is*, never use *it's* (see the first row above).
I, me or you	Avoid personal terms (*I* is the first person, *you* is the second person). Use the third person – *he*, *she* or *it*.

CONTINUED ▶

AVOID	REPLACE WITH
To justly decide	You should say 'to decide justly'. 'To justly decide' is a split infinitive. Please avoid splitting the 'to' from the active verb. *To* boldly *go* is the epitome of a split infinitive. We appreciate the thrust of the sentence might be lost if it said 'To go boldly'; so split infinitives are not banned completely; but use only if unavoidable please.
The issue being duty of care.	The issue *IS* the duty of care. The word 'being' is being increasingly used as an active verb in verbal communication. It is not accurate. Have you ever seen a green squiggly line under your work on the computer screen, but you cannot work out what 'Fragment (consider revising)' means? It means the sentence has no active verb; your sentence is not *doing* anything (and it certainly is not scoring you any marks).
Authorize, specialize	Authorise and specialise. The 'z' indicates an Americanism. (We do accept it is also very old English (for those of you who are grammatical pedants) but the 'z' is to be avoided in modern English, please.) Note: your spell check will not assist with this; and it may even tell you the English version is wrong! Ignore it and use an English dictionary.
Would of, could of, should of	This is wholly inaccurate and inexcusable use of the word 'of' as the past participle of the verb to have. You mean, for example: *The claimant should* have *known about the clause in the contract because . . .*

■ *Figure 7.7 Tips on grammar and syntax*

7.8 Using only relevant material

An essay title is never 'Write everything you know about . . .'; so please do not. Just because you know it and want the reader to know that you do, that does not mean it is relevant. The rule of thumb, as mentioned above, but worth repeating here, is that if it does not further your argument and help you answer the question, leave it out. It does not matter how accurate your answer is. If it contains irrelevancy, you cannot be given credit because to do so would be unfair to those students who did answer the question using relevant material only.

How do you decide what is relevant? First, use your lecture handouts to get an idea of the minimum content. If you are in doubt about the best structure to adopt, your lecture handouts may also provide you with good hints because your lecturers usually put the handouts in a logical order; progressing from the basics to the more complex issues. Remember to make a note of all case citations (doing this as you go along is tedious, but in the long run saves loads of time). Next, refer to a range of textbooks. Do you grasp the point each author is making? Can you express the issues in your own words? (If not, consider whether you need to quote the author, or merely attribute the ideas to the author – see below on referencing.)

Answer the question! This may sound like meaningless advice, but ask any of your tutors, and they will all tell you; they mark more formless, 'everything including the kitchen sink' essays consisting of no more than verbal diarrhoea, than essays where the knowledge has been brought to the question in a thoughtful and informed manner and where the answer clearly makes an effort to relate the content to the question asked.

Never forget that the reader will be looking for evidence to support your arguments. This evidence may be statutes, cases or books of authority.

First, cases. In courseworks, there is no excuse for not citing cases accurately. This means the reference *Donoghue v Stevenson* should *always* be *Donoghue v Stevenson* [1932] AC 562. You need not necessarily spend too long dealing with cases; and you certainly do not need to use an equal amount of words on each. For example, you could say:

> During the 1980s, the test used by the courts to establish a duty of care was very wide, limited only by public policy issues (*Anns v Merton* [1978] AC 728), but this was overruled in *Murphy v Brentwood* [1991] 1 AC 398 and the current test is found in *Caparo v Dickman* [1990] 2 AC 605. The new test is based on three elements, all three of which must be satisfied. The elements are foreseeability, proximity and whether it is fair, just and reasonable to impose a duty of care. It was intended that this test would be applied irrespective of the type of loss suffered.

Essays must not look like the table of cases from the start of a textbook. Listing cases is an awful habit. Clearly stating the law as decided (the better term is held) in those cases is far better practice.

If one of the sources of law is statutory, make sure you use the correct name for the Act (what is known as the short title) and the correct year. You are generally not required to cite the chapter number (the number given to the Act when it receives Royal Assent); nor do you ever cite the statute book you used to find the Act if you did. Acts are primary sources in themselves. When referring to legislation, try to be specific: If the law you are referring to is in a particular section, refer to that section. As a matter of technique, the word 'Section' is written in full at the start of a sentence. If it arises during a sentence, the abbreviation 's' is used. If more than one section is referred to, sections is abbreviated to 'ss'. Subsections always appear in brackets, eg, 's 1(3)', rather than 's 1 subsection 3'.

You do not have to reproduce the section in full – it is often a waste of words to do so – but you may wish to extract a few of the key words in the section with which you wish to make a point. For example:

> Section 43 of the Criminal Justice Act 2003 provided for judge-only trial where the judge was satisfied that the 'length and complexity' of the case warranted it. However, to come into force, the section required an affirmative resolution of both

Houses of Parliament, which the government was unable to obtain. The Fraud (Trials without a Jury) Bill contained a provision to abolish the affirmative resolution procedure, but it was postponed by the House of Lords in March 2007 for six months.

Everything mentioned in the essay must be relevant to the title to attract marks. For example, in the exemplar essay titles suggested above, the following would be irrelevant:

Title	ELS/M	Torts	Crime
Irrelevant	Historical development of the jury trial	Calculating damages for breach of duty of care	The meaning of the word reckless
Why	This has nothing to do with the right of a defendant to elect jury trial	This has nothing to do with the tests used to establish a duty in the first place; damages are assessed only if a duty of care exists	Be careful here: if you were to explain how the definition of intention differs from the definition of the word reckless, this certainly could be relevant; but merely explaining what it is without *making* it relevant to the title will not help you answer the question.

Figure 7.8 Irrelevant detail in essays

As you can see from the end column, sometimes the difference between relevant and irrelevant material is how you *use* the information. If you can adapt your explanation to the key words of the title, you can use the material to further your argument. Compare the examples below which might be parts of answers to the ELS/M title:

Jury trial has existed in the English legal system since the fourteenth century.

You might say; 'So what?'

All the writer has to do now is add a few words to make the sentence relevant:

Jury trial has existed in the English legal system since the fourteenth century, which shows it is a tradition, even if not a fundamental constitutional right.

Rather than wasting the 13 words in the first sentence completely, adding another 13 makes the point and makes it well. Word limits are tight: but it is not always what you say in essays that counts; sometimes it is how you say it. The reader knows you have a word limit and will assess the essay bearing this in mind. Note that word limits are not set randomly – the assessor decides how many words you should need to make the arguments succinctly, accurately and using only relevant information. Remember this: if you find yourself a long way over the word limit on your first draft; ask yourself:

- Are you sure all the information is relevant?

- Have you wasted words reciting unnecessary case facts?

- Have you wasted words in a long quote, when you only really need a few words?

- Have you waffled? Check you have made your points clearly and concisely.

- Have you repeated yourself? Even if you wish to emphasise a point, you do not need to say it more than once; you can presume the reader is intelligent and will follow your argument.

The first draft is never the final draft; and if you have ever submitted the first and only thing you have written on a topic as the final version, you should realise now why you did not do as well as you could have.

Once you have drafted the explanations, you are half way there. However, law essays are not purely explanatory. Most, if not all, titles indicate that some analysis of the state of the law is expected. So, do not just explain what the law *is*; you are also expected to say what is right and wrong with the law, provided your comments are relevant to the title of course. This is the analysis and evaluation element of the essay. You are not, however, expected to provide this analysis from your own personal view. You may do so if you wish (but never state 'I think . . .' or 'I believe . . .' because such a statement lacks objectivity), but if you cannot think of anything to say, most leading authors will be able to, and you can quote them.

NOTE

Can you, hand on heart, say 'yes' to the following question? *Would a person who picked up your essay answer, but not the title, be able to make a good guess at what the title is?* If not, you must go back and re-write your response!

☐ ☐ ☐

7.9 Quotations

Never forget to attribute a quote. Put the quote in quotation marks. Put the source information in brackets afterwards or in a footnote. Never pass off an opinion as your own if you have taken it from someone else (even if you happen to agree with it!). Doing so is plagiarism: it is cheating. It is bad academic practice at the very least; it could land you in the middle of an academic irregularity investigation and possibly lead to the Law Society or Bar Council being informed on a reference at worst. It is vital to remember: quoting is not cheating in itself; in fact, quoting well from authoritative sources shows good research skills which will increase your marks: but *failure to state the source (cite it) is plagiarism*. There is no excuse!

Plagiarism

ACTIVITY

Are you sure you know what plagiarism is?

Look in your course/module handbook. Find a definition online if you cannot find what you are looking for (for example, see www.jiscpas.ac.uk or enter 'plagiarism' into a search engine).

Answer either true or false to each of the questions below:

- It is not plagiarism if someone else's words are unintentionally reproduced.   T/F

- It is not plagiarism if I only take someone else's ideas but put them in my own words.   T/F

- It is not plagiarism if I copy someone else's diagram, only if I copy text.   T/F

- It is not plagiarism if I change the odd word or phrase from someone else's work.   T/F

- It is not plagiarism if the material I use is available on the Internet anyway.   T/F

- Most of my tutors don't recognise plagiarism when it is in front of them and they have no way of finding out that I have copied.   T/F

- It is not plagiarism if I quote a paragraph by placing it in inverted commas with the source cited in a footnote and in again in my bibliography.   T/F

All of the above statements are false except for the last one. Your tutors are very familiar with the textbooks on the market, and with most of the websites that deal with the subject matter that they teach. Each of the authors of this textbook have marked work containing unattributed material copied from their own published works! Even if the copying is not quite as blatant as this, tutors can still identify plagiarised work, and there are websites to which institutions can subscribe to assist tutors in running 'spot checks' on student work. The most well-known is called Turnitin (see http://turnitin.com/static/plagiarism.html). You might find this a useful site too. Students can also subscribe and run their own work through first to check nothing has been unintentionally copied.

Good referencing is a legal skill: poor referencing gets you in trouble, but well selected quotations enhance your work.

So what to quote? Avoid quoting explanations of the law. Try to express these in your own words so the reader can assess your understanding of the issue. So, for example, the following quote would be better expressed in your own words:

> 'Before the plea before venue scheme was introduced, research into defendants' reasons for choosing summary trial and trial by jury (where a choice is permitted) suggested that the major factor was the intended plea . . .'

> Smith, Bailey and Gunn on *The Modern English Legal System*, 4th edn, Sweet and Maxwell, 2002, p 919.

On the other hand, the following is more evaluative. It is making a comment on the state of the law, rather than merely stating what the law is, so would make a useful quote:

> 'The election for Crown Court trial is arguably a tactic to create further delay, therefore putting pressure on the CPS to accept lower charges, on the prosecution witnesses to drop the case and generally to avoid the "evil day" of trial.'

> Smith, Bailey and Gunn on *The Modern English Legal System*, 4th edn, Sweet and Maxwell, 2002, p 920.

Try to keep other people's comments in your answer to a minimum; it is, after all, your knowledge, understanding and commentary that the reader is assessing; not anyone else's. Remember, too, that however insightful a quote is, unless it helps you to answer the question, do not use it.

7.10 Engaging in a balanced discussion

There are at least two sides to every discussion and in your essay: you need to cover both to maximise marks. You may disagree with one point of view, but do not ignore it. Deal with it and counter the argument as best you can. At undergraduate level, this is rather more sophisticated than presenting a list of the advantages and disadvantages of a particular issue and you should certainly never use bullet points in essays. Write in continuous prose (ie full sentences and proper full paragraphs). Never express your personal opinion in the following ways:

✗ I think

✗ In my opinion

✗ It is not fair

There are better ways!

Try:

✓ There are good grounds for arguing . . .

✓ The better opinion is . . .

✓ It follows therefore that the law . . .

Many law students feel the need to make essays rather grandiose with flowery language. There is absolutely no need to do this. If you were a practising lawyer and spoke like this in court, the judge may wonder what you were talking about, and in a criminal trial, you certainly make no sense to the jury! Instead, keep it simple. You may agree that the law is sufficiently complicated without you adding to the complication of it in the language you use.

One practice that has found its way from the court into law essays is the term 'I submit'. A submission is usually made by counsel, when she is, rather humbly, suggesting to the judge that the law as decided in a previous case was wrongly decided. While this practice has its place in the court room, it is a rather convoluted way to say what you mean. Compare:

✗ I submit that this case was decided wrongly because . . .

With

✓ The decision can be criticised on the grounds that . . .

The second phrase has the benefit of maintaining a degree of objectivity and as a result it sounds more authoritative.

How to balance the discussion in your essay will depend on what you are being asked to discuss. The ELS/M suggested title above indicates the two views that need to be considered and a list of the advantages and disadvantages of jury trial is not going to answer the question. A reasoned debate considering (on the one hand) the constitutional right of a defendant to elect jury trial and (on the other) the higher acquittal rate at the Crown Court, will. Say, for example, it is your opinion that jury trial *is* a constitutional right; one technique to consider using is to deal with all of the arguments *against* your view first and then focus the remainder of your answer and your conclusion on what you think are your strongest arguments. In this way, you will persuade the reader that what you say is correct and you will be credited for a clear structure.

7.11 Reaching sensible and reasoned conclusions

Some tutors advise that new information may be given in a conclusion; others say the conclusion should only draw together the arguments already made. Neither is true, however, to the exclusion of the other. Your conclusion should, without doubt, be *based* on arguments made. An essay whose 'middle' part supports the view that oblique intent (the Criminal Law suggested title above) *is* merely a form of recklessness would lose marks if the conclusion stated it was *not*. But your conclusion must not *merely* repeat already arguments made – this is a waste of words and the marker will not credit the same point twice! The best conclusions are forward looking; this is not as odd as it sounds. Although it is the end of the essay, it is not the end of the matter and the law will continue to evolve and develop; so consider finishing the essay with a brief discussion about any proposals for reform in this area of law and what effect (if any) it might have on the topic discussed. Law Commission proposals are an invaluable source of information in this respect.

Alternatively, you may have a really strong point to make. You may have the winning argument in this discussion; and although it is related to the arguments already raised, you could decide to

Common comments made	What they mean	What you need to do about it
Sense?	Something in this part of your essay does not make sense. Is this a grammar issue, or have you made an assertion that is wrong in law?	Re-read and if necessary, say the offending paragraph out loud. If still in doubt, ask your tutor.
Structure!	Have you jumped from one point to a completely different point half way through a paragraph? This may have caused the reader to get confused. Alternatively, you might have repeated a point already made and the reader is calling your attention to this.	As part of the planning for your next essay, draw a flowchart showing how each point builds upon points already made. Make sure there is a logical progression from one issue to the next.
Citation/Source/ Reference?	The reader has highlighted here that a case has not been cited correctly, or you have not provided the correct reference for a quote or other source of information. This commonly arises where you have said that 'Many people think . . .' or 'The Report recommended that . . .' without stating where you obtained the information.	As you research your next coursework, keep a note as you go along of where you found the information *and* case citations. It will save you time in the long run.
Relevance?	You have included material that is either irrelevant or which you have not made relevant to the title.	No student ever submits an essay knowing there is information in it that is irrelevant. But, with hindsight, can you see why you thought an issue was relevant but which in fact is not? You may have to discuss this with your tutor, but do take the time to do so. Once the essay is returned, there is nothing you can do about it; but you can improve for next time.

Figure 7.9 Interpreting the marker's comments

There may be criticisms in the comments – do not take this personally, but learn from them. Now write yourself a checklist for future essays. Keep this handy and before you do another essay, double check you meet the action plan!

Further reading

Smith, Glanville Williams, *Learning the Law*, 13th edn, London: Sweet and Maxwell, 2006, Chapter 9.

Truss, L., *Eats, Shoots & Leaves: The Zero Tolerance Approach to Punctuation*, Profile, 2003.

chapter 8 COMPLETING COURSEWORK ASSIGNMENTS – 2 – PROBLEM QUESTIONS ■

AIMS AND OBJECTIVES

After reading this chapter you should be able to:

- Identify the key facts in a problem question

- Create a structure for your answer

- Use the assessment criteria to meet the demands of the assignment

- Use relevant material only, and discard irrelevant material

- Quote appropriately from and provide accurate citations to cases, Acts and academic authors

- Apply the law to the facts of the problem to reach a conclusion

Many of the remarks mentioned in Chapter 7 are also relevant here, for example, those regarding spelling, grammar, using relevant material and avoiding waffle. You are strongly advised therefore to read Chapter 7 (again or for the first time) before starting this chapter. However, if you do not have time, wherever the information does overlap, you are pointed to the appropriate part of Chapter 7.

8.1 What is a problem question?

Problem questions are a set of hypothetical facts. They look like a short (and for the parties involved usually an unfortunate) story.

- They look longer than essay titles, which usually ask for an analysis of one area of law for academic discussion, but the areas of law could be similar, as could the length of the answer required.

- The problem question could very well be the sort of problem that clients have when they first go to see a solicitor.

- You may recognise the facts as they might be a mixture of several decided cases in one big question, but more commonly they are similar to decided cases, but different in some important ways we will examine later.

You may feel the facts of the question are entirely unrealistic; do not worry about that. In the world of question-setting, the assessor realises the question is rather fantastical (you will see this from the examples on police powers and the criminal law below: Angela, Robert and Juan are having rather unusual days!) but the lack of realism may be necessary to enable students to get to grips with the legal issues that arise. That's not to say real cases are dull – far from it – just to get you to realise that problem questions are rarely dull either!

> **TIP**
>
> Before you start, a word of advice:
>
> **Do not be afraid of thinking.**
> **You may have to prepare yourself for some deep pondering about the law.**
> **Better thought-out responses score higher marks.**
>
> *This may have gone without saying, but it was worth a mention to the novice student.*

8.1.1 Why are so many questions on a law course problem based?

That's the nature of law. That's what lawyers and judges do. They problem solve. To be fair, that's not *all* that lawyers do – they may also be required to comment on and evaluate the law, so essay questions have an important role in a law course too, but most modules will use at least one problem-style question in the assessment regime. This is only common sense as it is preparation for the world of professional legal practice. It is vital that you start to develop the special skills required in problem solving as early as possible. We cannot state strongly enough that this reason alone should persuade you that full attendance at seminars is vital; without it, you are going to find answering problem questions tough. It does get easier with regular practice though, we promise.

The most crucial factor to remember from the start is that in answering a problem-based question, *you are the judge.* To illustrate this, read an appeal case: any case at all in any area of the law. Examine the process a judge goes through when delivering a judgment. The judge will identify the material or key facts of the case, will examine the law that governs those issues, will apply the law to the facts and will deliver his or her decision on who wins the case. That is exactly the process you have to go through when answering a problem question.

In fact, if you think about it, all cases are just legal problem questions, aren't they? The difference is that the court cases are real; your problem question will almost certainly be fictitious, but to one extent or another, it will be loosely based on real cases.

The second introductory point is to note that a problem question is not an invitation to write an essay. The facts of the question are important and they are there for a reason: to get you to apply the law.

We will consider the structure of a problem question answer in more detail below. Let's start at the beginning.

8.2 Identifying the area of law

Read the question. Read it again. Do not skim read it. Now do it again.

You should be getting the picture. A failure to grasp all of the issues raised in the question can usually be traced back to a failure to read the facts properly and completely. To give a real example: One student in a problem question kept saying in her answer 'If Bruce had been drunk'. This was amazing; *the question specifically stated Bruce had been drinking alcohol all day and was very inebriated*. Another, when considering a local authority's duty of care, discussed the remoteness of damage *had* his garden flooded; which, on the facts, it had! There is no excuse in courseworks – you will be given the question in enough time for you to be able to read the question regularly.

To identify the area of law in the question, you need to know your subject matter well. It comes back to attendance and preparation again. Presuming you have at least some knowledge of either the law of torts (exemplar question 1), police powers (2) or the criminal law (3), we will pick apart some examples.

8.2.1 The torts example

Sample question 1 (torts)

Angela still plays competitively for a woman's hockey team despite being seven months' pregnant. During a match an opposing defender, Becky, trips Angela with her hockey stick while trying to prevent an attacking move. Angela falls heavily, landing on her stomach, and also banging her head as a result of which she loses consciousness.

Angela is rushed to hospital still unconscious. Doctor Careless carries out an emergency Caesarian section on Angela to save the baby, but the baby is stillborn. During the operation the doctor discovers that Angela also has an infected womb. Although the infection is not life threatening, Doctor Careless performs a hysterectomy (removes Angela's womb).

When Angela is recovering in her hospital bed, Doctor Careless tells her about the hysterectomy. Angela is angry because she wanted to have more children. She shouts at the doctor 'I'll make sure that you never have children either!' Nurse Dowell calms Angela but when she leaves Angela's hospital room she locks the door in case Angela gets angry again and tries to find the doctor.

Fifteen minutes later Doctor Careless goes to Angela's room to give her a sedative but he finds it locked. He then tells Nurse Dowell to unlock the door. Angela is unaware that she has been locked in.

Advise Angela of any actions that she might take.

■ *Figure 8.1 Sample question on torts*

Angela is having a very bad day. While she is not real, there are some real legal issues that arise. The next step is for you to get to the detail of the problem. The clues for this will be in the question. Perhaps the most important piece of advice is for you to read every word of the question and read the question several times before you start to write the answer. This will help you identify the specific area of tort law that arises and ensure you do not accidentally omit a key issue. To find out, first use your lecture notes and tutorial questions to see if you recognise the issues. Certain 'flags' or pointers are put in problem questions (usually based on past cases so you can identify them); can you identify the flags above?

- She is playing a sport

- She is injured by contact with another player's hockey stick

- She is unconscious when she is taken to hospital

- The doctor carries out an emergency operation

- The doctor also carries out an operation that is not an emergency

- Angela gets angry because of this and threatens the doctor

- The nurse locks Angela in a hospital room for a short time

- Angela is unaware that she has been locked in.

What specific topics in torts have you learned that are relevant here? Do you recognise any cases that are similar? You are correct if you identified the question as dealing with the tort of trespass to the person. Within that area of law, however, there is more than one tort (assault, battery, false imprisonment) and it is very common in problem questions to have to deal with a number of issues. The main issues here are whether:

- Becky has committed a battery on Angela

- Becky has a defence of consent

- Doctor Careless has committed a battery on Angela with the emergency Caesarian

- Doctor Careless has a defence

- Doctor Careless has committed a battery on Angela with the hysterectomy

- Doctor Careless has any defence

- the nurse has falsely imprisoned Angela by locking her in

- it matters that Angela is unaware of the false imprisonment.

8.2.2 The police powers example

Some questions are very specific about what the assessor wishes the student to comment on. You will see from the instructing words in the question below that the tutor specifically points out the area of law to be considered:

Sample question 2 (police powers)

Robert, a law student, was walking home from the pub late at night. He desperately needed to go to the toilet and stood behind a tree on the pavement in order to urinate (this is an offence).

Police Constable Woodcock, a uniformed police officer, witnessed this taking place and, when Robert had finished, he approached him and asked him his name and address. Robert replied (truthfully), 'My name's Robert Redford and ha! believe it or not I live in a flat above the Sundance Pub.' (This is the name of a well-known actor who starred in the film *Butch Cassidy and the Sundance Kid*.)

'So you're a comedian are you?' said PC Woodcock. 'Let's see if you think this is funny. You're nicked'.

(a) Advise Robert on the legality of his arrest.
(90 per cent of the marks available for this question)

(b) The police have charged Robert with two offences; urinating in a public place and obstructing a police officer in the execution of his duty. Who will decide whether Robert should face trial for these offences and on what basis is this decision likely to be made?
(10 per cent of the marks available for this question)

■ *Figure 8.2 Sample question on police powers*

You will see here that the assessor wants the student to analyse the arrest and the prosecution of Robert, but that the marks for each are clearly specified. If this is the same in your question, relate the word limit to the mark allocation. So in a 1,500 word limited answer, try to spend no more than 150 words on part B (you cannot be given more than 10 per cent of the marks available for that part, however good your answer is).

Just like the tort, we need to identify the flags. Let's focus on the flags in part A. Can you identify the flags in the question?

- It is late at night
- Robert commits an offence
- Witnessed by a uniformed police officer
- The officer asks him for his name and address
- Robert supplies him with his name and address
- The police officer does not believe Robert's answer and he arrests him by just stating 'You're nicked'.

The major issue is the question of arrest. You can use the flags as a guide for the answer.

- What are the police powers of arrest?
- What are the procedures to be followed on arrest?
- Can a policeman ask an individual to provide them with his or her name and address?
- Can an arrest be made if a policeman does not believe a name and address that is provided?

8.2.3 The crime example

In criminal law questions more than in any other of law, students tend to be distracted by how the facts of the question could be proved. The answer is that:

- the facts are hypothetical; they are not real
- therefore ignore issues of proof; just accept the facts as stated, and
- you are not concerned with questions of proof, but with questions of criminal liability.

The facts of the question below are sacrosanct – you have to accept what you are told. The assessor has also informed the student which offences the defendants have been charged with; even if you think they have been charged with the wrong offence, or should not have been charged, that is irrelevant.

Sample question 3 (Criminal law)

Juan was shopping in Nottingham City Centre when he was approached by Maria, a campaigner for the 'Save the Trees' charity. Maria was going to ask Juan to sign her petition but Juan thought she was going to attack him and he shoved Maria away. Maria tripped on an uneven cobble stone and fell to the ground, suffering bruising to her hands and elbows.

Ronaldo, who witnessed the incident and who was very intoxicated, shouted at Juan. Juan went to run off, but Ronaldo, because of his drunkenness, thought Juan was going to hit him. Ronaldo punched Juan, causing Juan a concussion from which Juan fully recovered.

Discuss the liability, if any, of Juan who has been charged under section 47 of the Offences Against the Person Act 1861 and Ronaldo, who has been charged under section 18 of the Offences Against the Person Act 1861.

Figure 8.3 Sample question on Criminal law

There are two charges. By all means, make sure you do examine whether the elements of these offences are satisfied; but do not spend too many words on that part of the answer because the two offenders have made mistakes about the circumstances; they thought they were acting in self-defence but they were wrong (this is called mistaken or putative self-defence) and one of them was drunk. These are very important parts of the question to deal with and even though you have not been given a specific instruction to deal with them, the flags are clearly emphasised in the facts.

8.3 Sorting out the key facts

These are the 'flags' referred to above. What does this mean?

- No word in a problem question is there without a reason.
- The actions of the parties have been carefully thought out by the assessor to give you hints on the issues and to make sure you deal with the areas of law to be assessed.

- You must make sure you find all of these signposts, or indicators, and deal with the law applicable to each.

- The key facts guide you in identifying which issues of law arise.

As part of your preparation, to find the key facts, you might highlight the different issues in different colour pens, or underline the flags and put the relevant cases next to the underlined parts. Alternatively, you might find it useful to recite the facts of the question to a person who does not know the law and then you try to explain to them what area of law is involved. This technique can be surprisingly beneficial; sometimes just putting problems into words helps solve them.

So for instance, if we look at the tort problem again (see Figure 8.1) and do some highlighting of the key facts:

Sample question 1 (torts)

Angela still plays competitively for a woman's hockey team despite being <u>seven months' pregnant</u>. In a match an opposing defender, Becky, <u>trips</u> Angela <u>with her hockey stick</u> while trying to prevent an attacking move. Angela <u>falls heavily landing on her stomach</u> and also banging her head as a result of which she <u>loses consciousness</u>.

Angela is rushed to hospital still unconscious. Doctor Careless carries out an <u>emergency</u> Caesarian section on Angela <u>to save the baby</u> but the baby was stillborn. During the operation the doctor discovers that Angela also has an infected womb. Although the infection is <u>not life threatening</u>, Doctor Careless <u>performs a hysterectomy</u> (removes Angela's womb).

When Angela is recovering in her hospital bed, Doctor Careless tells her about the hysterectomy. Angela is <u>angry</u> because she wanted to have more children. She <u>shouts</u> at the doctor '<u>I'll make sure that you never have children either!</u>' Nurse Dowell calms Angela but when she leaves Angela's hospital room she <u>locks the door</u> in case Angela gets angry again and tries to find the doctor.

Fifteen minutes later Doctor Careless tells Nurse Dowell to unlock the door to Angela's room so that he can sedate Angela. <u>Angela is unaware that she has been locked in.</u>

Advise Angela of any actions that she might take.

Figure 8.4 Highlighted sample of question on torts

All of the words that are underlined are critical not just as pointers to what the problem is about but also in identifying the appropriate law that will determine any liability.

One point has already been mentioned above, but is worth repeating: *Do not make up facts.* Another point is about *omitted* facts.

In the criminal law question (see Figure 8.2), for example, you have been told that Ronaldo is drunk; but you are not specifically told that Juan is sober. It is acceptable in these circumstances to presume Juan is sober because if he had not been, you would have been told. (To play it safe, you could add a sentence that you infer that Juan is sober.) On the other hand, you are not told (ie the assessor has omitted to tell you) whether the mistakes made by each defendant are honest and/or reasonable. That is because in each scenario, you have to consider these alternatives. In order to assess the depth of your understanding, the assessor will often omit a key fact that in practice a solicitor would ask his client. That said, do not go off onto a flight of fancy. There is no indication that either defendant is insane, so you must not discuss this defence. If the assessor wanted the student to consider the defence of insanity, he would have added a fact (for example, Ronaldo was a diabetic and having forgotten to take his insulin, upon arrest said that he had not done anything wrong).

You might find it useful to relate this advice to another real example, so what follows (in Figure 8.5) is a full annotation of the criminal law question for you to see how we have identified the key issues.

Sample question 3 (Criminal law)

Juan was shopping in Nottingham City Centre when he was approached by Maria, a campaigner for the 'Save the Trees' charity. Maria was going to ask Juan to sign her petition but Juan thought she was going to attack him

HE MAKES A MISTAKE; THINKS HE IS IN DANGER. ISSUES OF SELF-DEFENCE? CASES: WILLIAMS (GLADSTONE), BECKFORD.

and he shoved Maria away.

ASSAULT/BATTERY? HE HAS ACTED ON HIS MISTAKE – IF ANY DEFENCE, PUTATIVE SELF-DEFENCE. SEEMS SOBER (NOT TOLD HE IS DRUNK).

Maria tripped on an uneven cobble stone and fell to the ground, suffering bruising to her hands and elbows.

CONSIDER SECTION 47 – ASSAULT (HE SHOVED HER), OCCASIONING (CAUSATION), ACTUAL BODILY HARM (BRUISING). CASES: SAVAGE & PARMENTER, ROBERTS, MILLER.

Ronaldo, who witnessed the incident and who is very intoxicated,

WHATEVER HAPPENS, I NEED TO REMEMBER HE IS DRUNK. NEW RULES OF LAW APPLY; MAJEWSKI. NEED TO THINK ABOUT BASIC AND SPECIFIC INTENT ETC.

shouted at Juan.

ASSAULT? DEFINITION? IS THE OFFENCE SATISFIED ON THE FACTS?

Juan went to run off, but Ronaldo, because of his drunkenness,

NOT A MISTAKE HE MIGHT HAVE MADE WHEN SOBER?

thought Juan was going to hit him.

PUTATIVE SELF-DEFENCE EXPLAINED ABOVE – SO NOW I NEED TO ADD DRUNKEN MISTAKEN SELF-DEFENCE – O'GRADY AND O'CONNOR – PERSUASIVE (OBITER).

Ronaldo punched Juan, causing Juan a concussion from which Juan fully recovered.

SERIOUS INJURY (HE LIVES, SO NOT A HOMICIDE QUESTION); CONSIDER GRIEVOUS BODILY HARM; SMITH.

■ *Figure 8.5 Annotated sample of question on Criminal law*

You might wish to adopt a similar method in preparing for tutorials. This will give you plenty of practice for answering problem questions in the coursework and in the exam.

The next stage in your planning is to make a note of precisely what you have been asked to do. Read the instructions. Are you told to discuss, advise one of the parties or examine only one area of law? By the way, if you are asked to advise one of the parties, that does not mean you give one-sided advice, or you bias your answer to suit that side. Imagine you are asked to advise the prosecution. You would be negligent if you did not advise them about the strengths and weaknesses of the defence case too. This is very important because in court, the lawyers must refer the judges to all of the relevant cases, even if they do not support their argument. Do not forget the first piece of advice we gave you; all problem questions require you to be the judge in the case even if the instructions are phrased in terms of advice. You need to present all arguments (even if you disagree with the law in the area, you need to explain and apply it). A really sophisticated answer would also state which argument wins and why.

Please note you should not give advice in the first or second person (I or you). Use the third person (he, she or it).

Reading the instructions in the question is a crucial activity as the commands in problem questions vary. This can be seen by the instructions in the three questions that are under discussion in this chapter.

TORTS	Advise Angela of any actions that she might take.
POLICE POWERS	Advise Robert on the legality of his arrest.
CRIME	Discuss the liability, if any, of Juan who has been charged under section 47, Offences Against the Person Act 1861 and Ronaldo, who has been charged under section 18, Offences Against the Person Act 1861.

The commands are different. Each question wants a different focus. The police powers scenario requires focus on the legality of arrest. The crime question wants a discussion on liability of two individuals. It is important that you focus exactly on the command given in the scenario. Focus on the following:

- Who are you advising? Is it one individual or is it a number of people?
- Is the advice from a particular viewpoint, eg the applicant or respondent?
- Is it offences, defences, liability or a combination?
- Does the question want focus on one area, eg arrest, or does it want general advice?

ACTIVITY

> Think about an area of law with which you are familiar. It may be something you have studied in the past or that you are studying now.
>
> Have you picked a topic? Now think of one aspect of that topic that interested you in particular. It might have been because of a case with funny or peculiar facts, or it could be because the teacher was very critical of the decisions made, or for some other reason.
>
> Got it? If you need to, take a minute and check you are confident that you know the law well.
>
> Now write a very short problem question on that topic. What you are trying to do is point to the law through the facts of the question without specifically stating what the law is. For example, if you chose the postal rule, your scenario would include Alf making an offer to sell something and Bert replying by post, but the letter not being received by Alf.

This activity should get you to think like an assessor does, and if you can *write* problem questions, you can answer them.

8.4 Time management

Refer to Chapter 7 (Section 7.4) for information on time management. Suffice to say here that there is no such thing as a 'spare' five minutes during coursework preparation time. Those five minutes (at the bus stop, waiting for your favourite soap opera to start, whatever) can be spent in thought. As we said above, a tutor can recognise a well thought-out answer. Do not be afraid of having a little thinking time. Consider: I am Maria and I have been hit. What arguments would I want the prosecution to present? The next time you have five minutes, think about how Robert feels: is having the same name as a famous person reasonable grounds to arrest him? If you can picture yourself as one of the parties and you will get a good feel for the issues involved.

8.5 Creating a structure

Unlike essays, where a logical and clear introduction is required, some tutors do not miss an introduction to a problem question. At all times, resist any temptation to write a general introduction to the area of law:

- A problem question on breach of contract does not need an introduction explaining offer and acceptance.

- A criminal law answer should not start with a definition of *actus reus* and *mens rea*.

- A problem question on the tort of negligence does not require a introduction to the meaning of the word 'torts'.

- Do not state 'This question involves complex issues relating to public law'. Of course it does. That is why it has been asked.

Second, never start an answer to a problem question with the phrase 'In this answer I am going to . . .' The marker knows what you need to do – answer the question set within the fact scenario of the question; so do not talk about doing it; just do it! The earlier you can start explaining and applying the law, the more marks you will attract and the better focused the answer will be.

There is no universal magic formula for writing good problem question answers. Examiners differ in their preferred practice. What follows is general guidance.

There are three regularly used methods to structuring a problem question answer and they have a great deal in common as you will see:

- The **IRAC** system
  - State the **I**ssues
  - Explain the legal **R**ules
  - **A**pply the law to the question
  - **C**onclude.
- The **IDEA** System
  - Identify the legal issue
  - Define the legal rule
  - Explain how the rule works
  - Apply the rule to the facts.
- In other books in the '*Unlocking*' series the authors use problem questions and refer to:
  - Key facts
  - Key law
  - Applying the law to the facts
  - Reaching conclusions.

Whichever way it is described, the process is effectively the same.

8.5.1 Planning

Once you have identified the key facts (the flags), next list the issues of law that the facts of the question facts focus on. For example:

TORTS	Becky trips Angela with her hockey stick	Is there a direct and intentional application of force without consent (battery)?
POLICE POWERS	Arrested	Legality of arrest – 'You're nicked' – adequate?
CRIMINAL LAW	Juan thinks Maria is going to attack him	Mistake – self-defence?

Do this for *each* key fact in the question. This is your plan.

> **TIP**
>
> You should never recite the facts of the question as your first paragraph of the answer – the marker wants you to get on with explaining and applying the issues of law. The flow chart in Figure 8.6 may help to focus your mind on what the question is all about.

There are certain universally accepted norms:

- in crime questions, never mix in questions of civil law
- in torts questions, never mention the overlap with the criminal law
- in crime questions, never deal with the defences until you have considered the offences.

So, to the plan. This is best done as a flowchart so you can see a pictorial representation of how the answer will progress (logically) from one point to the next. The first few points have been written in full in Figure 8.6, so you can also see how to explain what you want to say as clearly and precisely as possible. Each main arrow in the plan will be its own paragraph. Check:

- each paragraph deals with one issue
- each paragraph deals with that issue in full (including explanation and application; we will come to this below)
- the marker should not get confused from one paragraph to the next; there is a clear flow.

8.5.2 Explaining the law

Once you are satisfied with the plan, you need to start drafting the law. Be aware of the word limit, but do not try to write to the limit; you can always condense and refine your writing later. That said, you cannot afford to waffle so make sure your explanations are as precise and concise as you can as you go along.

> 'A bad answer to a problem, even though correct, will not earn many (perhaps not any) marks, because the [marker] cannot tell whether the student has knowledge or is just guessing. Reasons and authorities should, therefore, always be given. Pretend

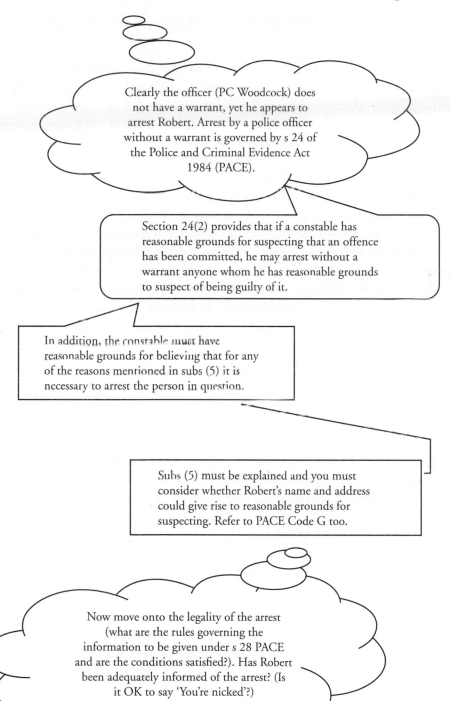

Clearly the officer (PC Woodcock) does not have a warrant, yet he appears to arrest Robert. Arrest by a police officer without a warrant is governed by s 24 of the Police and Criminal Evidence Act 1984 (PACE).

Section 24(2) provides that if a constable has reasonable grounds for suspecting that an offence has been committed, he may arrest without a warrant anyone whom he has reasonable grounds to suspect of being guilty of it.

In addition, the constable must have reasonable grounds for believing that for any of the reasons mentioned in subs (5) it is necessary to arrest the person in question.

Subs (5) must be explained and you must consider whether Robert's name and address could give rise to reasonable grounds for suspecting. Refer to PACE Code G too.

Now move onto the legality of the arrest (what are the rules governing the information to be given under s 28 PACE and are the conditions satisfied?). Has Robert been adequately informed of the arrest? (Is it OK to say 'You're nicked'?)

Figure 8.6 Flow chart on sample question 2 – police powers to yourself that the examiner will disagree with your point of view and set yourself to persuade by argument.

One of the most important of a lawyer's accomplishments is the ability to resolve facts into their legal categories. The student should therefore take pains to argue in terms of legal rules and concepts. It is a not uncommon fault, particularly in criminal law, to give the impression that the answer is based wholly upon common sense and a few gleaning from the Sunday papers.'

Smith, Glanville Williams, *Learning the Law*, 12th edn, London, Sweet and Maxwell, 2002, 151.

So the lesson here is that each proposition of law needs to be clearly explained and backed up by authority. Do not spend too long explaining the obvious; the assessor wants you to get to grips with the controversial areas, not spend a quarter of the essay dealing with points of law that are settled and accepted. For example, do not use a number of cases dealing with a single and uncontroversial area of the law such as the definition of the term 'actual bodily harm' in s 47, Offences Against the Person Act 1861. There may be solid criticism of the meaning of the term, but to spend more than 50 words in this answer where there are far meatier issues, would be a waste of words.

Uncontroversial issues should be dealt with quickly:

Sample question 1 (torts)

Technically any intrusive treatment by a doctor can be a battery unless it is carried out with the consent of the patient (*Re F (Sterilisation: Mental Patient)* [1990] 2 AC 1). However, in *Leigh v Gladstone* (1909) 26 TLR 139 it was established that consent can be implied in emergency situations where the patient is unconscious because of the doctrine of necessity. As a result the emergency Caesarian section operation on Angela is unlikely to lead to any liability.

Sample question 2 (police powers)

Once you have stated the power to arrest under s 24 (if a constable has reasonable grounds for suspecting that an offence has been committed, he may arrest without a warrant anyone whom he has reasonable grounds to suspect of being guilty of it) all you need to do is explain that PC Woodcock has watched Robert commit an offence and has clear reasonable grounds to believe Robert to be guilty of it. You do not need to enter into a debate about the elements of the crime of urinating in a public place. The assessor has told you only to consider arrest and you cannot get credit for anything else.

Sample question 3 (criminal law)

Miller [1954] 2 QB 282 defines actual bodily harm (ABH) as any hurt or injury likely to interfere with the victim's health and comfort. As a bruise clearly falls within this definition (provided it is not trivial or transient (*Brown* [1993] 2 All ER 75, HL), Maria has suffered ABH.

For more complex issues, you will need to state in full the rules of law that apply. There may be a number of rules and there will almost certainly be more than one source of law. Start with the statutory provisions (if there are any), but refer to the relevant section(s) rather than copy them out in full because that is a waste of valuable words.

If there is no statute governing the area of law, or after you have dealt with the statutory provisions, move onto the cases. Unless you are sure they are relevant, do not use old cases to answer a problem question; cite the authorities (the current leading cases) in each area. Do not merely mention the case name nor just the facts. The marks are awarded for explanations of the rule or principle of law established in that case. You may wish to discuss the case in great detail, perhaps arguing that it was wrongly decided, especially if the cases directly covers the factual situation but your view is that the decision should not be followed. It is more likely, however, that the facts of the question will fall directly between conflicting authorities. In this event, the marker will be looking for you to analyse which is the better decision.

Sample question 1 (torts)

In the case of Becky tripping Angela with her hockey stick, there are three key issues to discuss:

- Whether the tripping is intentional (which would be necessary for battery – but is not clear here so alternative possibilities would have to be discussed).
- Whether the application of force is in fact direct (again necessary for battery – but you would be able to show through cases such as *Scott v Shepherd* (1773) 2 Bl R 892 that the courts have taken a fairly broad view of the meaning of direct in battery).
- Whether Becky could claim the defence of consent which is common in a sporting context (but for the defence to apply you would need to consider whether Becky is acting within the rules and spirit of the game, which allowed the defence to be used successfully in *Simms v Leigh Rugby Football Club* [1969] 2 All ER 923).

Sample question 3 (Criminal law)

ACTIVITY

It is always worth finding the time to practise explaining complex areas of law. The more practice you get, the easier it becomes. If you have studied this area of criminal law, make some notes, citing the leading cases, on the operation of self-defence and the defence of voluntary intoxication. Then compare your explanations with the suggested content below.

The force used must be unlawful force, as is the case with all offences of violence. Thus Ronaldo may have used lawful and reasonable force in self-defence. Academic writers have long debated whether the 'unlawfulness' of the force is an element of the *actus reus* of the offence or is entirely a defence. If it is the latter, the force is a lawful justification (or possibly an excuse) which negates liability despite the commission of the *actus reus* with the requisite *mens rea*. Support for this view comes from *obiter* statements made in the House of Lords in *Brown* [1993] 2 All ER 75. However, contrary case law suggests that lawfulness would negate the *actus reus*, because the force used would not be unlawful force (*Beckford v R* [1988] AC 130, PC; *Williams* (1984) 78 Cr App R 276, CA; *Kimber* [1983] 3 All ER 316, CA; *B v DPP* [2000] 2 AC 428). In terms of criminal liability, whether or not unlawfulness is an element of the *actus reus* or a defence seems to matter only in cases of mistaken self-defence or mistaken consent (often called putative self-defence or consent). If the normal rules were applied in this case, Ronaldo would be judged on the circumstances as he saw them rather than as they actually were.

The leading case on the 'defence' of voluntary intoxication is *DPP v Majewski* [1976] 2 All ER 142, HL. This states that voluntary intoxication has no effect on criminal liability unless the accused is charged with a specific intent crime and the intoxication prevented him from forming the specific intent. Accordingly, as Ronaldo has been charged with an offence under s 18, Offences Against the Person Act 1861, since s 18 is a crime of specific intent and since the intoxication prevented Ronaldo having the necessary specific intent, he could not be guilty as charged. Conversely his intoxicated state would not negate liability for a basic intent crime such as s 20 even if it had prevented him from having the *mens rea* normally necessary for that crime. However, two Court of Appeal cases, *O'Grady* [1987] 3 All ER 411 and *O'Connor* [1991] Crim LR 135, asserted *obiter* that a drunken mistake as to self-defence always had to be ignored and could not be a defence to either a specific or basic intent crime. As each case contradicts the established House of Lords' doctrine in *Majewski*, it is suggested that they should be ignored.

TIP

Our advice on dealing with conflicting authorities and making critical commentary:

- Be courageous! Make informed arguments.

- Be prepared to argue your point.

- While an important chunk of marks is given for clear and concise and accurate explanations of the law, do not forget that you are also expected to deal with contradictory cases and misleading authorities.

8.5.3 The process of application

The second major chunk of marks is for application of the law to the facts. This means you have to relate the law to the facts of the question in turn.

DO NOT

Recite the issues

THEN

Explain all the relevant law on one go

THEN

Apply to the facts in one go – you will either repeat yourself and waste words or will miss something
important from this part of the answer

INSTEAD

Identify the first issue

Explain the law relating to that issue

Apply to the facts

THEN

Move on to the next issue

Explain the law relating to that issue

Apply to the facts

AND THEN

Move on to the next issue

Explain the law relating to that issue

Apply to the facts

And so on

AND REMEMBER TO

Conclude

Figure 8.7 Applying the law to the facts

Application does not mean copy out the facts of the question. It means you have to link the law to
the question.

Wrong	Right
Intrusive treatment by a doctor can be a battery unless it is carried out with the consent of the patient, *Re F (Sterilisation: Mental Patient)* [1990] 2 AC 1. Doctor Careless has performed a hysterectomy on Angela without her consent.	Although Doctor Careless felt that he was acting in Angela's best interests, it is clear that a doctor must obtain consent before any intrusive medical treatment, *Re F (Sterilisation: Mental Patient)* [1990] 2 AC 1. As a result, the hysterectomy carried out by Doctor Careless may well result in his liability for battery.

Even a correct statement of law followed by a mere repetition of the facts is not application to those facts:

Wrong	Right
The *mens rea* for a battery is intention or recklessness to apply unlawful force to the victim (*Parmenter* [1991] 2 All ER 225). Juan thought Maria was going to attack him and he shoved her away.	The *mens rea* for a battery is intention or recklessness to apply unlawful force to the victim (*Parmenter* [1991] 2 All ER 225). Juan clearly thought Maria was going to attack him and in shoving her away, he acted intentionally. The *mens rea* for battery is therefore satisfied.

8.5.4 Conclude as you progress

Notes:

- In a problem-style question, deal with the issues in chronological order.
- Use the word count carefully and stay within it.
- You are taking a law degree (of one form or another), so make sure your analysis is of the law, not the facts of the question – never repeat the question.
- There is no hard and fast rule about reciting case facts in answer to problem questions, but generally, do not spend too long explaining facts unless you are using them to distinguish the facts of the question itself.

 TIP | The magic word in all legal arguments, essays and problem questions is 'IF'.

There is no 'right' answer in most problem questions, there are just a range of possible outcomes. You may not have been given enough facts to form a firm conclusion, or you may have a number of conflicting authorities and no clear conclusion can be drawn. That is why **IF** is such a magic word. You could make it clear that *if* the court followed the case of X, the outcome would be . . . but if the court followed the case of Y, the outcome would be different.

Do not say *what* without *why*. Throwing cases names around and then concluding that D is liable or guilty is unlikely to attract a good grade. You need to have stated why first, then conclude. It does not matter if the reader disagrees with your conclusion. You will have achieved most of your marks already anyway and the assessor is not looking for the 'right' answer (remember there is not one in problem questions – that's why we call them problems!) but whether your conclusion is:

- well argued, and

- consistent with the law as explained and applied above, and

- has highlighted areas of law that are inconsistent, and

- has suggested reform to areas of law that are unsatisfactory.

Leave your options open if you have to; don't forget to use the *if*.

You may find it useful to use subheadings if they help. But do not overdo it! If subheadings assist the structure to your answer, use them. But if you feel that the answer flows logically without them, there is no need to use them. They will almost certainly form part of the word count. However, where there are a number of events that need dealing with, you may find the answer has a clearer focus if subheadings are used:

Sample question 1 (torts)

Becky tripping Angela

Doctor Careless performing the emergency Caesarian on Angela

Doctor Careless carrying out the hysterectomy on Angela

Angela threatening Doctor Careless

Nurse Dowell locking Angela in the hospital room

Figure 8.8 Subheadings which may be used for sample question 1 – torts

Alternatively, use subheadings when planning your answer, but once the answer flows well, delete them.

8.6 Using the assessment criteria or learning outcomes

In Chapter 7, we pointed out that the assessor marks your work by reference to assessment criteria. (See section 7.6.)

When answering problem questions, the assessor will make a specific reference to the demands of answering problem-based scenarios. Common examples are reproduced for you below. Make sure your answer meets those demands *before* you submit your coursework.

Example 1

When marking your coursework, particular regard will be had to the following matters:

- ability to analyse factual situations and relevant law

- depth of understanding of key legal principles.

Example 2

The student should be able to:

- demonstrate knowledge and understanding of the relevant legal principles
- demonstrate the ability to apply relevant case law to the facts above
- demonstrate that you have used research skills to locate paper or electronic versions of the principal cases and/or legislation.

8.7 Grammar, syntax and spelling

Refer to the Chapter 7 at section 7.7.

8.8 Using only relevant material

Case facts are not always irrelevant. They may be helpful as illustrations and you will certainly have to refer to them if you are distinguishing.

Sample question 1 (Torts)

For instance you might point out that the soldier in *Murray v Minister of Defence* [1988] 2 All ER 521 was unconscious when he was locked in a room but here Angela is merely unaware of having been locked in her hospital room by Nurse Dowell. In *Meering v Grahame-White Aviation Co Ltd* (1919) 122 LT 44 the claimant was unaware that security police were outside the room and would have prevented him from leaving, although he was obviously being detained for questioning. So the facts in neither of the leading cases that could be applied to Angela here are the same as those in her situation, but you will have to use the facts of the two cases (briefly) to make that point.

Irrelevant material is twice as bad – you cannot get credit for it *and* at the same time you are wasting words you could have used for credit-worthy explanations.

Do not discuss what you have not been asked to discuss. It would be superfluous to consider the legality of the stop and questioning of Robert; you have been asked only to consider the legality of his arrest. Similarly, you are told that Angela has only shouted at Doctor Careless; do not discuss what would have been the case had she jumped out of her hospital bed and hit him.

If it does not further any of your arguments and you feel you cannot apply it to the question, leave it out because it is irrelevant.

8.9 Quotations

Lengthy criticisms are less necessary in problem questions than essays. But a key critique that assists your argument may be persuasive. See section 7.9 for general advice on using quotes in law answers.

8.10 Balancing the arguments

See section 7.10 for general advice on balancing the legal arguments in law coursework. For problem questions, also note that you must check that:

* all the realistic but alternative possibilities have been considered

* the strongest points in favour of each side have been presented.

8.11 Reaching sensible and reasoned conclusions

Some tutors do not expect conclusions in problem question answers, but it is important if you have been asked to advise X, that you have done so. If you have been asked to consider Y's criminal liability, if any, you should. The problem may be that there are so many variables in the facts, it is impossible to conclude firmly one way or another. If that is the case and you are sure you have explained all of the alternatives, it is not imperative to have a vague repetition of this at the end.

8.12 Referencing

Refer to section 7.12.

8.13 Reflection and improvement

Refer to section 7.13.

Further reading

Smith, Glanville Williams, *Learning the Law* 13th edn, London: Sweet and Maxwell, 2006, Chapter 8.

chapter
9 COMPLETING
DISSERTATIONS OR PROJECTS■

AIMS AND OBJECTIVES

After reading this chapter you should be able to:

■ Decide whether, if you have the choice, you will achieve a good grade if you write a dissertation rather than take a 'taught' module

■ Create a structure for your project

■ Draft and amend an abstract as you proceed

■ Produce detailed research from a range of sources, noting the relevant citations as you proceed

■ Develop advanced time management and organisational skills

■ Appreciate fully and take advantage of the support of your project supervisor

■ Submit a well written and well structured project, on time

■ Prepare and perform well in any oral 'viva' that you may have

9.1 Introduction

Many law schools include a module that is assessed by way of dissertation or project only. In some, this module is compulsory, but in most it is optional. Word limits for the dissertations or projects vary from 4,000 to 12,000 words or more. If you have to write a dissertation, or if you wish to, we strongly recommend you read this chapter in full before you start, and then refer back to parts of it as and when the need arises.

9.1.1 What is a dissertation?

A dissertation is a long essay written on a single topic, which you research by yourself. Think of it as an independent learning project designed to improve your expertise of the law and develop your legal research, intellectual and organisational skills.

While projects may vary greatly in scope and topic area, most share a number of key characteristics. First, you determine the focus and direction of your work. Second, this work is carried out on an individual basis – although usually you will be given support and direction by a tutor. Third, there is a substantial research component to the project, requiring the collection and analysis of legal material. Finally, you will have a more prolonged engagement with the chosen subject than is the case with 'standard' coursework assignments such as essays or reports, with the work consequently expected to be more in depth. This provides you with an opportunity to show your originality and creativity.

In essence, a dissertation requires you to:

*   undertake an extensive programme of reading and research
*   demonstrate intellectual independence and originality by choosing your own subject of study and defining its nature and scope
*   engage in sustained analysis, interpretation and possibly comparison of a substantial body of data
*   present the results of your research in a clearly written, cogently argued, logically structured and properly referenced form.

This is excellent preparation for further study and research at postgraduate level. In addition, the skills described above are transferable skills that equip you as a law graduate to work independently and methodically in professional practice.

9.1.2 Choosing a dissertation as an optional module

Working on a dissertation is a different process from following a course. A taught module guides you through the relevant background material in a particular area of study, whereas a dissertation involves finding out yourself what is, and what is not, relevant to your own topic.

If the module is optional (usually in your final year), you are going to have to consider if it is the best use of your time or if you should elect a 'taught' module. Complete the following grid; being as honest with yourself as you can be:

Are you . . .	Yes	No
Hardworking?		
Self-motivated?		
An independent worker?		
A good time-manager, or able to find the time to complete the project and balance the other modules against it as the year progresses?		
A reasonable, if not yet an expert, researcher?		
Able to stick to a task for an extended period?		

■ *Figure 9.1 Choosing an optional module*

If you have said *no* to any of the above, think long and hard about choosing to do a project as an option. If you have said *no* to any of them, the skills mentioned are the skills that you are going to need; can you develop them? Realistically, do you have the time to develop them before the project starts? If you have said *no* to any of them, but really want to do a project, ask yourself why. Would a 'taught' module not be able to give you the subject knowledge you want to acquire? If not, then fine. By all means do a project. If it will, think seriously about taking the more traditionally taught course. We are not trying to put you off doing a project, even if it looks like that. Self-directed study is study in isolation. You will have spells when you cannot face doing work on it. You may lose motivation. You will hit 'writer's block' just as if you were writing a novel (in fact, a project of 12,000 words will feel like it is an epic!).

On the other hand, the keen and eager student may find his time taken over completely by the project. The dissertation must take up only a proportionate amount of your study time and no more (and no less). See Time management at section 9.6 on page 223.

9.2 Preparing the title and abstract or understanding the abstract supplied

9.2.1 Choosing a topic area

The first stage in preparing a dissertation is to decide what topic you wish to research in detail and write about. In this process, you should take advantage of the opportunity to pursue a particular personal interest or develop an interest from previous study.

Given the need to develop advanced research skills, it is easier for you to build on modules that you have followed in previous years. However, if a particular topic which has not been covered has caught your interest for some time, then you are also encouraged to follow your own ideas, if suitable. In certain ways, the dissertation reflects a direct development of the kind of skills that you have acquired through the writing of essays. You will find that your experience of writing undergraduate essays has prepared you for writing a dissertation.

During the first years of your study, your critical insight into the law developed. The dissertation builds on this foundation; it grows out of your own particular interest, both in terms of the material you choose to write about and the topic that provides the focus of your study.

Selecting a topic for your dissertation may not happen right away. You may have to do a great deal of background reading before you arrive at your topic. It may be helpful to talk to a member of academic staff about your ideas.

If the module is an option in your final year, you should really begin the process of considering the subject area during your second year to have made the decision before the end of that year. Then you can spend part of the long summer break identifying and reading around the subject matter, so that you get a good idea of the critical and scholarly material that is relevant to your discussion.

You need to choose an area that:

- will hold your interest for the duration of the dissertation (this is often a full academic year)

- is not so broad that it prevents you getting into the details of the law and is thus unmanageable

- is not so focused on a narrow area that it prevents you from reaching the word limit.

If you cannot decide, we have supervised projects on the following areas, one of which might interest you:

Freedom of contract	Legal professional privilege
Sport law	The defences available to battered spouses who kill
Tax and Revenue law	Autonomy
Drugs law	Fair trial rights
Euthanasia	The right to silence
Abortion	Regulation of the internet
The admissibility of confessions and unfairly obtained evidence	Crime/criminology
Corporate manslaughter	Crime and mass media
European Union competition law	Employment law
Sexuality and the law	Equal opportunities
Youth justice	Welfare law

Figure 9.2 Some suggested subject areas to choose from

9.2.2 Writing an abstract

Once you have decided the area of law that interests you, you will need to write a working title. This is a draft. Add an abstract of about 100–200 words after the title. The abstract is a summary or statement of the contents of the project which pinpoints the essence of your thoughts at this early stage. It is not going to be the only version that you write out during the course of the project; the question answered in the final dissertation will evolve over the course of your research and so will the abstract, so do not worry too much about your style here.

If you are having difficulties drafting the abstract, get a friend to write as you talk for about two minutes on what you would like the project to be about. This is your initial starting point, but it is not set in stone. It is important that this is done at the beginning of the project to serve the purpose of keeping you on track in your early research.

In your abstract, try to describe the dissertation's scope, possibly explaining your reasons for investigating your chosen topic. It may be easiest to write this as an action plan of what you aim to

Example 1

Working Title: Securing a conviction for corporate manslaughter was almost impossible at common law.

Working Abstract: Following disasters such as the sinking of the Herald of Free Enterprise, the Hatfield rail crash, and so on, prosecutions against companies were either not brought at all, or the few that were brought quickly collapsed. This project will investigate the apparent failings in the common law to bring defendants to justice, and will also consider whether a conviction in such a case is in any event a desirable outcome. The common law and Health and Safety legislation will be examined, as will the Law Commission's 1996 proposals for a new offence of corporate killing, which was ultimately enacted by the Corporate Manslaughter and Corporate Homicide Act 2007. The Act is controversial and was subject to extensive ping-pong between the Houses of Parliament during enactment. The Bill will be examined, and the sentencing structure under the Act will be evaluated, especially focusing on the nature of community penalties and adverse publicity as a deterrent tool.

 Figure 9.3 Example of a working title and abstract

achieve. Try not to anticipate the conclusions that you hope to reach in the process of your work. This might lead to confusion. Instead, you might simply say that you have identified certain features in a range of cases, journals or texts, or a particular issue that is represented in them. You may also say that your dissertation will examine the relevant material in order to demonstrate more precisely the relationships between them and whether the way they deal with the issue in question is satisfactory.

> **TIP**
>
> Do not forget that once you have completed the work on the main substance of your dissertation, you will have to return to the abstract and revise it in light of the final title.

9.3 Assessment criteria

It is vital that your project meets the learning outcomes and assessment criteria of the module. A couple of examples follow and the first is annotated with what you should be aiming to do to meet each of them.

Example 1

Intellectual skills

The student will be:

❖ able to analyse and synthesise by being able to recognise and distil information in terms of relevance and importance, collect and integrate information from a variety of sources, combine relevant issues in relation to a topic, analyse complex factual information systematically, utilise abstract ideas in an argument and reason logically

> You need to provide all the relevant primary sources of substantive law (statutes and cases) as well as deselecting irrelevant law and/or academic commentary.
> Make sure there is a range of statutes, cases, textbook and journal authors' views.
> Also ensure your project has a logical and fluent structure. Clarify conflicting arguments. You may wish to extrapolate (this means hypothesise, in other words to answer the question 'What if?' to expand the arguments).

❖ able to evaluate by being able to make informed critical and individual judgments and opinions, recognise and justify value judgments, be tolerant towards and handle alternative viewpoints and be perceptive to issues underlying legal principles.

> Provide a balanced but detailed commentary on both the substantive law and any academic views on the law.

Key skills

The student will be:

❖ literate in the English language, communicate in writing and orally, précis information, present information in a comprehensible manner and present a clear and logical argument

> Poor use of grammar, syntax, spelling and legal terminology will lose you marks. Use an English dictionary and a legal dictionary. Refer also to Section 7.7 above.

❖ competent in word processing, use the www and use relevant electronic legal information retrieval systems.

> Most students have this skill, but make sure you adopt a clear layout for the project and proof read; spell check (cheque?) cannot always be relied on. We have lost count of the number of 'statues' rather than statutes in law projects!

CONTINUED ▶

Graduateness; autonomy and ability to learn which leads to lifelong learning

The student will be:

❖ able to plan and learn independently, take responsibility for and be committed to his/her own continuous learning, be a reflective learner, be aware of the learning environment and initiate and make use of learning

❖ able to recognise and be receptive to all forms of feedback.

Undergraduate law schools have to prepare you for life in the 'real world'. The dissertation is an excellent way for you to show the accumulation of legal knowledge and skills developed throughout the programme. The project will be assessed in light of the final version which is submitted; but some law schools also give a mark for the whole process, including your supervisor's views on your willingness to learn, respond to feedback and open-mindedness. Independence does not mean you cannot ask for help: an independent learner knows when to ask and when to find the answer out for himself.

Figure 9.4 Annotated example of learning outcomes and assessment criteria

Example 2

A student taking this module will be able to:

• Show development of advanced legal research skills, applying those skills to a project generated on the student's own initiative.

• Show competence in the presentation of a dissertation in an appropriate legal scholarly style.

• Show evidence of virtually autonomous research underpinning self-directed learning, making full use of available resources including those of staff and other students.

• Produce a formal dissertation demonstrating the results of an independent project of autonomous research involving the selection, analysis and comparison of appropriate materials presented in a coherent, logical and perceptive manner.

• Demonstrate the ability to use information technology skills in the preparation and presentation of the work.

• Indicate the acquisition of skills relating to data collection and management and personal organisation including the ability to meet deadlines.

Figure 9.5 Example of learning outcomes and assessment criteria

9.4 Research

You must be willing to put a lot of effort into your research. To build a research trail, start with a textbook (or if your initial thoughts were stimulated by a case or journal article, start with those). That material will make reference to other books, cases and journals. Now read them. That is the start of the trail. From each researched case, extract or article, at least three new avenues should be produced. At some stage, of course, your research will take you off at a tangent. This is where the initial title and abstract come into use; make sure you keep on track and do not be tempted to skirt off into new areas that have no bearing on what you want to say.

We cannot over emphasise the importance of the following point. **Always keep a note of where you have been *and* how you have searched** – this will help you when you construct your bibliography and also if you need to retrace your steps at any time. It can also help you to avoid duplication of effort.

If you have a helpful librarian, be kind to them. They are going to be invaluable use to you because they will have more ideas than you about research; and they will be a good friend to you over the year, especially if the article you are desperate for is only available on an inter-library loan. They may also be able to advise if you are including a comparison with other jurisdictions in your dissertation.

9.4.1 Note-taking

Your notes are going to become the project, so always try to take notes which are precise, concise and accurate. Being precise means making a complete note of where you found the source in the event you have to go back again to edit or correct something. It also means you should be able to reproduce the exact information into the bibliography. Vague notes lead to vague ideas and then to a vague dissertation. However, do not merely reproduce everything you read. Being concise means reducing the key issues in what you have read (paraphrasing) to avoid waffle when you write up the dissertation. Remember to note where you found the sources – you may wish to return to find a good quote (fully attributed of course). Never paraphrase an author inaccurately. In a quote, you must be careful to reproduce the author's exact words, including punctuation. It is likely your supervisor will be aware of the author's views and their published work, so do not get caught out. Be faithful to what the author says and if the ideas you are expressing are not yours (even if you happen to agree with them) state the source.

There will never be enough time for you to read all and everything. So you are going to have to be selective. On the one hand, the assessor wishes to see evidence of wide reading, but you have neither the time nor the space to reproduce it all. You have to be realistic and you must try to keep your reading within some limits. Challenge yourself without giving yourself an impossible task. For example, if you were to find a reference to an article in an obscure journal which has not been peer reviewed (we call this a non-refereed journal) about how the law you are investigating is dealt with in an island in the Pacific, unless this is what your project is about of course, let it go. On the other hand, failure to cite from the leading textbook will not make a good impression.

Whatever we say, you will spend too much time reading. Ask every project supervisor and they will tell you that those students who come to their supervisors the very last minute always say that they have been reading a lot, but need more time to write it up. Such students show poor time management, poor organisational skills and poor independence. They also indicate an ignorance of the power of the supervisor to grant an extension. If you have a hard time being strict with yourself on how much more to read, remember that marks are available for making a reasoned *independent* argument – not simply for regurgitating the opinions of people you have read.

Refer to Chapters 4 and 5 on research and library skills.

9.5 Structure

There is an old saying about project writing:

> *Tell them what you'll tell them,*
> *tell them it, tell them what you've told them.*
> *Start with a plan.*

List the different stages of your argument and then use a flowchart to see in diagrammatic form how you want the final project to look. Select the material that you want to go into your introduction, followed by three or four longer chapters and then a conclusion. This process inevitably involves some de-selecting of material you have researched. As much as you will hate having to leave out material you have spent time and energy discovering, you must not include irrelevant material in your dissertation. Keep reading the title and the abstract to keep the focus.

Breaking the project into manageable sections by working to approximate word limits will help you to start. For an 8,000 word project, for example, this is a structure you might like to try:

- Abstract   200 words
- Introductory chapter   800 words
- Chapter 1   2,000 words
- Chapter 2   2,000 words
- Chapter 3   2,000 words
- Conclusion   1,000 words

Dividing the dissertation in this way means that all you have to do is write three 2,000-word essays, add an introduction and a conclusion and you are there. But do not be deceived – a dissertation is not simply four essays fastened together. It is a single argument with a logical progression from one issue to the next.

9.5.1 Drafting the project

The first draft is *never* the only draft. You may have to re-write parts of the dissertation several times; and then delete parts and start all over again. Your time management is vital to the process (see section 9.6 below).

The introductory chapter

The short abstract sets out what the project is going to investigate. The introductory chapter, which should account for no more than 10 per cent of your dissertation, will build upon this abstract and expand on what your question is asking and why it is important to answer it. This chapter should be written in an explanatory style, telling the reader what each chapter of the thesis will cover and the key claims that you will be presenting or defending to justify your arguments.

The body of the project

This accounts for about 80 per cent of the dissertation. The body is where you develop your argument. It should start with the simplest matters (such as definitions and the clarification of basic concepts). It should then build in clear and yet increasingly more complex stages until you arrive at your answer. This is the main basis on which your work will be judged. What the assessors will be looking for is a clearly expressed and argued thesis based on authority and hypothesis (the 'what if?' question). If you are not sure about the difference between an 'original' piece of work and an 'independent' one, note that 'original' means an idea no one has ever had before. It is very rare to come across an original argument and it is certainly not a requirement at undergraduate level that your arguments are original (although you will, of course, be credited if any of them are). It is sufficient to have an 'independent' idea; that is one where you gather what others have written and you string the ideas together to make a convincing case. Where you find other people have had the same idea already, acknowledge this in a footnote or endnote, pointing out that you thought of it independently.

For any project over 4,000 words, you must divide the body into chapters, each of which deals with a particular stage of your argument. Most dissertations of between 8,000 and 12,000 words should have no fewer than three chapters, and, if necessary, sub-sections too. The exact number of chapters depends on your particular topic. Your supervisor can advise, but each chapter should not be longer than 2,500 words.

You may structure your work so that each chapter or section is devoted to discussion of a particular aspect of your overall topic. The crucial thing is to show the reader that you have a good argument, which means that you must show you have good reasons for arriving at your answer. Cases should be cited correctly with the citation following the case name or in a footnote. Quotations should always be attributed. Remember that plagiarism leads to a zero mark, or even expulsion from your degree.

9.5.2 Suggested structures

Example 1

Title: **An investigation of whether the separate torts of negligence and nuisance should be brought under the single tort of negligence**

Abstract	Overlaps in the tests of reasonableness and proximity force us to reconsider whether two separate torts are needed. Should the same tests be used for both and if so, what is the best test?	200 words
Introductory chapter	Explain the nature of the torts of negligence and nuisance, highlighting areas of overlap. Focus on *Hunter v Canary Wharf* [1997] 2 WLR 684. Summarise contents of Chapters 1, 2 and 3.	1,500 words
Chapter 1	The tort of negligence. From basics to complex. From duty/breach/ damage to the basis of the reasonableness test and the rationale of the tort.	2,000 words
Chapter 2	The tort of private nuisance. From basics to complex. From reasonable user and locality to the *locus standi* of claimants in *Hunter*. Consider the nature of fault and strict liability within this discussion.	2,000 words
Chapter 3	Argue for and against the overlap in the torts. Should there be two separate tests or one that is not limited to type of claimant but purely on a test of reasonableness? Objectively assessed, but not strict liability.	2,000 words
Conclusion	Answer question raised in the Abstract.	800 words

■ *Figure 9.6 Suggested dissertation structure 1*

Example 5

Title: **Women who kill and their defences to murder**

Abstract	Focus on one or two key cases where the defences on a murder charge against a battered spouse have failed or have been unsatisfactory. Question whether the law's stance is adequate or fair. Indicate an investigation into, if not, why not.	200 words
Introductory chapter	Basic definition of murder (very brief) followed by a definition of battered spouse syndrome. Indicate the only defences are unavailable (self-defence and provocation) or inadequate (diminished responsibility). Summarise contents of Chapters 1, 2, 3 and 4.	1,000 words
Chapter 1	The defence of provocation. The need for a sudden loss of self control. Define (cases) and argue that battered spouses do not react immediately. Consideration of the 'reasonable person' test and how recent changes help, but cannot change the need for the sudden loss.	2,000 words

CONTINUED ▶

Chapter 2	The defence of diminished responsibility. The breadth of abnormality of mind and 'any inherent cause' limited by the effect of the defence – to name the defendant as abnormal and impaired in their responsibility. Consider use of Scottish cases as a comparative review as the defence is Scottish in origin.	1,500 words
Chapter 3	Self-defence. A possible solution to the problems raised by the other defences because leads to an acquittal except for the proportionality element (by their nature, such defendants over-react) and/or the 'imminence' of the threat *obiter dicta*.	1,500 words
Chapter 4	The Law Commission's Reports. Possible new offences, and partial defences. Pros and Cons. Political and academic reaction. Analysis of the suitability of the proposals for all defendants charged with murder (could the battering spouses also benefit from any changes?).	1,500 words
Conclusion	Answer question raised in the Abstract.	1,000 words

Figure 9.7 Suggested dissertation structure 2

The conclusion

This should be a 'mirror' of the Introductory chapter, in that it restates the question, reviews the key stages of your argument and shows that you have argued logically and convincingly for your thesis. There are no 'right' answers in law, but your mark will reflect whether your thesis is clear, shows a deep understanding of the issues raised by the question and the problems that arise when trying to answer it, as well as making a convincing case.

It is often advisable to leave not only the writing of the conclusion, but also that of the introduction, until you have written the rest.

9.6 Time management

At the outset, devise a timetable for the entire project, from initial research to submission, including interim deadlines as well as meeting the final submission deadline. For example, you should decide for yourself or agree with your supervisor deadlines for:

(i) carrying out your basic research (reading the primary texts, literature survey, and any required data collection)

(ii) producing drafts of chapters

(iii) producing a final draft of the whole dissertation and

(iv) producing the final version.

It is *vital* that you keep to these 'internal' deadlines.

Example 1	
Year 2 – spring	Decide topic area.
	Initial draft of a broad title and abstract.
	Complete module option form.
	Find/be allocated a supervisor.
Summer	Reading around the subjects. Take notes. Highlight areas for further investigation on start of new term.
Year 3 – September	First meeting with supervisor – agree a working title and discuss areas already researched. Get hints on other areas to investigate.
	Agree a timetable for the year. Check final submission date. Agree first draft deadline.
	Meet with the law librarian. Ask for support and guidance now and/or in future. Request an update on searching electronic databases.
	Continue with research.
October	Continue with research.
	Detailed plan of structure.
	Write 2,000 words for the supervisor's comments.
November	Early in the month – second meeting with supervisor for feedback on first draft and advice on progression. Revise original timetable if necessary. Show detailed plan for review. Agree next deadline.
	Continue with research.
December	Continue with research and start drafting each chapter. Do relevant bibliography on an ongoing basis. Case citations too.
	Possibly meet before Christmas break to agree action plan with supervisor.
January	Put all project work on hold: courseworks due in for other modules.
February	Return to project. Re-read all drafts and revise with fresh eyes.
	Continue with research. Continue to draft.
March	Meeting with supervisor for discussion on content and progress.
	Continue to draft. Project should be taking shape now.
April	Final re-drafting and refining.
May	Submission.
June	(Possible) oral presentation – see section 9.9 below.

■ *Figure 9.8 Devise a timetable at the outset*

Dissertations always take longer to write than students expect. Remember that it is not only writing that you are concerned with, but also with word-processing your text, inserting quotations, producing footnotes, appendices and a bibliography detailing all sources cited. Start early and revise as you progress. Never start writing a 10,000 word project with only a month to go before the submission date. Either you will not finish or you will omit something important.

9.7 The supervisor

Almost without exception, law schools will provide a dissertation student with the guidance of a supervisor. The role of your supervisor is very important in the development of your work. It is a different role from that of the lecturer. It is a one-to-one teaching relationship in which you are guided, rather than directed, in your thinking. Meetings between student and supervisor will be more or less regular depending on the nature of the dissertation and the amount of supervision judged necessary by the supervisor. You should, however, aim to meet your supervisor at least three times during the progress of the project.

At your first meeting, be prepared to show your supervisor your initial plan of action and your outline arguments. The supervisor may then set you a deadline for the production of an outline structure and one chapter from the work. If it is possible to do so, tape record all of the meetings. That way, you do not have to take notes, you can concentrate on what is being said, and you will have a fully accurate record of the advice given to refer back to later.

Your supervisor may agree to read a limited number of drafts of some sections of the dissertation. You should not expect though that the supervisor will read each chapter and certainly not that the supervisor will correct drafts of what you write. All supervisors will be as helpful as possible but can only offer advice as to content. They cannot become too closely involved in what you actually write because this is *your* project. In the end, what remains in and what is left out is your decision. The dissertation is ultimately your own work for which you take responsibility.

Please do not ask, because your supervisor will not be able to answer, what mark you will get. He or she will not be able to suggest a mark for what you have written in the drafts because the mark depends upon what you finally submit (and how you perform in the oral presentation if you have one). Even asking the supervisor to guess at the likely mark is inappropriate, considering the nature of the supervision relationship. After discussion you should make corrections you consider necessary and work on making the final presentation as neat and user-friendly as possible.

When you have received your supervisor's comments on the draft of any section, you should try to revise that particular section immediately. Prompt revision is likely to be easier to do while the advice of your supervisor is fresh in your mind. It also avoids a backlog of work, that is essentially finished but needs a redraft, from growing on your desk. This can be discouraging.

9.8 Presentation

The process of preparing your dissertation for final submission starts with a careful final drafting and proof reading of all your chapters. You need to check that your argument clearly and fluently develops from sentence to sentence and from paragraph to paragraph and from chapter to chapter. While you are proof reading, check the accuracy of your spelling and punctuation, and, if in doubt, use a dictionary.

You also need to ensure that your quotations from and references to both primary and secondary materials are clearly and consistently identified according to the conventions of your required referencing system. You will need to read your handbook on the preferred method used at your institution.

Common guidelines for the final presentation of the project might be, for example:

- your dissertation must be typed or word processed on A4 paper
- your own text must be double-spaced in a minimum size 11 font
- indented quotations must be single-spaced
- the pages of the dissertation must be numbered
- it must have a title page
- it should include an acknowledgments page
- it must have a table of statutes (short title and year in alphabetical or chronological order, including secondary legislation if relevant) and a table of cases (in alphabetical order, including citations)
- it must have a bibliography of texts, journals and web pages (include the full address and the date you accessed the site)
- do not consider submitting the project until it has been read and re-read at least four times.

Checklist

Are you sure that your introduction states the problem clearly?

Does it make clear what the major stages of your argument will involve?

Does the structure of your argument reflect what you say in the introduction?

Have you divided it into chapters in the best way?

Is every sentence necessary? If not, then eliminate the unnecessary waffle.

Does each paragraph make only one point?

CONTINUED ▸

Is your style of writing clear, logical, precise and fluent?

Is your use of technical and legal language accurate?

Are all of the references and citations complete?

Does the conclusion bring your argument together effectively?

TIP If you have to have the project bound before final submission, you will have to leave a few days for that to be done. You may need to book in advance. Do not forget!

9.9 The oral presentation

Some marks are sometimes available for an oral presentation based on the dissertation. This is called a viva. Not all law schools have the time, staff or facilities to make this part of the assessment, but in the event that you do have to do a presentation (and do please check!), the following advice is for you.

First, find out the structure of the viva. How long will it last and for how long do you need to talk? Will you be asked questions? Who will be present? And (of course) when and where is it? The date of the presentation will be set so that the supervisor and often a second marker will have read and discussed your project.

9.9.1 The structure of a viva

Example 7

Peter submitted his dissertation on 2nd May. His oral presentation is on 1st June, after the date of his last exam. Between the submission date of the project and the date of the viva, the House of Lords decided an appeal contrary to the arguments he made in his dissertation.

The viva will last for 20 minutes. He is required to present his findings for no more than 10 minutes, after which the panel (comprising the supervisor and a second marker) may ask questions.

Structure	Minutes	Contents
Peter's presentation	1–2	Peter explains why he chose to do the project on that subject matter and he shares with the panel what he anticipated his findings to be.

CONTINUED ▶

Structure	Minutes	Contents
Peter's presentation – *contd*	3–6	Peter talks though each chapter of his project, noting the key cases/statutes/academic writings incorporating an evaluation of the material. Peter is far more subjective than he was in his writing; he expresses his personal opinion about the material and why he holds that view.
	7–10	Peter explains the recent decision of the House of Lords. He has left plenty of time to recite the key facts, the *ratio decidendi and* his views on the decision.
Panel's questions	11–20	First, the panel asks Peter about one of the arguments raised in the project with which they happen to disagree. Peter stands his ground and submits that his view is correct and why. He acknowledges the panel's contrary view has merit, but criticises it nonetheless because of certain weaknesses he discovered.
		The panel then ask whether Peter was surprised by any of his findings. This gives Peter an opportunity to show his open-mindedness and reflective approach to his studies.
		The panel then refers to the recent House of Lords' decision.
		They happen to agree with Peter's opinion of the decision, but in an effort to challenge Peter, they express support for it. Peter is required to go into more detail about why his thinks the decision was wrong (he is happy to do so – he did not have time in the first 10 minutes to say all he wanted to).

Figure 9.9 Example of the structure of a viva

If you have to do an oral presentation, please remember the panel is not trying to catch you out. The questions are being asked to see if you can rise to the challenge of a higher level of evaluation. Many panels ask questions starting with 'What if . . .?' This method encourages students to hypothesise in a way they may not have thought of doing in the project. It is a very sophisticated educational technique (it is called synthesis) and if the student can rise to the challenge, he or she will be given a great deal of credit.

Further reading

Smith, Glanville Williams, *Learning the Law*, 13th edn, London: Sweet and Maxwell, 2006, Chapter 12.

chapter 10 MOOTING ■

After reading this chapter you should be able to:

- Describe a moot

- Decide whether, if you have the choice, you will enjoy and be good at mooting

- Participate with confidence in a moot

- Appreciate the importance of the rules governing mooting

10.1 What is a moot?

A moot is a mock appeal.

You may have heard of mock *trials*, where students act the parts of the lawyers, the judge, the jury and the witnesses in a case. A *moot* is where a complex point of law is (or more commonly, two complex points of law are) argued as if the case was a real appeal in a Divisional Court of the High Court, the Court of Appeal or, sometimes, the House of Lords. It is always a problem-based scenario. Students take the roles of the advocates (the barristers, called counsel) in the case. The role of the judge is sometimes taken by other students, but is more commonly taken by law tutors or sometimes visiting solicitors, barristers or real judges. Moots might be assessed as part of a module. Some law schools also put forward teams of student volunteers to moot externally on behalf of the law school, either in an informal moot with another university called a friendly, or as part of a national mooting competition such as The Weekly Law Reports Mooting Competition, or as part of an international moot such as the Jessup or the Telders moots.

There are two parts to every moot. First, there are the written arguments. Second, there is the oral presentation of the arguments.

Written pleadings

There are two types of written arguments. The first are the skeleton arguments, which are usually no more than half a side of A4, summarising the submissions on the ground of appeal under consideration, and listing the authorities to be relied on to support that submission. Rarer than the skeletons are the pleadings, also called memorials. The pleadings are a full argument of the law.

You may have to submit skeletons, or pleadings, or both, or even neither. It is your responsibility to check the rules governing your moot.

Oral presentation

In the oral presentations, you act as the barristers (referred to in court as counsel) appearing in a hypothetical case, either in the Court of Appeal or the House of Lords, or another appeal court, such as an international court. There are usually four students in each oral presentation. The orals often last for one hour which is broadly divided to allow each mooter equal 'speech time.'

There are strict rules governing acceptable behaviour in a moot, which are explained below.

10.2 Who is involved in mooting?

In many law schools, moots are arranged and organised by the student law society or council. In others, there is a member of academic staff who runs the moots. Moots may vary in format, length and organisation, but the following information is true of most moots. If you are involved in mooting, you must find out the exact format and rules that your institution adopts.

10.2.1 The Master of Moots

The person with overall responsibility for organising the moots within a law school is called the Master (or Mistress, or, for a more gender neutral term, Director) of Moots. This role may be taken by a member of academic staff or a student. The Master's role is to:

- organise or write the moot question
- find a suitable time and place for the moot
- find or act as the judge (and if the latter, to deliver judgment in the case at the end of the moot)
- publicise the moot so there are people in the audience
- enter the teams for moots against other institutions or in the national mooting competitions.

10.2.2 The judge(s)

The Master of Moots will often be the judge in an internal or friendly moot. You can be assured the judge will be familiar with the case and the previous case law. The role of the judge is not to sit and listen to your arguments like an oral presentation. Judges interrupt mooters and ask complex questions and push the mooter for an answer.

The questions are not designed to put you off, but test your ability in the powers of persuasion and your ability to think on your feet. Questions are also a useful way for the judge to indicate to counsel which points of law they should focus on. For example, a judge may ask a question in order to draw out of you a piece of information which he feels may assist your case, but which you have not yet mentioned. If you have not anticipated this question, take a couple of seconds to allow the question to sink in, take a deep breath and then give a calm answer. The judge is not timing you for a quick response; he will be far happier with a considered and thoughtful answer. If you do not understand a question politely ask the judge to repeat or rephrase it. Something along the lines of 'I should be obliged if your Lordship could possibly clarify that question' or 'I am having a little difficulty following your Lordship's meaning' will usually suffice.

In preparation for your moot, try to consider what questions might be asked and try to have an answer ready. Use both the skeleton arguments of the other side to prompt your thoughts and any dissenting/minority judgments or academic authors with which your argument conflicts to anticipate the questions.

If a judge asks you for information that you plan on coming to later in your arguments, you can point that out ('If it pleases your Lordship, I do intend to cover that exact point a little later in my submissions'), but do be prepared to deal with the question there and then if the judge insists ('As your Lordship pleases . . .').

10.2.3 Counsel

Most moots have four students as advocates. Two of the students are acting for the appellant (the party bringing the appeal) and two for the respondent (defending the appeal). In each team there is a lead and a junior. The leading counsel for each side argue on the first ground(s) of appeal and junior counsel for each side argue on the second ground(s). For each ground, a number of arguments may be presented, but do not think that quantity is a substitute for quality. One or two well argued points are invariably better than four or five less strong points.

10.3 What work should I do before my moot?

Typically, a moot question will consist of a background to the facts of the case and a decision made at first instance from which two points of law arise. Each of the pairs of mooters on each side takes one of the points of law for debate in the moot as explained above. Before the moot, each team must inform the other side of the main points in their argument and the authorities to be relied on. This is usually done by submitting the 'skeleton arguments'.

Leading Counsel for the Appellant (name)

Junior Counsel for the Appellant (name)

The first ground of appeal (paste it or copy it from the moot question)

Summarise your first argument briefly stating why the trial judge was incorrect at first instance and citing a case for each proposition or statement of law, such as:

The trial judge misdirected the jury as to the meaning of the word 'intent' in the definition of the offence of murder, *R v Moloney* [1985] 1 AC 905, *R v Woollin* [1999] 1 AC 82

Summarise your second point

And so on for each ground of appeal

■ *Figure 10.1 Sample of a skeleton argument*

There may be rules limiting the number of authorities that can be cited in a moot (commonly the limit is three or four). Decide carefully. Choose cases with the highest authority (House of Lords if possible or Court of Appeal). Consider Privy Council decisions too. Choose unanimous judgments if you can. This does not mean you cannot rely on minority or dissenting judgments, but be prepared to make strong arguments why your judge should follow a persuasive precedent. On the whole, ignore citing textbooks and articles in the moot. Rely on the cases mentioned by the authors and use the authors' arguments in your oral submissions.

The skeleton arguments should be sent to opposing counsel, the Master of Moots and the judge (if another person) within the time limit as laid down by the rules of your moot. You may also have to provide photocopies of the cases on which you are relying (you may highlight the relevant passages) and do not forget to have copies for opposing counsel and the judge.

You need to be very familiar with each case you cite. The judge will ask you questions on the facts and the *ratio decidendi* and possibly also *obiter dicta* in the case. Your ignorance of any of these key parts of the judgment will soon become apparent; to the frustration of the judge and your acute embarrassment.

A detailed knowledge of the rules governing precedent and statutory interpretation is also vital. You are likely to be submitting that the judge in the moot follows, reverses, distinguishes or overrules previous case law. You need to be able to tell the judge the circumstances in which each *can* and (in your view) *should* occur. A common mistake with the novice mooter is to inform a moot judge hearing an appeal in the Court of Appeal that he has the power to overrule a previous House of Lords' decision, which is clearly incorrect. Similarly, you might be trying to persuade a judge to interpret legislation in such-and-such a way. Let us imagine you wish the judge to adopt a purposive construction. He or she will obviously ask why a literal interpretation is not to be preferred. Make sure you can answer.

Your understanding of legal reasoning must be as good as it can be. Refer to Chapter 6 on legal reasoning, and other textbooks on the English legal system if you are in any doubt.

10.4 What is the order of events?

The judge(s) will be absent at the start. When he or she enters (or they enter) the court room, all counsel and the audience must be upstanding. The judge(s) will walk to his or her bench, bow and tell the court to be seated. Unless you have a physical difficulty or disability and cannot stand, it is of the utmost importance that you stand when the judge(s) enters. To do otherwise shows disrespect.

The judge may then start the proceedings by referring to the case in question, or may nod at leading counsel for the appellant to commence.

Leading counsel for the appellant must introduce the parties first.

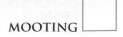

'May it please your Lordship(s); I (name) appear with my learned junior (name) for the appellants. My learned friend (name) appears for the respondents with his/her learned junior (name).'

It is also good practice for leading counsel for the appellant, after making the introductions, to ask the judge if a brief statement of the facts of the instant case would help the court. The judge(s) may or may not agree to such a suggestion, but if the court indicates a brief summary would indeed be helpful, you must ensure that the summary is unbiased and objective. This is not an opportunity for the legal arguments to be asserted; that comes later.

After a summary of the facts of the case, or if the judge indicates no summary is needed, leading counsel for the appellant will then present the legal arguments on the first ground of appeal and will often commence by summarising the points of law made in the skeleton. After this, proceedings differ from institution to institution. The next person to speak could be:

- leading counsel for the respondent to respond to those arguments on the first ground
- or it could be junior counsel for the appellant who then presents arguments on the second ground of the appeal
- followed by junior counsel for the respondent who responds to those arguments.

In the latter, it is leading counsel for the respondent who will close the moot. There is sometimes a right to reply built into the moot structure to give the last word to counsel for the appellants, but time constraints or the moot rules may prevent this.

Another order for events might be:

Leader for the appellant 20 minutes
Junior for the appellant 15 minutes
Leader for the respondent 20 minutes
Junior for the respondent 20 minutes
Appellant's right to reply 5 minutes (not obligatory)

Figure 10.2 Possible order of events 1

On an occasion where the moot takes the form of an appeal and cross-appeal, the order and timing of speeches might be as follows:

| Leader for the appellant 20 minutes |
| Leader for the respondent 20 minutes |
| Junior for the cross-appellant 15 minutes |
| Junior for the cross-respondent 15 minutes |
| Reply by the appellant 5 minutes |
| Reply by the cross-appellant 5 minutes |

Figure 10.3 Possible order of events 2

Court etiquette

- Always stand up when addressing the court.
- Remain standing if being asked questions by the judge.
- If interrupted by your opponent, sit down and stand up to respond at the judge's direction.
- Refer to your team member as your 'learned leader/junior'.
- Refer to your opposing counsel as your 'learned friend, lead/junior counsel for . . .'
- Address the judge as 'My Lord' (if you would, for example, call him by name in a sentence) or 'Your Lordship' (instead of saying 'you').
- Female judges are always addressed as 'My Lady' or 'Your Ladyship'.
- Never confuse the 'my's' and 'your's' – My Ladyship, or My Lordship are not recognised terms.
- If you have a mixed bench (male and female judges) do not refer to the Bench as 'Your Lordships'. Acknowledge that there is a female judge: 'Your Lordship and Your Ladyship'.
- In a criminal case, refer to the prosecution as 'The Crown', not 'The Queen'.
- Never express your personal views ('In my opinion, the defendant is innocent/the claimant is clearly in the right'). You may make submissions and, at the most, suggestions to the judge. You should certainly not tell the judge how you think the case should be decided.
- Cases must have full citations. This applies both in the skeletons (see above) and when referring to the case in the moot. For example, you would *not* refer the judge in speech to
  - 'Duncan versus Cammell Laird and Co, from 1942, AC 624'.
  - But you *would* say:
  - 'Duncan and Cammell Laird and company, reported in the Appeal Cases Law Reports for 1942 at page 624'.

- If you are not familiar with any of the citations before the moot, sort that out beforehand; or risk the embarrassment of the judge's rude comments.

- When you introduce a case in your arguments, ask if the judge would like to hear a brief summary of the facts of the case. If he says that is not necessary, do not do it.

- When referring to a judge, use his or her correct title. Never say 'Judge LJ'; say 'Lord Justice Judge'. When referring to the judge in the lower court of the case which you are mooting it is polite to refer to him/her as 'The Learned Judge', or 'The Trial Judge in this case'.

- If you are mooting in the Court of Appeal then the court should be referred to as 'The Court'. However, in the House of Lords it is referred to as 'The House'. For instance, 'In the case before the court today . . .' becomes 'In the case before the House today . . .' in the House of Lords.

- Never interrupt the judge. If the judge asks you a question wait until he has finished speaking before answering. Do not butt in, in the hope that you can put him off!

- Do not gesticulate wildly while you are speaking. This may look very good on television but in a moot it will simply detract from what you are saying. Hands and feet are still.

- Dress in a suit or smart clothes if you do not have a suit. Appearance is important as it indicates the respect with which you regard the proceedings.

While all this may seem old fashioned and 'stuffy' you should remember that a court is a very formal setting and follows a lot of historical tradition. For example, referring to someone as '*learned*' is not only polite, but is recognition of the fact that they are learned in the law.

The importance of time limits

If the rules of the moot at your institution include time limits; stick to them. It may seem unfair to you if you think your arguments are too complex to be dealt with in only 15 or 20 minutes (including questions), but the proceedings do need to be of a reasonable length, and one of the aims of a moot is to enable students to develop the skill of expressing themselves concisely and succinctly. Do not repeat yourself and you should be able to stay within the time limits.

At the end of counsels' arguments, the judge will deliver the judgment.

10.5 What if I think I am going to lose the legal argument?

- **Do not worry** – there are two decisions the judge makes when determining a moot; a decision on the law and a decision on the moot. So even if you think your legal case is weak, it is certainly possible for you to win the moot. It is how you make your arguments and how convincingly you express your points that wins the moot.

- **Good technique** – speak clearly and slowly. If you rush speech, you will lose the power of your argument. Do not rush even if you are quoting from a case and the judge has an extract of the passage in front of him. You are quoting for a reason; do not hurry through it.

- **Pause regularly** – and always at the end of a submission.

- **Make eye contact with the judge** – make sure he is keeping up with your arguments. Ask at the end of one point for his permission for you to proceed to the next. He may merely nod – and you would miss it if you were not looking up.

  Unless quoting from a case or other extract, try not to recite your arguments from a prepared script.

- **Be expressive** – make sure there is intonation in your voice. A judge is not going to be persuaded by counsel who sound bored by their own submissions.

- **Be brief** – make your submissions as intelligible as possible, avoiding excessive use of legal jargon.

- **Do not refer to authorities for the sake of it** – because the judge may question you in detail on any particular case mentioned. Therefore be prepared to recite a precise proposition of law for which you think any case cited is an authority.

It is also helpful to have a closing sentence prepared. If the worst happens and you are so thrown off your argument that you cannot carry on, it is useful to be able to deliver a closing sentence before sitting down rather than simply mumbling and sitting down red-faced! In any case, something along the lines of '*For the reasons I have given I would ask that this appeal be allowed/dismissed*' is usual.

10.6 Why should I moot?

Mooting enhances your overall understanding and knowledge of particular areas of law and also enhances overall confidence in public speaking, general research and presentation skills. Application forms for legal professional courses, solicitors' firms and barristers' chambers often demand that a candidate has, and can provide evidence of, their advocacy or mooting experience while at university (over and above any of the more traditional areas of advocacy such as debating). However, all lawyers need to develop the skills of fluency of expression and clear enunciation. Whether your intended career path is to be a barrister, solicitor or member of another profession, having advanced advocacy and legal reasoning skills mean that people will listen to you. If you can express yourself concisely and succinctly, your audience in any setting will be influenced by your powers of persuasion. Good mooters rarely lose arguments or debates (outside the moot room at least). A moot is the best way to develop these practical and transferable skills to be enhanced for your later professional life.

10.7 Where can I get further information?

How to Moot: A Student Guide to Mooting, by John Snape and Gary Watt, published by Oxford University Press, October 2004.

chapter 11 PREPARING FOR EXAMINATIONS – REVISION ■

AIMS AND OBJECTIVES

After reading this chapter you should be able to:

- Understand the difference between learning and revising

- Know when to start revising

- Understand the importance of time management

- Understand a variety of different revision aids

- Understand the importance of practising past exam questions

- Manage time effectively during revision

- Prepare revision aids that suit you personally

- Apply techniques to revise effectively

- Feel confident and prepared before exams

Revision is a dreaded time for many students. It is time consuming and stressful. But it is an unavoidable task. Being a law student requires memorising many cases and legal concepts. What makes an excellent law student is the ability to reproduce this information in the required format. It is therefore critical that the revision process goes well.

It also must be remembered that revision is an individual process. What works for one person may be a poor approach for another. It is important to experiment to find the right mix of techniques that work for you. For example, it is important that you are in the right environment. Think about the time of day, noise levels, the materials you need and the timing available. Using a mixture of techniques may be more effective than using just one. Failing to take these issues into account could mean you are wasting your time.

Revision should not be the start of your learning but a way of making what you already know and understand available to you in the exam. Revision can take up a lot of your time and for the best use of that time it should be organised and you must make use of effective techniques.

11.1 When to start

Revision is of course the last stage in the process before you actually sit your exam, although it may actually start a long time before the exam. In fact if you are going to achieve the most you can in the exam then you must prepare for your revision just as the revision itself is a preparation for the exam.

NOTE

> If you are working effectively during the course you will be preparing for both the exam and the revision that precedes it all the time during the course. You do this by keeping your notes up to date, and making sure you amend what you have written down in lectures with what you learn also from text books and other sources. ☐ ☐ ☐

In terms of when to start, very often you will be having lectures right up to a couple of weeks before the exams. You are learning new information at this time but you cannot ignore the need to revise what you learnt earlier in the course. Remember, if you leave everything until the last minute then this gives you little chance of doing your revision effectively. If you suddenly realise how long revision is taking and that you have very little time left to do it all then it will only add to your anxiety.

Revision is to a law student as training is to a sportsman. Sportsmen train regularly to get their bodies in the appropriate physical condition to be able to take part in competitive events. This is really no different to the studying that you do throughout your course. The athlete trains his or her body and you must train your mind. Of course anyone who has been to a football or cricket match or watched an athletics meeting will see the competitors out on the field going through various exercises prior to the start of the contest. This is as vital as all the preparation done before. If the sportsman is not warmed up before the start of the event then he is unlikely to perform well because his muscles will be not be toned for the contest ahead. This is just the same as your preparation for the exam. If you have not exercised your brain sufficiently before the exam it may let you down. Just like with sports people and their training, the earlier you begin your programme the fitter and more finely tuned your mind will be. A span of short sessions spaced over a longer period is much more useful than 'burning the midnight oil' and cramming viciously at the last minute. So begin early.

11.2 Collecting materials

During your course of study you will have learnt a lot of detailed information on the law. It is almost inevitable that your sources of information will not have been broken down into manageable proportions for the purposes of revision. Many if not most textbooks are written mostly in lengthy prose. Until you are very proficient at note taking your notes also are unlikely to be in a form that is most useful for revision purposes.

Your revision is what helps your memory in the exam to sift through all the detailed knowledge that you have and then to reproduce only the relevant parts from it. You need to be able to focus on the relevant areas of law from the limited information that you are given in the questions.

 TIP One of your first tasks then at the start of your revision is to go through all of your notes and text books and to prepare condensed versions of the important key points.

So before you start your revision you have ensured that you have all of the materials necessary in order to be able revise rather than learn from scratch. Make sure then that before revision you have done the following:

• You have read the necessary sections or chapters of text books and have made notes from them to supplement your lecture notes if you need to do so.

• All of your lecture notes are up to date and in a methodical order fully amended with any additional information that you needed to supplement them with from other sources.

• If you intend to use in your revision any essays which you have written for your tutors during the course, or any materials that you have prepared for seminars, that you have amended them to include any comments made by your tutors, or that you have corrected any errors which were identified in them.

• If there are any important handouts that you have missed or lost, you have asked your teacher for replacements. Even if this makes you look inefficient it is far better than being without important information that is critical to your effective revision.

• If possible you have some revision aids already prepared such as those identified in section 11.5 below.

One of the key aspects of your revision is that it is carried out in a methodical rather than a random way. That is one of the great benefits of a revision timetable as that identified in section 11.4 below.

You also need to be just as methodical about the materials you are using for revision. If you merely have a collection of books and notes in no particular order then you are less likely to be cohesive in the planning of your revision.

You will be revising more than one area of law. You should therefore have kept your notes in separate folders from the start of your course. Even within the different subjects you should consider your materials as a series of files. If you go on to work in a legal office you will certainly have to get used to working with files that are cohesively structured so that you can easily put your hand not only on the appropriate thing that you are working on but also even within the file move smoothly through it to the precise document you need at the time.

You should adopt the same approach to each subject you are studying.

- Treat each topic of the subject as a sub-file within the overall file that represents the subject as a whole.

- If you are keeping your materials for a subject within the same folder then it is a very good idea to use the cards (or dividers) that are provided with ring binders or something similar to separate the different topics.

- Have the name of the topic clearly written on this divider so that you can go straight to the topic you are currently revising.

- Within each sub-file representing a topic area separate your revision aids out into type with the most detailed to start and the more visual and punchier aids towards the end. This is so that you can revise first by reading through the most detailed information and then test yourself against the most abbreviated aids.

11.3 The difference between learning and revision

Learning is the process of gaining knowledge for the first time. Revision is a re-examination of knowledge already learnt to improve that knowledge for an examination. If you know that you have spent too little time preparing for tutorials, contributing in classes and reflecting and refining your knowledge, then you must be prepared for what should be the revision process to be a learning process. Accept that your mark in the exam will inevitably reflect this fact. It will be lower. This is true unless you notice this early enough to remedy the problem.

How can you tell whether you need to learn a topic or revise it?

ACTIVITY

> Take a piece of paper and choose a topic that you think will come up in the exam.
> Break it into down into elements and list as many as you can. If the sheet is blank,
> you are going to have to learn it. If the sheet has a few vague comments and many
> gaps, that indicates a learning process is needed. If there are a few gaps, say of a couple
> of the elements and a few of the key case names for example, you should be ready to
> start your revision.

If you have lecture handouts or a module pack to hand, use the lecture outline as a starting point and identify which areas are your weakest. Do not fall into the common trap of learning and re-learning topics about which you are already confident. As comforting as it is to spend time reviewing law you already understand, it will do you no good if that topic does not come up in the exam.

Anyone who has ever sat an exam will know that revision is hard work and time consuming. However, as with everything, it is effective use of time that counts. Revision is not the same as learning afresh. It should be the final stage in the process. While you may be realising things during your revision that you had not thought of before, the process should essentially be about fixing in your mind in a methodical way things that you have already learnt.

11.4 Time management

One of the most important aspects of revision is managing your time effectively. Of course this can be said for any aspect of your study, whether it is in making sure that you are punctual for your lectures, organising your time in reading and following up lectures or being aware of the opening times of libraries and resources centres, and it even applies to the day of the exam itself. Time management is a critical factor in any area of your life, not just study.

Time management then is one of the most important aspects of your revision. If you merely sit in front of your book or notes and randomly select topics to read then this is likely to leave you unprepared for the exam, and it is likely that you will have no idea of how well or how poorly prepared you are.

11.4.1 Timing

Revision is often seen by many students as a period of intense cramming of case names and key concepts two to three weeks prior to an examination. This approach has many pitfalls. These include:

- **Lack of understanding of key cases and concepts** – On average a student will forget 80 per cent of information in a lecture within 48 hours.

- **Stress** – Cramming creates pressure as there is only a short space of time to memorise a significant amount of information.

- **A lack of resources** – Leaving revision late leaves little time to prepare revision notes and prepare and review past questions.

- **Focuses heavily on memorisation** – Leaving little time to consider other important examination techniques/factors such as making sure you can answer the question (not the question you want, but the question asked).

In order to make best use of your time you should prepare a revision programme for yourself and you should also make sure that you work to it. If you can start your revision four or six weeks before the exam then you have time to break it down into manageable sessions rather than wearing yourself out at the end. You can begin by identifying what are the harder areas you need to learn because you will need to spend more time on these.

ACTIVITY

On a blank sheet of paper, write out the cases and the concepts that were explained to you in your most recent lecture. Compare your response with your lecture notes.

Repeat the process above, but now choose a lecture from four weeks ago.

There will be gaps, not only in terms of your ability to remember the cases and concepts, but you may also have found difficulty understanding some issues. It is important to realise that failing to review course material soon after it is delivered will result in the information not being retained. This can mean that in a short space of time you may not be able to recollect the important cases and concepts. The normal cycle of intensive revision prior to an exam will not compensate for this. Can you really memorise six months of lectures in four weeks when you have little familiarity with the subject content?

Revision is therefore an ongoing process. There are three key phases:

* long term
* medium term
* short term.

11.4.2 Long term

Review your lecture notes as soon as possible. Highlight and fill in any gaps within your course notes. Review and research the areas that you do not fully understand – using tutorials and set texts as the basis to seek clarity regarding cases and materials will help with this process. Put your lecture notes in a format that is accessible to you. Collect the necessary case and journal materials and organise them in a logical and accessible order. Then, for each topic produce an overview. See Figure 11.1 overleaf for an example. This will provide you with an accessible overview of the key issues and cases and will be a useful tool for revision.

By doing this you are:

* improving understanding
* improving the retention of information
* preparing revision aids.

11.4.3 Medium term

Your objective is to refresh your mind on prior learning. You therefore need to review the information you prepared in your long-term phase. This process is not time consuming – it should only take 20–30 minutes per topic.

Precedent

Key Terms
Stare Decisis
Ratio Decidendi
Obiter Dicta
Overruling
Reversing
Distinguishing

Court structure	
Criminal	**Civil**
ECJ	ECJ
House of Lords	House of Lords
Court of Appeal Criminal Division	Court of Appeal Civil
Queen's Bench Division	Divisional Courts
Crown Court	High Court
Magistrates	County Court

System operates by decisions in higher courts having to be followed by lower courts.

Key Concepts

1) Practice Statement 1996 – allows **House of Lords** to move away from past decision when right to so

Cases Relevant

London Street Tramways v London County Council
Conway v Rimmer
Herrington v BRB
R v Shivpuri

2) **Court of Appeal's** role
Cases Relevant

Young v Bristol Aeroplane
R v Gould
Gallie v Lee
Miliangos v George Frank Textiles

3) **Human Rights Act** section 2(1)(a)
Cases Relevant   *Re Medicaments No.2*

Figure 11.1 Example of an overview sheet

ACTIVITY

Suggested tasks

1 Use the overview sheet and try to explain the issues it mentions. Where there are gaps, revisit the subject content that you have difficulty remembering.

2 Look at past examination questions on the topic and prepare some responses. This may highlight a lack of information in certain areas and prompt the need to revisit the subject content or carry out further research.

3 Produce a concept map on this area. (See section 11.5.7 (page 266) for concept maps.)

This can:

- improve your memory of key cases and concepts
- highlight specific areas of memory loss
- build your confidence in applying these areas of study.

11.4.4 Short term

This is the last process before the exam. In terms of timescale, it normally relates to the two to three-week period prior to the exam. The aim is to commit the required knowledge to memory. The first task is to produce a revision timetable. This is not a work of art and should not be time consuming. It is important that it is an effective aid. The revision plan should therefore be:

- **Specific** – The revision plan must include not only what you are going to revise but when and for how long.
- **Measurable** – You need to be able to measure the success of the memorisation process. This can be done by getting somebody to test you on the cases and materials you have revised, or by attempting past questions related to your revision topics.
- **Achievable** – There is no point in setting unrealistic targets and goals. Can you really fully understand the whole of EU law with two hours?
- **Realistic** – The plan must focus on how you work. Do not set a start time of 6.30 am if you are not a morning person. You need to take into account of a number of factors that will dictate the plan.

Time out

Certain times or days need to be blocked out due to other commitments, for example lectures, playing sport, part-time jobs, etc. This may highlight the need to reduce your commitments or extend the length of the short-term revision phase.

Location

Where are you going to revise? You need to consider access to resources, potential distractions and noise levels.

Ongoing

Your revision plan is a working document, for instance it changes as you progress. Certain topics could take longer than others, while you may find some relatively easy to absorb. It is also important to tick or cross areas you have covered. It will provide a motivational boost through giving a sense of completion.

Time related

There needs to be a time context. Timing relates to two issues:

* the length of time for the short term revision phase, and
* how long you are spending on individual topics. There is no set time for these two issues.

They are dictated by:

* the success of the long and medium-term revision process
* individual memorisation skills
* number of exams or topics requiring revision.

It is important not to underestimate the time needed in this phase as you could find yourself in the unfortunate position of not completing the required revision before the exam. It is necessary to leave free space at end of the cycle as a contingency.

Revision timetable example

Time	9–10	10–11	11–12	Lunch	1–2	2–3	3–4	4–5
Day 1	Omissions	Omissions	Causation		Causation	Lecture	Lecture	Seminar
Day 2	Seminar	Lecture	Murder		Murder	Plan answers to causation, omission and murder	Watch TV	Meet friends
Day 3	Review prior topics for gaps	Provocation	Provocation		Play sport	Play sport	Play sport	Play sport
Day 4	Provocation	Lecture	Seminar		Diminished responsibility	Diminished responsibility	Work	Work
Day 5	Lecture	Lecture	Work	Work	Work	Work	Work	Work
Day 19	Contingency		→					
Day 20	Contingency							→

Figure 11.2 *A section of a sample revision plan*

Task

- Make a list of the modules on which you will be examined

- For each module make a list of the examinable topics

- Estimate how long it will take to memorise and apply these topics and record this on the table

- Work out the number of days available for revision

- Select your start and finish times

- Make a list of the times and activities that prevent revision in those slots

- Place all the information into the plan. This may call for an adjustment by either increasing the days or removing certain leisure activities

- Leave two days at the end of the plan blank to give flexibility in case certain topics cause delay.

You should in any case prepare your revision programme a long time in advance of your actual revision. Then you will be able to make a note as you go along how much time you need to give individual areas.

11.5 Preparing revision aids

The key to good revision is to bring your existing knowledge and understanding into a form that can stay in your mind and be easily remembered during the exam itself. Reading your text books over and over again is very time consuming. In any case, you can only read to remember in short bursts and chapters of most law textbooks take a long time to read. Besides this you are unlikely to remember large and detailed bodies of information effectively. The proper time to read your text books is during the course. This is also the time when you should be extracting key points of information as we have already seen in Chapter 3.

As the exam gets closer it will be very time consuming continuously to read over your lecture notes time after time. Once you have the essential knowledge you need to reduce the time you spend looking at each individual area. For this you need to prepare revision aids that will have sufficient information to jog your memory and to focus your attention on things that you do not so easily remember so that you can go back to these in your books or lecture notes. However, they do not need to be extensive. Students do this 'reducing' in many forms and there are even books on the market that do the same very effectively, such as the *Key Facts* series published by Hodder Education. However, even those may be quite detailed and be more lengthy to read through than you may want or need.

Revision aids are the means of unlocking your knowledge. They are a system of mapping knowledge. If you were to go into any office, legal or otherwise, and look at the filing cabinets you would find little cards on the front of each drawer. If they are only arranged 'A–C', 'D–G', 'H–L' etc you would know to look in the file 'H–L' if you wanted for instance to look for the file on Mrs Huxley-Binns. Within that file you would then be able to find all the information you have on that particular client.

A good text book will operate in exactly the same way. You can look in the contents list and see for instance that the chapter on Occupier's Liability in Tort is for example Chapter 8. Even within that contents list you can find more particular information because a good text will have sub-headings as well as chapter headings. So you might find for instance that Liability to Lawful Visitors under the Occupiers' Liability Act 1957 is in Chapter 8, section 8.2. A good text will go even further so that you can find that section 8.2 has sub-sections also. You might be able to find section 8.2.1. Potential claimants; section 8.2.2. The scope of the Act – the common duty of care; section 8.2.3. Liability to children; section 8.2.4. Liability to persons entering exercising a calling; section 8.2.5. Liability for the torts of independent contractors; and section 8.2.6. Avoiding the duty. If your question in the exam involves some children injured on premises and also that this has resulted from some faulty work done on the premises by some independent contractors, then you would very quickly realise that what you need to know is in sections 8.2.3. and 8.2.5.

You should be able to operate this methodically in the exam, getting right to specific aspects of your knowledge that relate to the questions in front of you. Revision aids can help this process. They act as the list of letters on the front of the filing cabinet or the contents list of the text book. For this reason they all involve reducing the information that you already have to a manageable amount. They should contain the essential pointers but never be overloaded with information.

It may be helpful to develop the skill of producing your own example of the art. This can be done in different ways as long as you end up with something that has a brief reference to all the relevant and necessary information and it is an effective memory jogger for you personally.

There are numerous examples of revision aids that can be used and you should always aim to choose a type of aid that suits the way that you remember. Below are a number of different examples. This is by no means an exhaustive list. There are as many ways of producing revision aids as there are students who have to revise.

11.5.1 Repetition and review

On the face of it this is one of the simplest ways of revising and it certainly involves the least preparation. This involves the reading of notes constantly. Periodic reviews are undertaken to test the absorption of information into the memory. Variations on this method involve rewriting notes. The merits and defects of this method of revision are outlined below.

Merits	• simple • needs no resources other than the notes or books that you already have.
Defects	• lack of focus on certain skills, eg exam timing • takes a significant amount of time • it is passive method and some learners may become easily bored • it is not systematic.

11.5.2 Revision aids: making key cards

Perhaps the most common example that we see students produce is in the form of a key card, reducing the information to its barest form. In fact listening to students and learning from the ways that students choose to revise is at the heart of the *Key Facts* revision books. Key cards are a very personal thing. You should practise getting just the right amount of information into these aids with just the amount of detail that you think is necessary. Different students will want to include different amounts of detail but you should never include too much detail so that it becomes like reading your notes or reading your text book.

Criminal law is a classic example of where you have to remember sections of Acts as well as the appropriate cases, as well as having a clear understanding of how the law applies. In the exam you will need to remember all of this. Below is an example of a key card on the area of provocation in voluntary manslaughter, which can be quite a difficult area but can still be reduced to some essential elements. Try practising the same for all of the offences and defences but remember to include the appropriate cases and sections as this does. You should use the key cards as a constant means of memorising the area on the card. Try to use them as we have looked at already, not just to memorise the specific details on the card but as a way of remembering other detail not contained. If you cannot remember specific details when you are testing yourself or being tested go back to your notes on that detail and look at them again.

Provocation

Definition – section 3, Homicide Act 1957:
- Things said or done
- Caused D to lose self-control
- And a reasonable man would have reacted the same

Roles of judge and jury
- Judge decides whether there is provocation for jury to consider – Acott
- Jury decide whether D was provoked

The provocation
- Provocation can be things said, eg taunting about D's addiction to glue sniffing – Morhall
- (Though this did not apply in common law before the Act – Holmes)
- Or it can be by things done, eg homosexual advances – Newell

The loss of self control
- Loss of control must be temporary and sudden – Duffy
- 'Slow burn' is generally not accepted – Ahluwhalia
- And a cooling off period defeats the plea – Thornton

D's characteristics
- Jury entitled to take into account characteristics of D relevant to the provocation, eg age, sex, etc – Camplin
- Now jury cannot take into account characteristics relevant to D's loss of control – Holly

---

Figure 11.3 Example of a key card for provocation

11.5.3 Cue cards

This is a more specific type of key card and can be used for instance as a memory jogger for individual cases. It involves putting cases and their important issues on cards. Cards are normally placed in date order or information order. Learners then memorise by continuously reviewing the cards. This allows you to memorise the law as it progressed or is logically explained.

Take the example below. Both the brief facts of the case are indicated as well as the key issues arising from the case. A brief recitation of the facts of the case is important for being able to apply the law in problem questions.

Example

R v Cunningham

Facts
D broke into a gas meter to steal the money. Gas leaked out of the damaged meter and seeped into the house next door. The next door neighbour became seriously ill. D was charged with maliciously administering a noxious substance so as to endanger life.

Key issues – relevance to revision
- is the leading case for recklessness
- made recklessness a subjective test
- there have been tests different to this but this was seen as the most acceptable.

Figure 11.4 Example of a cue card for R v Cunningham

Key cards and cue cards are really just different names for the same type of aid, although as they are presented here they are achieving slightly different ends. It is an entirely personal decision how you use them and what amount of detail you include. The merits and defects of both the above aids are as follows:

Merits
<ul><li>quick to prepare</li><li>portable so you can test yourself on the move</li><li>easy to use</li><li>can involve others to test you.</li></ul>
Defects
<ul><li>lack of focus on certain skills, eg how to use the information to answer the question within the time restraints of the exam</li><li>it is passive and certain learners may become bored</li><li>it is easy for the cards to become muddled. You will need strong organisational skills to ensure different topics are categorised appropriately.</li></ul>

11.5.4 Revision aids: reducing statute law to key elements

Again textbooks rarely reduce law to its essential elements. Criminal law is a classic example of where the law can be quite hard to remember simply in the form in which you usually find it. You will have to know all of the various aspects of many sections of different Acts and this can be quite frightening if you are simply trying to remember the sections off by heart as was traditionally demanded of law students. A better way is to reduce the lengthy wording of the sections to simple key elements. You must of course understand the wording of the sections before you can do this. Put in a simplified form a statute may prove to be a much quicker and easier way to revise than trying to learn all of the various sections from the Acts themselves.

Essential elements of crimes

The following are the essential ingredients of many of the major areas of crime studied on most degree courses.

Offences against the person

Murder

1. A sane person over the age of 10
2. Unlawfully cause the death of
3. A living human being
4. Within the jurisdiction of the English courts
5. With intent.
   a) to kill; or
   b) to commit GBH

Constructive manslaughter

1. A sane person over 10
2. Intentionally or recklessly
3. Does an unlawful and dangerous act
4. Which causes the death of
5. A living human being
6. Within the jurisdiction of the courts

Gross negligence manslaughter

1. A sane person over the age of 10
2. Acting under a duty
3. Does an act or omission which is so negligent that it goes beyond mere compensation and amounts to a crime
4. That causes the death of
5. A living human being
6. Within the jurisdiction of the courts

Wounding with intent – contrary to s 18, Offences Against the Person Act 1861

1. Unlawfully and
2. [Maliciously]

CONTINUED ▸

3. a) wounds; or

   b) causes GBH

4. To any person

5. With intent to

   a) cause GBH

   b) resist lawful arrest

Unlawful wounding – contrary to s 20, OAPA 1861

1. Unlawfully and

2. Maliciously

3. a) wounds, or

   b) inflicts GBH

4. On any person

Assault occasioning actual bodily harm – contrary to s 47, OAPA 1861

1. Does an act (assault or battery)

2. That causes another

3. Actual bodily harm

4. a) intending to cause apprehension/inflict violence

   b) reckless as to whether apprehension/violence is caused

Common Assault – s 39, Criminal Justice Act 1988

1. Does an act

2. a) causing another apprehension of immediate and unlawful violence

   b) inflicting violence on another

3. a) intending to cause apprehension/inflict violence

   b) reckless as to whether apprehension/violence is caused

Offences against property

Theft – contrary to s 1 Theft Act 1968

1. Dishonestly

2. Appropriates

3. Property

4. Belonging to another

5. With the intention to permanently deprive the other of it

Robbery – contrary to s 8, Theft Act 1968

1. Steals (*actus reus* and *mens rea* of theft)

2. Immediately before or at the time of the theft

3. Uses force or puts in fear of force

4. For the purpose of stealing

CONTINUED ▸

Burglary with intent – contrary to s 9(1)(a), Theft Act 1968

1. Enters
2. A building or part of a building
3. As a trespasser
4. With intent to
   a) steal
   b) inflict GBH on a person therein
   c) cause criminal damage

Burglary – contrary to s 9(1)(b), Theft Act 1968

1. Having entered
2. A building or part of a building
3. As a trespasser
4. a) steals
   b) inflicts GBH
   c) attempts either

Making off without payment – contrary to s 3, Theft Act 1978

1. A person knowing payment on the spot is required
2. Dishonestly
3. Makes off without having paid as required or expected
4. Intending to avoid payment

Criminal damage – contrary to s 1(1), Criminal Damage Act 1971

1. Without lawful excuse
2. Destroys or damages
3. Property
4. Belonging to another
5. a) intentionally
   b) recklessly

Recklessly endangering life – contrary to s 1(2), Criminal Damage Act 1977

1. Without lawful excuse
2. Destroys or damages
3. Property
4. Belonging to himself or another
5. a) intentionally, or
   b) recklessly
6. a) intending to endanger life, or
   b) reckless as to whether life is endangered

CONTINUED ▸

Inchoate offences

Attempt – contrary to s 1, Criminal Attempts Act 1981

1. With intent to commit an offence

2. Does an act

3. More than merely preparatory to the commission of the offence

Conspiracy – contrary to s 1, Criminal Law Act 1977

1. Agrees

2. With another person or persons

3. To pursue a course of conduct

4. Amounting to or involving an offence

5. Intending to play a part

Incitement

1. Communicates encouragement or persuades

2. Another person

3. To commit an offence

4. Intending an offence is committed

■ *Figure 11.5 Example of the key elements of an area of law*

Although the defences are mostly creations of the common law rather than Parliament, they are still difficult to remember if you are trying to do so from the chapters of text books. Just as we have created a simpler version of the elements of the offences themselves, we can do the same for the important elements of the various defences.

The following are the essential elements of the major defences studied on all courses. In their simplified form they should prove to be a quicker revision aid than learning the definitions supplied in the judgments of cases or even sometimes than the rather lengthy explanations given in some text books.

Essential elements of defences

Incapacity through age (infancy)

1. Based on irrefutable presumption

2. That a child under the age of ten

3. Is incapable of forming criminal intent – so no *mens rea*

Insanity

1. Available to all crimes

CONTINUED ▶

2. Can mean defendant:

   a) is incapable of pleading; or

   b) was incapable of forming *mens rea* at time of crime

3. Based on a legal rather than a medical definition

4. Defendant is:

   a) labouring under a defect of reasoning

   b) caused by a disease of the mind (internal factor)

   c) and does not know the quality of his act

   d) or if he does, he does not know that what he did was wrong

Non-insane automatism

1. Defendant

   a) has no voluntary actions – so is not responsible for the *actus reus*; and

   b) is unconscious of his deeds – so has no *mens rea* either

2. So based on

   a) an act done without any conscious control

   b) such as a reflex, spasm, convulsion

3. Will be caused by an external factor, eg

   • concussion

   • attack by a swarm of bees

   • anaesthetic

   • but not sleepwalking

Intoxication

1. Covers alcohol and drugs

2. Voluntary intoxication is not a complete defence

   a) but can be a defence to specific intent offences, eg murder if *mens rea* not formed

   b) but not in basic intent offences where voluntary intoxication will be recklessness

3. Involuntary intoxication

   a) is no defence if D had necessary *mens rea* when committing the offence

   b) but can be a defence where D does not have the necessary *mens rea*

Consent

1. In some ways not really a defence since if the victim consents there is no offence

2. In theft consent to appropriation does not necessarily remove liability

3. In assault the consent means the action is not unlawful – so is common, in eg contact sports

4. Not generally available to wounding or GBH on public policy grounds

5. But consent to assault in a domestic context may be accepted

6. A genuinely mistaken belief in consent may be accepted

CONTINUED ▶

Duress

1. A 'concession to human frailty'
2. D has a defence when he committed the crime under threat of violence to himself or his family and a person of reasonable firmness would have done the same
3. But there must be a connection between the threat and the crime
4. Not available as a defence to murder, attempted murder, being an accomplice to a murder
5. Not available if D
   - could have escaped but did not
   - voluntarily associated with the maker of the threats knowing of his violent character

Duress of circumstances

1. Available as a defence if from an objective view the accused acted reasonably and proportionately to avoid the threats
2. Available to all crimes except murder, attempted murder, being an accomplice to a murder
3. There must be
   - imminent peril of death or serious injury to death or others within D's responsibility
   - the jury must be satisfied that the threat overbore D's will at the time of committing the offence
   - execution of the threat need not be immediate

Necessity

1. Traditionally not considered to be available for any offence
2. And this could work unfairly
3. Now linked to duress of circumstances
4. Possible now in rare cases – but only if
   - the act is needed to avoid inevitable and irreparable evil
   - no more is done than is reasonably necessary for the purpose to be achieved
   - the evil inflicted is not out of proportion to the evil avoided

Mistake

1. To be a successful defence the mistake must be one of fact not law
2. So that if the facts were as D believed
   - there would be no *mens rea*; or
   - D would have been able to rely on another defence
3. The mistake need only be an honest mistake – it does not have to be reasonable
4. A drunken mistake may negative the *mens rea* of the offence

Self-defence

1. Available as a complete defence on the basis of justification
2. Can use self-defence to protect self, others or property
3. But only possible where the defendant has used reasonable force

CONTINUED ▶

Where murder is charged there are also some partial defences that have been identified in the Homicide Act 1957. They are not complete defences because they merely reduce the charge to one of manslaughter and remove the mandatory life sentence. They also can be represented in a simple form.

Diminished responsibility

1. Section 2, Homicide Act 1957
2. Defendant suffered from
   - an abnormality of the mind
   - caused by
     - arrested or retarded development of mind; or
     - any inherent causes; or
     - induced by disease or injury
3. This substantially impaired his/her mental responsibility

Provocation

1. Section 3, Homicide Act 1957
2. Defendant
   - was provoked
   - either by things done or things said
   - so as to lose self-control
   - and any reasonable person
   - sharing the relevant characteristics of the defendant (ie that would affect the provocation)
   - would have reacted in the same way
3. The jury is satisfied
   - that the defendant was provoked; and
   - that a reasonable person sharing the same relevant characteristics as the defendant would have reacted in the same way

Failed suicide pacts

1. Section 4, Homicide Act 1957
2. Defendant
   - agreed with one or more people
   - to carry out a course of action that would result in their deaths
   - and the other person(s) died
   - but the defendant did not
3. The defence can satisfy the court that there was in fact a suicide pact

Figure 11.6 Example of the key elements of defences

The merits and defects of the above aids are as follows:

Merits	
	• more portable than text books or even your notes so you can test yourself on the move • quite easy to use and to memorise in this form • less bulky than key cards and reasonably easy to organise • other people can test you.
Defects	
	• lack important detail that you still need, ie the case law • you must understand the sections well to be able to complete such a list so it may be time consuming to create • lack of focus on certain skills, eg exam timing.

11.5.5 Revision aids: diagrams and charts

Most complex information can be reduced into diagram form and there is no end to the types of diagram that you might use. Diagrams are visual so they are a good stimulus for memory.

The following is a very basic diagram from tort illustrating the essential elements required for proving an action in negligence:

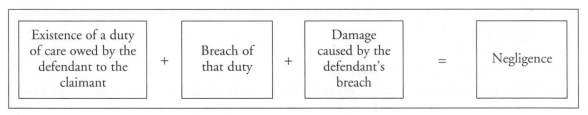

Figure 11.7 The basic elements of an action for negligence

The following is another simple diagram from Contract Law illustrating the difference between the past consideration in operation and its exception from the rule in *Lampleigh v Braithwait*:

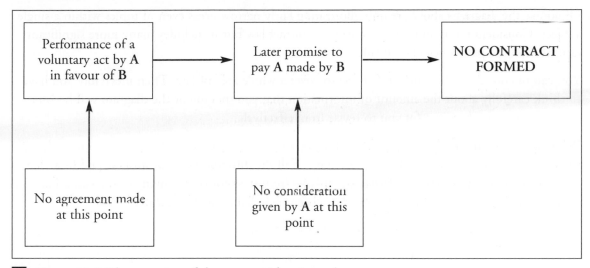

Figure 11.8 The operation of the past consideration rule

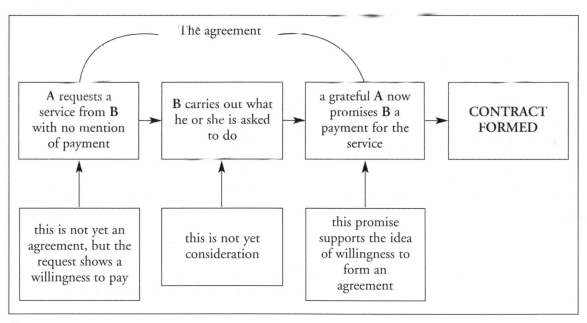

Figure 11.9 The exception in Lampleigh v Braithwaite *in operation*

Of course the diagrams above are only illustrating fairly narrow areas even of topics within a single subject. Consideration is an important area in contract law but it includes many more significant aspects than the past consideration rule.

You can of course use diagrams and charts to cover a whole area of law. Then inevitably you have to think carefully about the amount of information that you include or the diagram will become too big or too cumbersome for you to revise from effectively.

Below is a chart that in effect covers the whole of a large and quite complex area in contract law, the law of mistake. It gives a full understanding of all the different types of mistake and how they differ in their essential elements. What are missing from it of course are many of the cases that you would also need to learn, although some have been included as an illustration.

The class of mistake	The character of the mistake	The legal consequences of the mistake

Common mistake
 	
• *Res extincta*
  (Couturier v Hastie)
 	
• *Res sua*
  (Cooper v Phibbs)
 	
• **Mistake as to quality**
  (Bell v Lever Bros)
	The same mistake is made by both parties:
	
	• The mistake concerns the existence of the subject matter at the time the contract is made
	
	• The mistake is about who owns the subject matter at the time of contracting
	
	• Mistake is merely as to the quality of the bargain made
		• The mistake is 'operative' and the contract is void
		
		• The mistake is 'operative' and the contract is void
		
		• The mistake is not 'operative' – contract continues but may be set aside in equity *(Solle v Butcher)*

Mutual mistake	Both parties make a mistake but not the same one – they are at cross purposes	• If performance is impossible then the contract is void *(Raffles v Wichelhaus)* • If the court can find a common intent then the contract may continue *(Smith v Hughes)*

Unilateral mistake
 	
• **Mistake as to terms**
  (Hartog v Colin and Shields)
 	
• **Mistaken identity not face to face**
  (Cundy v Lindsay)
 	
• **Mistaken identity face to face**
  (Lewis v Avery)
 	
Non est factum
	Only one party is mistaken – the other party knows and takes advantage of the first party's mistake:
	
	• (i) One party mistaken over a material detail;
	  (ii) Other party knew of mistake;
	  (iii) Mistaken party not at fault
	
	• (i) Mistaken party intended to contract with someone else;
	  (ii) Mistake material to contract;
	  (iii) Mistake known to other party.
	
	• Party contracts in person with someone who claims to be someone else
	
	• Mistake concerns nature of the document being signed
	• The document is
	  (i) Materially different to what it was represented to be;
	  (ii) There is no negligence by the person signing it
		
		• If all three mistake is 'operative' and contract void – if not then may be voidable in equity
		
		• If all three mistake is 'operative' and contract void – if not then may be voidable in equity
		
		• Not an 'operative' mistake – mistaken party deemed to be contracting with person in front of him
		
		If both are present then there is an 'operative mistake' – the contract is void – but if not then there is no effect on contract *(Saunders v Anglian Building Society)*

![] *Figure 11.10 The different types of mistake and their legal consequences*

Another way in which a diagram can be useful as a revision aid is when you need to understand the differences or connections between different areas of law. This may be appropriate because you could be called on to make a comparative analysis in the exam. It may even be useful for you in understanding problem questions on areas that seem fairly similar. You may then more easily work to the correct area, as the diagram has helped your basic recognition in reading the scenario.

Below is an example of a chart of that type on the basic differences between the various torts concerning land.

	Trespass to land	Private nuisance	Public nuisance	*Rylands v Fletcher*
Claimants	A person in possession of land	A person with a proprietary interest in land	A member of a class of Her Majesty's citizens	A person harmed by the escape of the dangerous thing
Defendants	Any person carrying out the trespass	A landowner, or a person creating or adopting nuisance	A person creating nuisance	A person in control of land from which thing escapes
Duration of interference	A single trespass is enough	Must be continuous	A single interference is enough	A single escape is enough
Directness	Must be direct	Must be indirect	Could be direct or indirect	Could be direct or indirect
Need to prove fault	Actionable *per se* – so no need to prove fault	Requires unreasonable use of land – which is similar	Fault need not be proved	*Cambridge Water* says foreseeability is required – so suggests fault
Locality of interference	Not relevant	Relevant unless damage is caused	Could be relevant, eg to losing client connection	Could be relevant in deciding what is non-natural
Availability of damages	Any damage related to the trespass – and no need to show damage	Physical harm, personal injury to proprietor, economic loss	Physical harm, personal injury, economic loss	Physical loss and personal injury
Defences	Customary right to enter, common law right, statutory right, consent, necessity, licence	Statutory authority, prescription, consent, act of stranger, public policy, over sensitivity of claimant	General defences	Consent, common benefit, act of a stranger, or God, statutory authority, contributory negligence
Whether also a crime	Yes – possible under some Statute	No – unless statutory	Yes – can be	No

■ *Figure 11.11 The similarities and differences between the torts relating to land*

11.5.6 Revision aids: using flow charts

Particularly in the case of problem questions in an exam where you have to apply the law, often in sequence, flow charts can be a very useful way of preparing yourself. A good flow chart is one that asks and then answers the type of questions that you would need to ask yourself in the exam in order to tackle the problem.

If you understand the major elements of the particular area of law then they are reasonably easy to prepare and you can find examples in a number of student focused text books.

In the exam if you apply the type of checklist that comes from a good flow chart then you should be able to go methodically through the question and answer all parts of the problem effectively.

The first example below is a very simple flow chart still explaining the difference between an offer and an invitation to treat, something you will learn very early on in your contract law course.

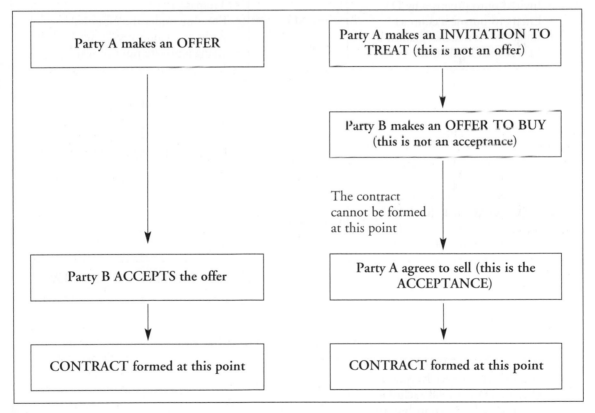

Figure 11.12 *Showing the point at which a contract is made in a standard offer and acceptance, and where there is firstly an invitation to treat.*

You can develop flow charts for information that involves one relatively simple aspect of a topic as above. You can also use them to cover a whole topic. The example below from tort on occupiers' liability under the Occupiers' Liability Act 1957 is an example of that.

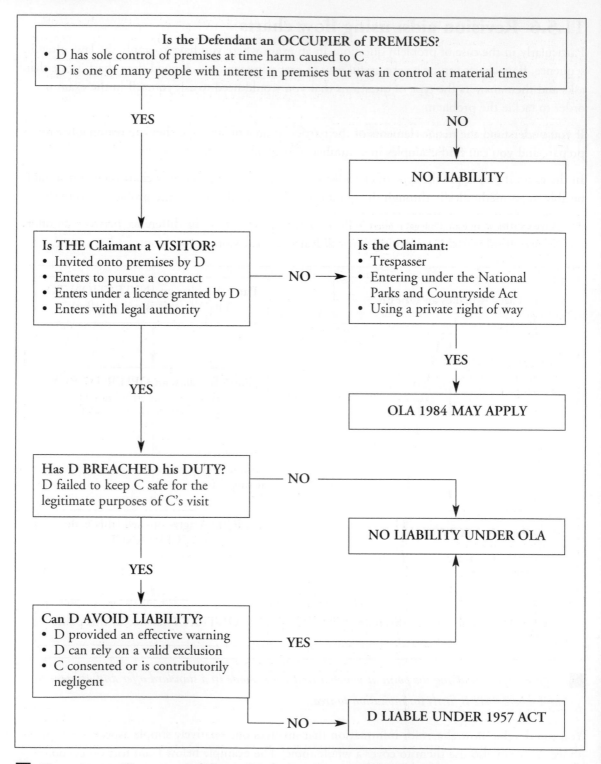

Figure 11.13 Illustrating liability under the Occupiers' Liability Act 1957

One of the things that is missing from the above is the cases that you need to use in illustrating your answer, but you can use your key cards to include that information. The above flow chart is still relatively simple because the information is not that complex. But you can use a flow chart for even very complex information as in the example below on registering land charges in land with unregistered title. This is an area of land law that students often find very daunting.

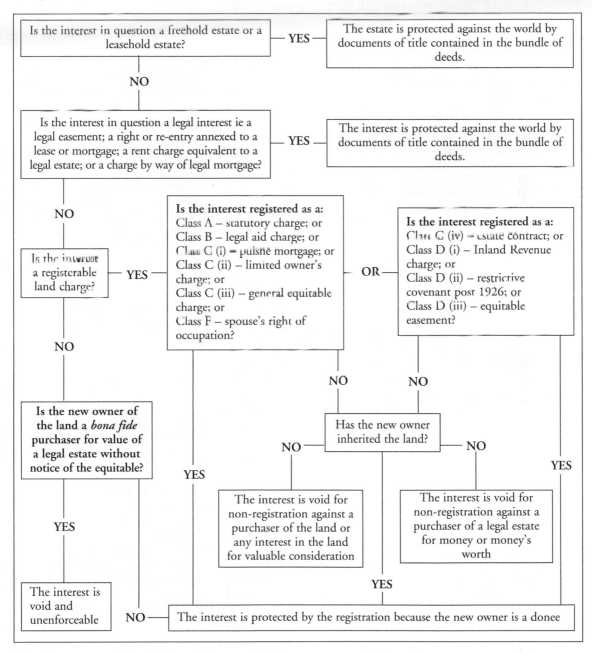

Figure 11.14 Unregistered land

.7 Concept/mind maps

This involves producing a graphic overview of a subject. It is not about recording every detail within a set topic. It is a summary chart showing the logical links. This can be done freehand or by computer. The use of various colours can improve the memorisation process and words can be substituted for pictures to give memory links.

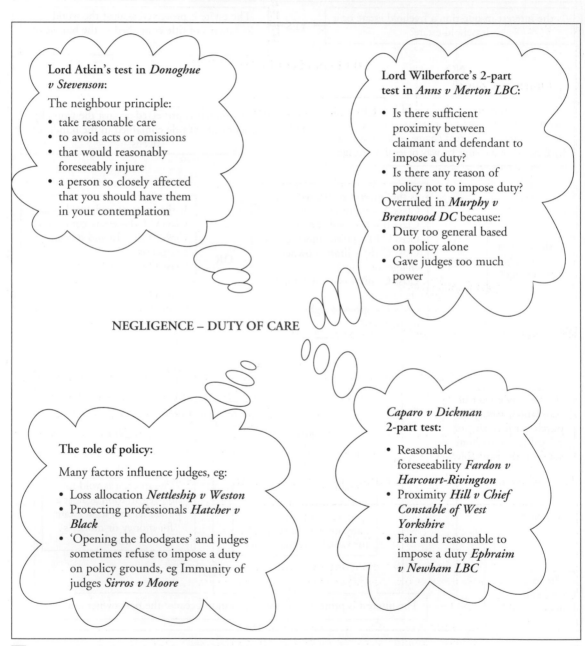

Lord Atkin's test in *Donoghue v Stevenson*:

The neighbour principle:

- take reasonable care
- to avoid acts or omissions
- that would reasonably foreseeably injure
- a person so closely affected that you should have them in your contemplation

Lord Wilberforce's 2-part test in *Anns v Merton LBC*:

- Is there sufficient proximity between claimant and defendant to impose a duty?
- Is there any reason of policy not to impose duty?

Overruled in ***Murphy v Brentwood DC*** because:

- Duty too general based on policy alone
- Gave judges too much power

NEGLIGENCE – DUTY OF CARE

The role of policy:

Many factors influence judges, eg:

- Loss allocation *Nettleship v Weston*
- Protecting professionals *Hatcher v Black*
- 'Opening the floodgates' and judges sometimes refuse to impose a duty on policy grounds, eg Immunity of judges *Sirros v Moore*

***Caparo v Dickman* 2-part test:**

- Reasonable foreseeability *Fardon v Harcourt-Rivington*
- Proximity *Hill v Chief Constable of West Yorkshire*
- Fair and reasonable to impose a duty *Ephraim v Newham LBC*

Figure 11.15 Example of a mind map on negligence

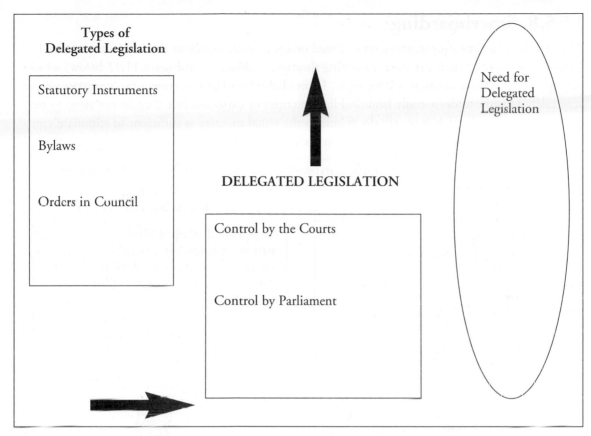

Types of
Delegated Legislation

Statutory Instruments

Bylaws

Orders in Council

DELEGATED LEGISLATION

Control by the Courts

Control by Parliament

Need for
Delegated
Legislation

■ *Figure 11.16 Negative factors of delegated legislation*

The above are two examples of mind maps both produced in different but very visual forms. They also allow you to incorporate different levels of detail. The first (Figure 11.15) is a simple map detailing some of the significant aspects of the duty of care in negligence and a useful pointer for a number of different essay titles. The second (Figure 11.16) is more specific and deals with some of the more contentious aspects of delegated legislation from your English legal system course.

The various merits and defects of using mind maps are indicated below:

Merits
• allows you to see the topic as a connected whole • easy to produce • can be individualised making them specific to your needs • it is an active process and particularly effective for visual learners.
Defects
• lack of focus on certain skills, eg exam timing • gets more complex with the more detail that needs to be included.

11.5.8 Storyboarding

This involves putting a topic into a set of visual images, which represent the key issues involved. This can be a quite broad storyboard running through a subject (as in Figure 11.17 below) which may give you a thread through a large topic. It could also be a fairly narrow area. Some people are very talented and can draw really beautiful little pictures or cartoons, but they do not need to be masterpieces. Simple stick men will do as long as the visual imagery is sufficient to stimulate your learning process and activate your memory in the exam.

Figure 11.17 below shows a fairly simple storyboard explaining the basis of the duty of care principle in negligence.

Negligence developed from Lord Atkin's 'narrow principle', in *Donoghue v Stevenson* – a manufacturer owes a duty of care not to harm users or consumers of his products.

But Lord Atkin also identified a 'broad principle' (the neighbour principle) – you owe a duty of care to anyone who might foreseeably be affected by your acts or omissions.

Now, following *Caparo v Dickman*, a duty will be imposed by a three-part test:
- is damage foreseeable?
- are the parties legally proximate to each other?
- is it fair just and reasonable to impose a duty?

CONTINUED ▶

And duty of care has developed incrementally, situation by situation. So it has been applied to fellow road users as in *Froom v Butcher*.

And it has been applied to doctors in relation to their patients, for instance to examine them as in *Barnett v Chelsea and Kensington Hospital Management Committee*, but in many other aspects of their work too, including diagnosis, treatment, advice, etc.

Figure 11.17 An example of a storyboard

The relative merits and defects of this type of revision aid are indicated below:

Merits
• a good technique for those who have a visual learning style
• student illustrations can be replaced with magazine images for those learners who have weak artistic skills.
• it is an active process and should negate boredom.

Defects
• drawing images can deter some individuals
• lack of focus on certain exam skills, eg timing
• difficult to cover technical issues.

11.5.9 Remembering the 'buzz words' for problem questions

Many students think that problem questions are more difficult than essay questions. This is actually understandable because one of the first things that you have to do with a problem question is to identify the area of law that the problem is concerned with. Learning to recognise areas of law from the factual circumstances in a problem is indeed a skill that you need to master and it can be quite baffling to start with.

Doing this confidently is a skill that only develops with time. The more confident you are with the law the more that it will become second nature for you. However, practising the art of examining the wording of problems for the key words or 'buzz words' is also a useful means of developing the skill. The more examples of problem questions on past papers that you see and tackle, the more familiar you will get with the skill.

Below are just some examples of key wording in tort problems on various key areas of any tort syllabus that you might study.

Occupiers' Liability Act

- A key feature here will be someone visiting the premises of another person, for example *Gemma has been staying at the Crest Hotel.*

- Remember though that premises can be a variety of things, for example *Richard was taking Valerie for a cruise down the river in his motor launch.*

- The occupier is the person in control of premises so there may also be clues as to who the potential defendant is, for example *Gareth has fallen and cut himself on broken glass in the Victoria Precinct. Westchester Corporation are responsible for cleaning the precinct.*

- Since children are treated differently under the Act there will usually be some reference to a child also, for example *Terry, aged seven, went to fetch his ball from Gordon's garden and fell in a trench which Gordon had dug, injuring himself.*

- And remember also that trespassers are protected under the 1984 Act so somebody being on premises unlawfully is a straightforward clue, for example *Rod was stealing lettuces from George's allotment one night when he tripped over a barrow left unattended and injured himself.*

Nuisance

- Here the obvious clue is that nuisance is indirect interference so it will involve things like smells, noises, vibrations, etc for example *Des is building an extension. He drills and hammers often into the early hours of the morning. As a result Derek and Mavis, his neighbours regularly lose sleep.*

- It also involves an unreasonable use of land which is measured by things such as location, but what is a nuisance in one location may not be in another, for example *Stan is annoyed because his car is always dirty from the dust which drifts from the quarry.*

- Continuity is also a factor, so a one-off will not usually be a nuisance, for example *Sid and Ada had no sleep on the Friday night when the rock festival was held in the field behind their house.*

- Malice is also a factor which can affect the outcome of an action and therefore is commonly included in a problem, for example *Hattie became so annoyed by the constant crying of the baby next door that whenever it did cry she turned her stereo and her television up to full volume.*

Vicarious liability

- Here the immediate clue is that the tortfeasor is doing work for someone else, for example *Ralph is repairing Sam's guttering. He leans too far on the ladder and falls onto a passer by, Andrew, injuring him.*

- One point which will usually be in a question is whether the tortfeasor is an employee or an independent contractor, so a problem will include, for example *Horace makes his own tax and NI contributions, but is not allowed to accept work from anyone but Bodgitts Co.*

- The other key issue will be whether the employee commits the tort in the course of the employment or not, for example *Fred was injured when Dave gave him a lift home in the works van. Dave was taking an unofficial lunch break to go to see his wife.*

Nervous shock

- Here the obvious clue is the type of injury suffered by the plaintiff, for example *since the car crash Gail has suffered a complete personality change, has regular flashbacks of the accident and is too afraid to go out.*

- Another common feature of such problems is distinguishing between primary victims and secondary victims so a question would include, for example *Harriet suffered shock when the racing car bounced off the barrier, flew into the air and came over the fence towards her –* compared with – *Raj was shocked when he was rushed to the hospital to find his daughter dead and still covered in blood.*

- Rescuers are a class of claimant who are also commonly referred to in a problem, for example *Eric, a fireman, had struggled hard to release trapped people but had been forced to jump clear when the petrol tank exploded, and had suffered shock when the passengers burnt to death in front of him.*

Some other negligence issues

- Standard of care – look for phrases indicating factors such as practicability of precautions, for example *despite the golf club erecting a thirty-foot high fence, Cyril was still injured by a sliced ball.*

- Causation – look for the possibility of *novus actus interveniens*, for example *when Tania arrived at the hospital her injury was not immediately diagnosed, but she was left waiting on a trolley for two hours.*

- Remoteness – look for damage which is not foreseeable, for example *Ali, who was trapped in his car after the crash, was actually killed when another driver, Colin, collided with the wreckage.*

ACTIVITY

Making revision aids

The box below is the basis of a very simple chapter on a quite easy area from contract law, the intention to create legal relations. Read through the extract and then try to create a revision aid from the examples you have seen in the sections above.

Remember it can be in any form as long as you abbreviate it sufficiently while keeping the essential knowledge

---

Intention to create legal relations

Introduction

We all regularly make arrangements with each other, and we may even be doing things in return for something, and this seems as though there is consideration too.

However, we do not always intend that if we fail to keep to an agreement the other party should be able to sue us. Nor would it be sensible for the courts to be filled with actions on all of the broken promises that are ever made. My children may expect their pocket money regularly but would you want them to be able to sue if I forget to give it to them one week?

The law makes a sensible compromise by assuming that in certain situations we would usually not intend the agreement to be legally binding, while in others we usually would. The first covers social or domestic arrangements where it is presumed there is no intention to be legally bound. The second concerns commercial or business agreements where an intention to be legally bound is presumed. In either case the facts can show that the presumption should not apply. So intention is very much decided on the facts in individual cases.

Social and domestic agreements

Arrangements between family members are usually left to them to sort out themselves and are not legally binding.

Balfour v Balfour [1919] 2 KB 571

A husband worked abroad without his wife who had to stay in England due to illness and promised an income of £30 per month. When the wife later petitioned for divorce her claim to this income failed. It had been made at an amicable point in their relationship, not in contemplation of divorce. It was a purely domestic arrangement beyond the scope of the court.

Where husband and wife are estranged an agreement between them may be taken as intended to be legally binding.

Merritt v Merritt [1970] 1 WLR 1211

Here the husband had deserted his wife for another woman. An agreement that he would pay her an income if she paid the outstanding mortgage was held by the court to be intended to create legally binding obligations.

CONTINUED ▶

272

Sometimes of course families make arrangements that appear to be business arrangements because of their character. In such cases the court will need to examine what the real purpose of the arrangement was.

Jones v Padavatton [1969] 1 WLR 328

A mother provided an allowance for her daughter under an agreement for the daughter to give up her high paid job in New York, study for the bar in England and then return to practise in Trinidad where the mother lived. When the daughter was finding it difficult to manage on the allowance the mother then bought a house for her to live in, and part of which the daughter could let and supplement her income. They later quarrelled and the mother sought repossession of the house. The daughter's argument that the second agreement was contractual failed. The court could find no intent.

If money has passed hands then it will not matter that the arrangement is made socially. It will be held as intended to be legally binding.

Simpkins v Pays [1955] 1 WLR 975

A lodger and two members of the household entered competitions in the lodger's name but paying equal shares of the entry money and on the understanding that they would share any winnings.

If parties put their financial security at risk for an agreement, then it must have been intended that the agreement should be legally binding

Parker v Clarke [1960] 1 WLR 286

A young couple were persuaded by an older couple to sell their house to move in with them, with the promise also that they would inherit property on the death of the old couple. When the two couples eventually fell out and the young couple was asked to leave their action for damages succeeded. Giving up their security was an indication that the arrangement was intended to be legally binding

Commercial and business agreements

An arrangement made within a business context is presumed to be intended to be legally binding unless evidence can show a different intent.

Edwards v Skyways Ltd [1964] 1 WLR 349

An attempt to avoid making an agreed *ex gratia* payment in a redundancy failed. Although *ex gratia* indicates no pre-existing liability to make the payment, the agreement to pay it once made was binding.

The offer of free gifts where this is to promote the business can still be held to be legally binding.

Esso Petroleum Co Ltd v Commissioners of Customs and Excise [1976] 1 WLR 1

Esso gave free World Cup coins with every four gallons of petrol purchased. The customs and excise wanted to claim purchase tax from the transaction. Since Esso were clearly trying to gain more business from the promotion there was held to be intention to be bound by the arrangement.

The principle has also been developed to cover situations where prizes are offered in competitions. The purpose of such events is generally to promote the body offering the prize so there is intention

CONTINUED ▸

to create a legal relationship which is binding and can be relied on by members of the public who enter the competition.

McGowan v Radio Buxton [2001]

The claimant entered a radio competition for which the prize had been stated to be a Renault Clio car. She was told that she had won the competition but was given a four-inch scale model of a Clio. The defendants argued that there was no legally binding contract. The judge held that was intention to create legal relations. The claimant entered the competition as a member of the public and that 'looking at the transcript of the broadcast, there was not even a hint that the car would be a toy'.

However, it is possible for the agreement to contain no intention to be legally binding where that is specifically stated in the agreement itself.

Jones v Vernons' Pools Ltd [1938] 2 All ER 626

The pools company inserted a clause on all coupons stating that '. . . *the transaction should not give rise to any legal relationship . . . but be binding in honour only . . .*' When a punter claimed that the company had lost his winning coupon and sought payment he failed. The clause prevented any legal claim.

The same type of principle applies with so-called comfort letters. Although such letters are worded so that they appear almost to amount to a guarantee, they do not and will not give rise to legal obligations.

Kleinwort Benson Ltd v Malaysian Mining Corporation [1989] 1 WLR 379

Kleinwort lent £10 million to Metals Ltd, a subsidiary of MMC. The parent company would not guarantee this loan but issued a comfort letter stating their intention to ensure Metals had sufficient funds for repayment. When Metals went out of business without repaying Kleinwort the latter's action based on the comfort letter failed. If they had wanted a guarantee they should have insisted on one.

Figure 11.18 Extract on intention to create legal relations

11.6 Practising past papers

The revision process is not complete until you have practised an examination question on that topic from a past paper or from one of the books on the market (for example Blackstone's/Oxford University Press publish a series called *Q&A*). Two of the unavoidable problems with the published books are that:

(a) students may skip over practising the answer and jump straight into reading the suggested answer which means they do not learn as much as they could from the process

(b) the cases used as illustrations of legal issues may differ in the text from that followed on a programme, causing the student to become confused or undermining their confidence.

The best way to practise is to complete as much revision on a topic as you can and then find the time (make the time) to complete a question under exam conditions. We always found parents and housemates to be very supportive of this process ('Please do not disturb me for 45 minutes: I'm doing an exam question').

Do not try to assess your answer straight away. Leave it for at least an hour and preferably longer if you have time and then using your revision notes as a marking scheme, read your work and assess:

- what was well expressed?
- what was well structured?
- how well were the case/statutes incorporated?
- what was omitted (why, did you think it was not relevant and on reflection you have changed your mind, or did you forget it)?
- what was waffle?
- what mark would you give the answer?

Now consider if you are unhappy with the answer what you could do in the future to rectify the situation.

Think about this: Is there any other activity you do only on an annual basis? For me, that is skiing. I know for a fact that the first run is always pretty dreadful. I seem to have forgotten how to turn, stop, bend my knees and it always takes me a few runs to get back into the swing of things. So many students seem, however, to think that sitting an exam is something that does not have to be practised from one June to the next. It is common sense that practice makes perfect.

So what can you get out of timed past paper practice?

- It can highlight areas of weakness that need to be revisited
- It can highlight areas of strength that do not have to be revisited, producing more efficient revision
- It can indicate where there are time management issues (for example, on reflection you spent too long explaining very basic information and ran out of time before you could get onto the complex areas which attract higher marks)
- It is a safe opportunity to make mistakes (you learn from the mistakes and you are unlikely ever to do the same mistake in the exam)
- It can build confidence (there is nothing as confidence-building as knowing when you walk into the exam that you can write for 45 minutes on each topic that can come up on the paper).

chapter 12 SITTING EXAMINATIONS ■

In many cases you will have completed assessment through coursework. While coursework may seem quite comforting because you do it at home and usually have many weeks to do it, it can still be quite demanding trying to complete lots of coursework assignments with the same deadline.

It is unlikely, however, that you will be able to complete a whole degree course in law without taking some exams. Most students seem to think that exams are pretty horrible things and yet, if you remember what an exam is, you should not really be scared of it. An exam is the culmination of a particular part of your course. Like all assessments, it is nothing more than the means of you showing the people who have taught you the level of understanding that you have gained from the course and demonstrating some of the skills required by the subject.

It is a way of showing that you are competent in the subject. If you are competent and if you are prepared then the exam should not be a frightening experience. In fact you should see it as your opportunity to show how good you are.

There are three important aspects to sitting exams successfully:

- being properly prepared for the exam

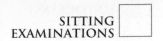

- knowing how to respond to the paper (which means reading the questions properly, selecting appropriate questions, and planning your answers)
- using your time effectively.

12.1 Preparing for the exam

12.1.1 Final preparations

It is surprising how quickly an exam is upon you. If you have not got into a panic during your course then there is no reason why you should get into a panic now if you are fully prepared.

Chapter 11 dealt with everything that you can do to make sure that you are properly prepared and to use what you have learnt during the course in the exam. This was revision. If you have understood the information that you have been given during the course and you have revised effectively so that the information is stored properly in your mind to be used in the correct way during the exam, then you should have done enough to cope with the questions on the exam paper, whatever they are.

It is important to remember that there are more things that you need to do to prepare than just know your subject well.

Being healthy

As with any testing experience it is vital that you are in good physical and mental health to gain the best out of the experience. You are unlikely to perform well at anything if you are feeling unwell or under the weather. You can do things to try to keep healthy for the exam:

- **Get plenty of exercise in the weeks and days before the exam** – this need not be a physical training programme; regular brisk walks are as good as anything and you get the benefit of fresh air to balance out the times you spend cooped up in your room revising.
- **Eat well and eat properly** – try to avoid junk food, eat plenty of fresh food, vegetables and salads. Eat sensibly.
- **Avoid artificial stimulants such as coffee** – these make it much more difficult for you to relax and in fact caffeine actually increases rather than reduces nervous tension which you are trying to avoid in the exam.
- **Try to get enough sleep** – our periods of unconsciousness are the times when we are not consciously focusing on the stress of the exams.
- **Take some time out for relaxation** – as we have said in Chapter 11 on revision, you will do yourself more harm than good spending all of your time working. Work should be broken up with times of relaxation to unwind, on the night before the exam try to avoid last-minute cramming, take the night off and enjoy yourself and be more fresh and relaxed going into the exam.

- **On the morning of the exam try to eat some breakfast** – even if you do not usually eat breakfast, because this will maintain your energy levels during the exam. Some eggs or meat are a good idea because protein is generally better for your digestion.

- **If you are allowed, take a drink and perhaps some sweets into the exam** – tension makes your mouth go dry and you feel dehydrated so some water is good for you, sucking a sweet may help you to concentrate.

Being organised

All of your hard work during the year and through your revision will be wasted if you are taken by surprise by the unexpected on the day. So as well as preparing on a subject basis you should make sure that you are fully organised for the exam in every other way. Again there are a number of things that you can do to ensure that the day goes smoothly:

- **Make sure you know the correct time of the exam** – sometimes exam schedules change and you certainly cannot take it for granted that because one exam starts at 2.00 pm that all of them will. There is nothing worse for your nerves than finding that you have arrived late, apart from the fact that it is robbing you of time you could have spent writing.

- **Make sure that you know the correct exam room and are familiar with where it is** – again exam rooms may change from the original schedule so you should keep checking it. You may take your exams in rooms that you have never been taught in, so if the exam timetable shows that the exam is in a room outside your experience, take the time to find it before the exam so that on the day you can go straight to it.

- **Prepare a checklist well in advance of all the things that you need to take into the exam room** – in law exams this is unlikely to be more than a pen, a highlighter and a ruler, but there may be other things you need, for instance you may be allowed to take in a case book or a Statute book, and always take a spare pen or even two or three.

- **Set out in plenty of time to get to the exam** – public transport is not always reliable and, even if you have your own transport, allow plenty of time to use alternative transport if you should break down.

- **Try to avoid taking anything unnecessary into the exam room with you** – this particularly applies to your notes and text books. Students seem to think that there is merit in revising right up to the exam door but that is not the case. If you do not know it by then you are unlikely to remember it in the exam and this last minute cramming can drive other things out of your memory. Try to reduce any distractions in the few minutes before the exam.

12.1.2 Dealing with exam nerves

As senior examiners of many years, all three of us appreciate that an exam is a nerve-racking experience. This is inevitable because your skills, knowledge and understanding are all being tested.

Whenever we test ourselves, in whatever context, the adrenaline begins to flow. This is both normal and healthy.

The nervous tension that exams create is often compared to the way an athlete builds up to a competitive event. Athletes prepare their minds as well as their bodies for the competition. They will have done all of the training to make them able to do well. That is the same as the learning that you have done during the course of study. The revision has sharpened your mental faculties in the same way that a training programme builds up towards the event. If you are prepared, just as the athlete is prepared, then you have the means to succeed. An athlete still has nerves as the contest is about to start. However, these nerves are productive and healthy; they are to help rise to the challenge of doing well, rather than the fear of taking part. This is the mental focus that you should have when you go into the exam and you should be able to use it to your advantage if you are properly prepared.

You can in any case prepare for these nerves in advance of the exam and be able to control the apparently uncontrollable impulses to panic. We have already identified the importance of leisure and relaxation during your revision. If you are in a reasonably relaxed state going into the exams you are more likely to be able to think clearly, recall what you need, and perform well.

Panic and anxiety, the so-called 'flight or fight' syndrome is the body's natural biological reaction to uncomfortable situations. However, you need not 'fly' from the exam nor 'fight it'. What you really want to do is to take part in it successfully. Relaxation is also the body's natural way of combating anxiety. It is a simple fact that the body cannot be both anxious and relaxed at the same time, different chemical reactions are involved. What you need to be able to do is to be capable of controlling yourself into a relaxed state.

There are several methods of relaxation and you can buy tapes that help you to relax, not just through peaceful music, but through repeated positive affirmations. Quite simply if you lie relaxed, let your body go limp and tell yourself that you are relaxed, you will be.

Although it seems strange to think of it as something to learn, learning to relax is certainly a lot easier than learning one of your legal subjects. The important point is that once you have mastered the practice of relaxing yourself you can use it in any stressful situation, not just the exams but also before interviews, when you are playing sport, or even in those awkward situations when you want to ask somebody to go out with you but you feel too anxious.

You can apply whatever techniques you learn long before you go into the exam room. Just shut your eyes and imagine the exam room, sitting at your desk, listening to all the instructions from the invigilator and then turning over your paper. Then practise your relaxation techniques, tell yourself to be calm, to relax. Do this again and again leading up to the exam. Imagining the experience of the exam in advance and dealing with your nerves will help to diminish the shock of being in the exam room when you get in there. Then when you are confronted with the real thing it will be easy to tell yourself to relax and to stay relaxed during the exam. In a reasonably relaxed state you will cope and perform much better than if you are tense.

12.1.3 Remembering what the exam is all about

Remember that an examination is simply a test of your knowledge, understanding and skills. The key to a successful exam is the preparation prior to it. However, the work done before the exam can be undone by poor examination technique. It is important that you are as calm as possible and refreshed before and during the exam.

You must approach the exam in a methodical manner in order to avoid mistakes and you must ensure that you attempt the most appropriate questions for you. A vital part of choosing the appropriate questions is to read the exam paper thoroughly and to be certain of what the questions are. You should never assume that because you recognise a subject from a quick read of the paper that you are really aware what the question is about. You must always read the question paper properly.

12.2 Reading the questions

12.2.1 Reading the paper

Note what instructions you are given. In particular, check the time allocated for the paper and the number and combinations of questions to be attempted. The time allocated to the examination paper will allow you to work out the time needed per question. To work out the average time per question, simply divide the total time by the number of questions.

For example, a three-hour exam with four questions means that you have 45 minutes of planning and writing time. This, therefore, indicates an extensive piece of writing is required per question.

However, note this assumes that all questions carry the same mark total. If you have questions with different numbers of marks allocated, you need to calculate how long is needed per question. To do this, divide the number of minutes allocated by the maximum mark of the paper. This will give you the number of marks per minute. Then, for each question, multiply the mark per question by the marks per minute. It is also important to note the number – and any potential combination of – questions that are requested. It is disheartening to see a number of exam candidates each year who do not read the instructions and, consequently, make mistakes. Some papers require all questions to be answered. Others require the candidate to answer a set number of questions from one section and a set number of questions from another.

For example, you must answer one question from part A (which attracts 30 marks) and one from part B (which attracts 70 marks) in two hours. You should aim to spend 36 minutes on part A and the remainder of the time on part B.

12.2.2 The questions

First scan the paper reading the question or selection of questions fully. This allows you to become familiar with the areas under examination. It is then important to re-read the paper. Your objective is to identify what each question wants you to discuss. Take each question in turn. This will allow you quickly to identify the key concepts and to ensure that the subject content matches what you originally thought was being asked. In exam conditions, it is easy to confuse what is being asked.

This is the point at which you are beginning to be selective about what you are going to write. You must make sure that you do not just assume what the title demands. For instance, in an exam question a few years ago on offer in contract law the question was 'Critically examine the circumstances in which an offer terminates'. The question was not asking for all of the rules on offer. In fact it was asking for an answer in depth on a fairly narrow area of the topic. Many candidates, used to seeing offer and acceptance as a single area, not only wrote a lot of unnecessary detail on offer, but also wrote extensively on acceptance which was not called for at all. The candidates did not lose marks for writing on unnecessary material. However, they did in effect cost themselves marks by writing on something not called for when they could have spent the same time writing on things that would have earned them marks.

NOTE

Reading the questions accurately and establishing what they call for without assumptions is vital – even in selecting questions.

☐ ☐ ☐

12.3 Selecting questions

12.3.1 Selecting the questions

For examinations that involve a choice, you will need to select questions which you feel will offer the most success. In an ideal world you should be able to complete every question. If this is the case then put the questions in order of preference. Start with the questions you believe are the easiest. This allows you to build confidence and puts you at ease.

Some or all of the questions might not be possible for you to tackle. This could be due to:

- a lack of revision
- a lack of focus on certain aspects of a topic
- failure to understand the question.

If you cannot complete the number of questions required by the exam (eg it may be that the examination is asking for three responses, but you believe that you can only attempt two); again, start with the questions which you feel are the easiest. This will give you confidence because you are completing part of the exam. The remaining time can be dedicated towards the questions that you are having difficulty with in the time you have remaining.

For the question(s) that you have perceived a difficulty with, it is important to approach them in a methodical manner. It may not be due to the fact that you have not memorised the relevant cases and concepts. You maybe misconstruing the question or stress may be causing a memory block. If this occurs:

- reread all the questions
- make a note next to the question of the subject content, for example parliamentary sovereignty, offer and acceptance, etc
- try to remember the cases that are relevant and the points of law and write them down
- compare your knowledge per question and select the question(s) that show(s) you have the greatest awareness.

Although this process will not result in a fully developed response that is capable of a first class standard, it will result in you achieving marks. This could make the difference between pass and fail or improving your overall mark. This process may also remove the mind block or stimulate the mind regarding the issues that you are having difficulty with.

12.3.2 Understanding the questions

Law exam questions tend to be one of two types: the essay question or the problem or scenario-related question. They each need a different approach, but there are common issues to both: understanding the focus of the question and identifying the relevant subject content (see Figure 12.1 below). An indication of the question's focus is given by its command words. These are the descriptors that dictate how you should focus on the subject content. See Chapters 7 and 8 for common command words.

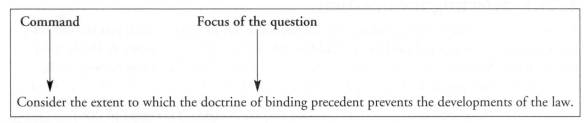

Figure 12.1 Identify the command and focus of the question

Many students look at the subject content of the question and write everything they have memorised about that topic. In effect, what they are writing is an answer to a completely different question – in fact, a 'what is' question (for example, '**What is** the free movement of workers?'). How the question is phrased is critical because it dictates how the question will be marked. A failure to identify the emphasis of the question will result in a significant loss in marks.

It is important to identify the questions subject content. From there you need to use the skills discussed in Chapters 7 and 8 to produce relevant answers to the set questions

12.4 Planning your answers

12.4.1 Planning

In exams always prepare a plan. A plan has a number of key benefits:

- it gives you an indication on how well you can answer the question

- it acts as a guide

- it creates an order

- it stimulates the mind into thinking how to answer the question

- it is useful when a memory block occurs because it acts as a reference.

A plan will normally use about five per cent of the time allocated to that question.

The key steps of an effective plan are as follows:

- identify the question's main issues

- jot down the key cases and concepts related to the issues identified

- work out an order to present the information.

However, it should be noted that it takes longer to plan a problem-style question than an essay.

There is no fixed way of producing a good plan. It is an entirely personal thing. Some students will plan in the form of a list while others use spider charts and others use more elaborate diagrams. The key point is that you should produce a plan that enables you to organise your thoughts best and gives you sufficient points of reference for you to get everything down that you want to in answering the question.

If you write a list it should also be done in a way that represents the order in which you are going to write. This is important because a good structure to an answer makes it more readable, more accessible and therefore more easily understood for the reader. Since this is the examiner who is giving you marks it is vital that he is able to pick up the points very easily and follow the thread of your discussion also with ease.

12.4.2 Producing plans for essays

Let us take the example of a simple essay title on the legal professions. Such an essay would obviously appear in an exam on an English legal system paper. However, the actual title could take a number of forms.

- It could be a simple knowledge-based essay on the qualifications and training needed to become a lawyer, either barrister or solicitor or both.

- It could be an essay on the contrasting roles and organisation of the two leading professions, barristers and solicitors.

- It could involve critical comment on the ways in which the two professions are disciplined, or on the ways in which a disgruntled client may take action against or resolve a dispute with a lawyer of whichever profession.

- It could also be an essay calling for a discussion of the various reforms that have occurred over recent years and asking for speculation on the future of the professions.

Of course the approach to each would be different and this should be reflected in the planning so that you do not engage in time wasting by discussing aspects of the legal professions that are not called for in the question.

Below is a fairly full checklist on the legal professions in a diagram form of the type that we have already used in Chapter 11, section 11.5.5, page 261. The benefit of having a revision aid in this form is its visual impact and in writing the plan you can selectively remove from your mind all but the relevant information. So you would know that if the question referred only to solicitors, you could ignore the references to barristers. It is a good way of focusing your mind in the exam to have the material you will use broken down in a systematic way in your mind.

Then you can plan your answer in the exam by reference only to the material that is relevant.

	Barristers	Solicitors
Training and qualification	*Three stages of education and training:* 1. **Academic stage** – law degree OR any degree and Common Professional Examination (CPE), a conversion degree in core areas of law. *Must then join an Inn of Court (and dine a number of times or go to weekend schools before call)* 2. **Vocational stage** – Bar Vocational Course (BVC), formerly only at Inns of Court School of Law in London now available in some regional centres – skills based, eg advocacy, drafting *Students can be called to the Bar after this* 3. **Professional stage** – Pupillage – shadowing a practising barrister (Pupil Master) for two periods of six months. *May accept a fee after first six months' pupillage*	*Three stages of education and training:* 1. **Academic stage** – again a law degree OR any degree plus (CPE) OR non-graduate route is possible through qualification as a Legal Executive 2. **Vocational stage** – Legal Practice Course (LPC) again a skills based course including, eg client counselling, account management, etc 3. **Professional stage** – two year Training Contract working in a solicitors' office and paid at minimum rates *Not enrolled on Solicitors' Roll and entitled to practise until third stage complete*

CONTINUED ▶

	Barristers	Solicitors
Organisation and role	*More than 10,000 practising:* • self-employed, sole practitioners • work from chambers and share services and costs of a clerk • members of an Inn of Court (Gray's Inn, Lincoln's Inn, Middle Temple or Inner Temple) Work is of three types: • advocacy (fighting cases in court) • writing 'counsel's opinion' on cases for solicitors • drafting legal documents *Some barristers are employed and others (about 2,000) are 'non-practising'*	*More than 80,000 in private practice:* • usually work in partnerships as partners or associates • solicitors have the first contact with clients Work is very varied: advocacy, particularly in lower courts though with an Advocacy Certificate they may now appear in higher courts; conveyancing; wills and probate, registering companies, general advice and litigation; contract *About 20 per cent are employed solicitors working for companies, for local authorities, Crown Prosecution Service and as Magistrates' Clerks*
Discipline and complaints	Senate of Inns disciplines as does General Council of the Bar. Complaints can be made to either and there is also a Complaints Commissioner and the Legal Services Ombudsman	Law Society controls and disciplines solicitors. Complaints are to Office for the Supervision of Solicitors, run by the Law Society, or to Legal Services Ombudsman

Critical comment – The future of the professions

'Fusion' of the professions was formerly an issue – due to problems caused by restrictive practices of professions.

Courts and Legal Services Act 1990, Access to Justice Act 1999, and other provisions have removed bar's monopoly on higher court advocacy and the solicitors' monopoly on conveyancing. Training and Continuing Professional Development is also required in both cases. Bar is most under threat with extended rights of audience to solicitors and employed lawyers, eg CPS. Solicitors have lost work to licensed conveyancers, and under threat from increased use of 'paralegals' (around 25,000), one for every three solicitors. Also Lord Chancellor has introduced procedures for his greater control of the professions.

Figure 12.2 The legal professions: checklist

Plans in list form

Looking at the area of the first point in Figure 12.2, let us imagine a very simple question (probably a part question) *'Discuss the qualifications and training needed to practise at the Bar'*. In picturing your checklist you only need to repeat the top box on the left hand side of the chart. So your list on scrap paper or before your answer would simply look as follows:

> *Three stages of education and training:*
>
> 1. **Academic** – law degree OR any degree + CPE (seven core areas)
> 2. **Vocational** – BVC (skills based, eg advocacy, drafting)
> 3. **Professional** – Pupillage (2 × 6 months shadowing practising barrister)
>
> Must join one of four Inns of Court (Inner Temple, Middle Temple, Lincoln's Inn, Gray's Inn) + keep term (dine 12 times or weekend course) before being called
>
> May accept a fee after first six months' pupillage
>
> **Difficulties** – cost, number of places, competition, limited tenancies, etc

Figure 12.3 *Planning your answer in list form*

Of course so long as you know your own form of abbreviation it could be cut even shorter and will take very little time to jot down if it is in your memory.

Plans in a chart or diagram form

Many students like a more visual reference to get everything they need down and tie it all together. Charts are popular where there is a contrast called for. A common plan in a diagram form is a 'spider chart'. This is useful because you put the central theme in a box of some kind at the centre and have the various sub-themes radiating around that box like the legs of a spider.

So let us take the example of the second theme in the second bullet above. This calls for a comparison between the roles and organisation of the two professions. A simple way of identifying the contrast is to merely repeat that part of your revision chart that is appropriate, that is the section for both barristers solicitors. So it would look like the following.

More than 10,000 practising:	*More than 80,000 in private practice:*
• self-employed, sole practitioners • work from chambers – share services and costs of clerk • members of Inn of Court (Gray's, Lincoln's, Middle Temple, Inner Temple) *Work =* • advocacy • writing 'counsel's opinion' • drafting legal documents. *Some are employed, about 2,000 'non-practising'.*	• work in partnerships as partners or associates • first contact with clients Work varied Advocacy (in lower or with Advocacy Certificate in higher); conveyancing; wills and probate, registering companies, general advice and litigation; contract; *About 20 per cent employed by companies, or local authorities, Crown Prosecution Service and as Magistrates' Clerks.*

Figure 12.4 *Planning your answer in chart form*

We can also reproduce the same information in the spider chart which would look something like the following:

10,000 + work from chambers use clerk belong to Inn of Court		80,000 + partnerships high st offices

barristers — Lawyers – role and organisation — solicitors

| Advocacy
Counsel's opinion
Drafting documents | | first contact for client litigation
advocacy (mainly lower)
contract, family, crime, etc |

Figure 12.5 Planning your answer in a spider chart

Remember the above examples are essay titles that call for little more than factual information. In reality, most essays require you to write critically. You should plan your critical comments just the same as you do your information. It may be that you can write a brief reference to a critical comment next to each piece of information in your plan. It may be preferable to make a bullet list of comment and refer to it as you go along.

12.4.3 Producing plans for problems

Producing a plan for a problem question is more complex because it is not just a case of jotting down information. You need first to look carefully at the facts in the scenario and sort out in your mind what law they are leading you to examine. Then you sort through your knowledge to make a plan with the appropriate law so that you can apply it.

Consider the following fairly simple problem on offer and acceptance in contract law:

Problem

On 11th May Andy wrote to his friend Brian offering to sell Brian his Cup Final ticket for £150. Brian posted a letter on 12th May which said:

'Dear Andy,

About the Cup Final tickets. £150 seems a bit on the steep side. I don't mind paying a bit over the odds but I'd be happier paying £100. Or could I pay you £100 now and the other £50 when I'm paid again at the end of the month?

Yours Brian'

Later in the day Brian wrote again to Andy:

'Dear Andy,

I've thought again about that ticket. I really want to go and it's cutting it a bit fine to get one from anywhere else. I'll pay you the £150.

Yours Brian'

He posted the letter the same night.

Andy received Brian's first letter on the morning of May 13th and sold the ticket to another friend Chris at work that day.

When Andy returned home that evening Brian's second letter had been delivered in the later post.

Brian missed the Cup Final and now seeks your advice.

Figure 12.6 Example of a problem question in contract law

In planning your answer there are obviously two things that you would have to do:

- First, you would need to have a clear idea of the critical facts on which the resolution of the problem depends. (This may mean that you have to organise them in your mind, particularly where there are a number of issues or a number of different people involved. You can do this in a number of ways – you can highlight key points on the paper, or you could put arrows next to key points so that you can then list the law next to the arrows, or you could make a brief list of key factual points.)

- Second, you will need to think what the law is that you need to introduce. That should then be applied to those facts – this is where your ability as a law student comes in and where recognition is so important.

The two boxes below represent a brief plan identifying the key facts and the appropriate law needed for answering this question.

The facts

1. Andy made an offer to Brian on 11th May of a Cup Final ticket for £150.

2. On 12th May Brian replied that he would prefer to pay £100 to £150, and alternatively asked if he might pay £150 in two instalments.

3. Later on 12th May Brian sent a straightforward letter of acceptance.

4. Andy sold the ticket to Chris on 13th May after receiving Brian's first letter.

5. Andy received the second letter later the same day.

6. All of these communications were carried out by post.

The law

We know that the problem concerns formation of contracts because the facts are all about whether Andy is obliged to sell the tickets to Brian or not that. In particular, the rules governing offer and acceptance are required (indeed the word offer is used in the situation).

The appropriate law would appear to be:

*   a contract can only be formed if there is an agreement, which is a valid offer followed by a valid acceptance

*   an offer must be communicated – *Taylor v Laird*

*   an offer can be withdrawn any time before acceptance – *Routledge v Grant*

*   but this must be communicated to the offeree – *Byrne v Van Tienhoven*

*   a contract is formed once the offer is accepted

*   the acceptance must be communicated to the offeree – *Felthouse v Brindley*

*   where the post is the normal, anticipated method of accepting then the contract is formed when the letter is posted not when it is received – *Adams v Lindsell*

*   a counter offer is a rejection of the offer that is longer open to acceptance – *Hyde v Wrench*

*   but a mere enquiry has no such effect – *Stevenson v McLean*.

Figure 12.7 Planning your answer to a problem question

Whatever way you choose to make a plan it should be methodical so it can train your thoughts on the structure of your answer to either essay or problem and contain the appropriate amount of detail for you to remember to write everything you want to write. It should not be like reproducing the essay or the problem itself.

12.5 Answering the question set

The following is a statement that students everywhere no doubt get very bored with since it is one that examiners repeatedly say in their reports or that teachers constantly remind students of before exams. However, it is worth repeating because it is absolutely true to say that the best exam answers are the ones that actually answer the question that was asked. Another way of saying this is to say that one of the biggest failings of students sitting exams is not answering the question set.

Sometimes in presenting conferences with students on exams I have used transparencies on the OHP like the following:

> Repeat all of your lecture notes on breach of duty in negligence

This seems silly on the face of it, and sometimes the students laugh. However, when they do I am able to say to them *'Well I've never actually set that as an exam question, but I've seen it lots of times as an answer, and you can only get limited marks even if you do it very well'*.

Another one I often use is the following:

> Write the answer to last year's question on nuisance

Again the students think that I'm being rather silly and may laugh. But again I am able to say to them *'Yes, sounds silly but I have seen this answer written many times and again you are not going to get many marks for it'*. Students often look at past question papers in preparing for exams. Indeed teachers often use them as exercises or even give students prepared answers to past questions. This is perfectly legitimate. It is a good way of getting a feel for what questions are like in the exam and it is also good to be able to see how you would go about answering a particular question.

However, both approaches to answering exam questions lose you marks. You MUST read the question and answer the specific question asked.

- **Do not** – assume that it is sufficient to give all your knowledge on the particular area of law identified in the question. (Essay questions will demand that you show critical awareness so you have to pass comment on the law. Problems demand that you apply the law effectively so you have to be able to use the law to deal with the factual scenario in front of you.)

- **Do not** – just trot out all the law you know on the particular area. (You have to be selective. It may well be that an essay on negligence, for instance, is only demanding that you discuss the development of the idea of 'duty of care'. There is little point in this instance in discussing either breach or causation, although you might briefly mention them as elements of negligence.)

- **Do not** – assume that because a question has been asked in one way on previous exam papers that it is going to be asked the same way on the paper you are sitting. (This can also mean that you must not assume that a particular area will always come up as a problem or another area as an essay.)

- **Do not** – learn only the main aspects of a particular topic. (Sometimes examiners will ask you about the fringe areas of the subject – so know those too.)

- **Do** – always read the question carefully. (You can only really know precisely what you need to write about if you have read the question thoroughly and established exactly what aspects you have to write on.)

- **Do** – always plan before you write. (You can eliminate at this stage knowledge that you have brought into the exam room but that is not called for in the question. It will not gain you marks if you write about it.)

- **Do** – always maintain a clear focus on the question itself when you write. (One way of doing this is to keep referring back to the question in what you write. But remember to do this only if you have made a point that justifies your assertion that you are answering the question. We sometimes see candidates who keep repeating the question but are actually doing so only after giving some factual information rather than some critical comment.)

12.6 Time management

One of the most significant points about exams as a means of assessing your knowledge, understanding and skills is that it is a time-constrained affair. In coursework assignments you may look ahead over the weeks or months until the coursework is due and think that you have plenty of time for both the research and the writing. In fact this is rarely the case when you analyse the time you have to spend at university, the number of other assignments that you probably have to complete at the same time and the fact that you need some time for relaxation and other pursuits.

12.6.1 Following the rubric

As a student on a law course at university, it is most probable that you will have already experienced both coursework and exams. You will already know then that however long you are given to complete an exam (three hours is usually the longest in exams such as A-Level GCE) the time goes very quickly in the exam room and most candidates will be struggling to get down everything that they want to say within the time allowed.

Accordingly, organising your time in an exam is crucial. In this respect one of the first rules to follow is to **KNOW THE RUBRIC** and if you are not aware of the structure of the exam before you get into the exam room you must at that point make sure that you **READ THE RUBRIC**.

12.6.2 Key features of the rubric

The rubric is the instructions on the front of an exam paper that tells you exactly what you should be doing during the exam. There are three critical points that you must know in order to make maximum use of your time in the exam room:

The length of the exam	*You should also take note of any reading time available. This is not uncommon in certain exams.*
The number of questions that you are required to answer from those on the paper	In certain exams you will have to answer all of the questions. In others you get a choice from a larger number. This is very useful because it has given you the opportunity in advance to focus on certain areas and in the exam room it means that you get the opportunity to select the questions that you think you will perform best on.
The number of marks available for each question	Very often the marks for each question are the same. Sometimes, however, different questions attach different marks and this is useful in making choices on which questions to start with and also if you are running out of time where to get the most marks from.

Figure 12.8 Key features of the rubric explained

You may have a subject that you are bursting to write about, that you know absolutely everything about and could spend the whole exam writing about, but it is very bad exam strategy if you do so. If you have to answer three questions and you only provide an answer to one then you have lost two-thirds of your marks. This is an extreme example of bad management, but as an experienced examiner, I have seen it happen and other strategies that are just as dangerous.

Even if you answer all three questions, if you spend (let's say) half the time available on that one question, you are still losing valuable time on the other two. That might prevent you from getting the marks that may otherwise have given you the grade of which you were capable, or at worst the pass of which you were capable.

It is a simple truth about exam questions that it is easier to get the first 50 per cent of the available marks than it is to get the next 50 per cent. Many if not most pass marks in exams are set at 40 per cent. In this way making sure that you answer all the questions that you must and ensuring that you give equal time to answering them is the surest way of achieving the pass mark.

A simple understanding and rigid adherence to the three points above give you the best chance of doing as well as you can.

12.6.3 Keeping to a schedule

Let us take the example of an exam lasting 2 hours and 15 minutes where you have to complete three questions out of five. This is a fairly standard timescale. The mathematics is easy: 3 into 135 minutes (2 hours and 15 minutes) = 45 minutes for each question.

Forty-five minutes is also a fairly standard time for both essays and problem questions. Remember the examiner has devised the questions so that they can be answered accurately and effectively within that timescale. In other words allocate yourself 45 minutes to each question and try not to exceed it.

Take a watch into the exam with you (this is not absolutely vital because usually invigilators have brought a clock into the exam room with them – but you should still make use of this).

If your 2 hour 15 minute exam starts at 9.00 am and finishes at 11.15 am then you can set yourself, right from the start of the exam, a schedule.

A simple schedule might be as follows:

•	9.00 am–9.45 am	question 3
•	9.45 am–10.30 am	question 5
•	10.30 am–11.15 am	question 1

Of course it may be possible for you to work to this type of schedule but it in fact hides the reality of working in an exam. There are a number of things to consider:

- First, before you can answer any questions effectively you must know which questions are the ones that are appropriate for you to answer. This means reading all the questions effectively and this takes time – probably at least five minutes.

- Second, before you start writing your answers you should be prepared for them (see Sections 12.3. and 12.4. above). Your plan for the answer can take a variety of forms as you have already seen, but whichever type of approach you use, this is going to take time – probably about five minutes each, or 15 minutes in total.

- Third, you should leave some time aside to read through your answers to check that you have not made any silly mistakes that would cost you marks, or that you have not missed some important points that could be added, or even to add in the names of cases that you have now remembered but sensibly moved on from while writing – again this is probably going to take another 15 minutes.

This means that of your 135 minutes you are likely to use about 35 minutes of that in reading and selecting questions, planning your answers and reviewing what you have done. You are left with 100 minutes or about 33 minutes each answer for the actual writing.

Your new schedule, taking all this into account then could look something like the following:

• 9.00 am–9.05 am	reading questions and selecting
• 9.05 am–9.10 am	writing plan for question 3
• 9.10 am–9.43 am	answering question 3
• 9.43 am–9.48 am	writing plan for question 5
• 9.48 am–10.21 am	answering question 5
• 10.21 am–10.26 am	writing plan for question 1
• 10.26 am–10.59 am	answering question 1
• 10.59 am–11.15 am	reading through answers

Alternatively, you may write all three plans at the start when your mind is fresh and you are full of energy and adrenalin.

• 9.00 am–9.05 am	reading questions and selecting
• 9.05 am–9.10 am	writing plan for question 3
• 9.10 am–9.15 am	writing plan for question 5
• 9.15 am–9.20 am	writing plan for question 1
• 9.20 am–9.53 am	answering question 3
• 9.53 am–10.28 am	answering question 5
• 10.28 am–10.59 am	answering question 1
• 10.59 am–11.15 am	reading through answers

Of course it would be silly to write down your schedule in such detailed terms since this is taking up more of your precious time. Nevertheless, it is possible to make a quick check list of the times that you need to finish each stage by so that you can stick to it during the exam.

It is almost inevitable that you will start with the question that you feel most confident about. This is a good strategy. The quicker you can get writing the more relaxed you will feel since you are busy and do not have time to worry there and then about any nerves you are feeling. It is also good strategy because if you feel confident about the question you are likely to make a reasonable job of the answer and this will give you confidence as you go through the rest of the paper.

However, the temptation is for you to carry on writing the answer to this question no matter how long it takes. This is not good strategy. Remember the point above that the first 50 per cent of available marks are earned much more quickly and much more easily than the final 50 per cent. The chances are that by the time your 33 minutes is up, you have already earned some pretty reasonable marks. It certainly is going to be the case that if you carry on writing for too long after that the time that you spend is going to be picking you up fewer and fewer marks per minute.

The sensible strategy is to finish where you are at the 33 minutes and move on to the next question. If you still have things to say then you can always come back to it later. Remember you have already accounted for a review time in your calculations. It may also be that when you answer another question, perhaps your final answer, that you have more time than you need because you have less to say. Again, you can pick up where you left off in the first question. You are far more likely to fail to gain marks by not answering a question through running out of time, than by failing to drag every last morsel out of what you could have written on one.

Remember the golden rule: the examiner has set the question in such a way that it is possible to give a good answer in the time given. If you find that you have masses more to say than you can get down in the time then you are probably straying off the point and not really answering the question set. A common fault here is to try to write down everything you know about the area, when in fact you are being called on to be selective within that topic.

Of course, it is also possible that you sit an exam where the weighting of the different questions is not equal. You can still make effective use of your time by following the same formula.

Let us say for instance that the examination has within it a compulsory question worth 50 per cent of the marks and that the exam is three hours long with you having a choice of questions from a second section of which you have to complete two.

Again you are looking at two questions which you have 45 minutes each to complete, as in example above, but this time you also have one question which you must devote half of your time to, or 90 minutes (one and a half hours).

Taking the formula above you would still use at least five minutes of your time reading the questions and five minutes on each of the two questions from the second section for preparing a plan. However, because the compulsory question is so much bigger the chances are that you would need extra time for preparing your plan, say ten minutes. If you add 15 minutes for final reviewing, you will use up 40 minutes of your time on reading the questions, making plans and reading over your answers. This leaves you 2 hours and 20 minutes for writing, or 140 minutes. Half of this should be used for the compulsory question, or 70 minutes. This leaves you 70 minutes for the other two, or 35 minutes each. This is an example of how longer exams actually work in the students' favour. It may seem to you as though you are under more pressure because of the longer question, but in fact you are under less. It is usually sensible to complete the larger, compulsory question first, as it is clearly more demanding.

If the exam started at 9.00 am and finished at 12.00 noon, the schedule this time would be as follows:

• 9.00 am–9.05 am	reading questions and selecting
• 9.05 am–9.15 am	writing plan for question 1 (compulsory)
• 9.15 am–10.25 am	answering question 1 (compulsory)
• 10.25 am–10.30 am	writing plan for question 5
• 10.30 am–11.05 am	answering question 5
• 11.05 am–11.10 am	writing plan for question 3
• 11.10 am–11.45 am	answering question 3
• 11.45 am–12.00 pm	reading through answers

Another possibility is that you have a first section where you have to complete, say, ten small questions each worth five per cent of the marks rather than one big compulsory question. Again you would need to follow the same rules and leave yourself half the time for the compulsory section and divide the other half between the two larger questions. A schedule for this type of exam would be as follows:

• 9.00 am–9.05 am	reading questions and selecting
• 9.05 am–9.15 am	planning for ten compulsory questions
• 9.15 am–10.25 am	answering compulsory questions

9.15 am–9.22 am	Question 1
9.22 am–9.29 am	Question 2
9.29 am–9.36 am	Question 3
9.36 am–9.43 am	Question 4
9.43 am–9.50 am	Question 5
9.50 am–9.57 am	Question 6
9.57 am–10.04 am	Question 7
10.04 am–10.11 am	Question 8
10.11 am–10.18 am	Question 9
10.18 am–10.25 am	Question 10

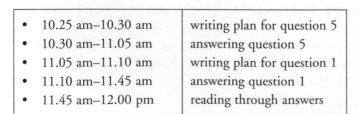

• 10.25 am–10.30 am	writing plan for question 5
• 10.30 am–11.05 am	answering question 5
• 11.05 am–11.10 am	writing plan for question 1
• 11.10 am–11.45 am	answering question 1
• 11.45 am–12.00 pm	reading through answers

The basic point is that whatever the character and structure of the exam it is easy enough, if you are prepared for that structure beforehand, to create a disciplined schedule to work to in the exam.

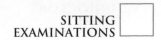

Remember the schedules indicated above are nothing more than a guide to how you can organise your time in the exam. You do not need to write down anything as elaborate. Something as simple as follows will suffice, as long as you remember in your mind to include time for reading the questions, planning each question, and a bit of checking through after.

So in an exam of three hours with four questions to do with equal weighting you might just jot down:

```
9.00–9.45
9.45–10.30
10.30–11.15
11.15–12.00
```

The important thing is to not overrun.

12.6.4 Avoiding time-wasting during the exam

Remember exams are assessments where you are bound by a time constraint. You cannot perform at your own leisure in an exam; you have to get on and work productively all the way through it.

You should also remember though that the people writing the exams are not just dreaming up any old questions without giving a second thought to it. The whole idea of producing a successful exam is that the answer can be given in the time set. An obvious example of how examiners have to think within time limits is where you have compulsory questions worth half the marks and then two or three other questions. In producing the paper the examiner is obviously including different demands for the different questions so that the compulsory question is designed to take you two or three times the amount of time of the other questions.

TIP

So the message is – never take too long over one question at the expense of what you could be writing and getting marks for on another.

Students inevitably want to give the examiner the benefit of all their knowledge. This is clearly a good thing, but do not let this eagerness to please cause you problems. A classic example is not being able to remember the name of a particular case that you want to use and no matter how hard you try it will just not come to you. We have all been there (yes, remember we sat law exams once). The problem is that you can become obsessed by one tiny bit of information that is going to be worth actually very few marks to you. As invigilators we have seen it many times: students scratching their heads and becoming very distressed. Their pens go down, they look around them for inspiration, they go to their scrap paper writing down little lists trying to take them to the case they want. More importantly two things happen:

297

- First, they are not writing. It is a simple truth in an exam that you do not get any marks for not writing and you could be taking up time writing other things that you could be getting marks for.

- Second, and much worse, you are distracted from your overall purpose and the clear danger is that trying to concentrate too hard on one little piece of information can drive other more important things out of your mind. You are also just making yourself more nervous.

- The proper thing to do in the circumstances is to move on. You can always come back and write the case name in afterwards if you remember it. Besides you can always write 'In a case in which . . . happened' and make the point that you want to make. The examiner will know that you know what you are talking about. You may not get all the marks available but you are only missing a tiny proportion of the marks by not getting the case name.

TIP

So the message is – never allow yourself to get over distracted by a missing piece of information, move on and come back to it later if you can.

We have already said in section 12.1.1 in 'Final preparations' that you should make sure that you are prepared in advance so that you can be in the room on time and with all the equipment you need. You do not want to waste time by arriving late when you could be gaining marks by writing. Neither do you want to waste time in the exam sharpening pencils or filling fountain pens when you could be writing.

TIP

So the message is – do not waste time in the exam room doing things that you could have prepared for beforehand.

Sometimes things happen during an exam that could be distracting. This is unfortunate for you but it can often not be avoided. People coming into the exam room late is an obvious distraction, as is people who are not so well prepared as you and leave early. A person may be taken ill during the exam and sometimes this can be quite dramatic. The first sort of example is annoying, the second you may feel very sympathetic to the person who is taken ill. Whichever it is does not matter. You should not concern yourself with either. There are other people, the invigilators, to deal with the disturbance. Your complete focus must be on what you are doing yourself, not on what is happening to others around you.

> So the message is – do not waste time in the exam by getting distracted by anything happening in the exam room.

Particularly with well-prepared students, it is possible that you may need more pages than you are given in the answer booklet in order to complete your answers. You should not wait until you have finished writing on the last page before you put your hand up to ask the invigilator for more paper. You then have to wait for him to get to you and you might be in a big hall. He may not see your hand straightaway and you may be unlucky and he comes to see what you want and then goes back to get you more paper. This is all time wasted when you could be writing.

> So the message is – when you turn onto the last page of blank paper put your non-writing hand up straight away to get more paper and keep writing while you wait.

One final point is also worth noting. It applies particularly while you still have other exams to sit, but applies also even when you have sat your last exam. Once you have finished the exam and left the exam room you have done everything that you can to complete that exam successfully. After that you simply have to wait for it to be marked and to get the results. Students often engage in post mortems after the exam either with their friends or by trying to extract from their teachers whether they said the right thing in the exam or not. This is wasteful of your emotional energy and can create even more stress than you would suffer already. It is a practice that is best avoided. Relax after the exams and forget about them until you get the results.

Good luck!

APPENDIX

Chapter 1

Answers to Activity on page 9:

1) A prosecutor.

2) Magistrates' Court, High Court, Court of Appeal, House of Lords.

3) The claimant must prove his claim on a balance of probabilities.

4) He or she is acquitted.

5) The defendant.

6) Damages usually, or equitable remedies such as injunctions.

7) To keep order in society and to punish wrong doing.

Answers to Activity on page 16:

1) (c)

2) (b)

3) (c)

4) (b)

5) Beyond all reasonable doubt is **criminal**   Liable for a claim is **civil**

   Prosecutor is **criminal**   Balance of probabilities is **civil**

   Theft is **criminal**   Damages is **civil**

6) (d)

Chapter 2

Examples

Summary Sheet

Lecture: Precedent – Practice Statement	Date: 20/10/07

Key cases:
London Street Tramways v London County Council
DPP v Smith
Conway v Rimmer
Herrington v BRB
Pepper v Hart
R v Shivpuri

Key comment and analysis:

- Needed to stop rigidity.
- House of Lords reluctant to use it.
- Reluctant to use it. Note date of *Pepper v Hart*

Links to tutorial activities:
Refer to tutorial manual to compare

Academic references:
See reading list

	House of Lords
What is the role of the House of Lords?	This is the most senior domestic court. When matters do not involve Europe it has the final decision on the case. This court binds all courts below it. It does not bind itself due to the Practice Statement 1966.
Why was the House of Lords bound by its own decisions?	*House of Lords & the Practice Statement* Originally the House of Lords had flexibility and could change its mind about its own past decisions but in 1898 the court decided that certainty in the law was more important than flexibility so in *London Street Tramways v London County Council*, the court decided that the House of Lords were bound by their own previous decisions.
What problems did this create?	*This created a rigid system, .as seen in DPP v Smith* A man murdered a police officer. The House of Lords made a mistake by giving a poor definition as to the mental test for murder. Due to this mistake, Parliament passed the Criminal Justice Act 1967 to replace the mistake
What is the criterion of the Practice Statement?	1966 Lord Gardiner issues a Practice Statement. This allows the judges in the House of Lords to depart from past decisions when it is right to do so
What case illustrates its first use?	It was first used in *Conway v Rimmer*. This was not seen as a major use as it only involved a technical matter.
	Examples Civil
What civil examples highlight the Practice Statement?	*Herrington v British Railways Board overruled Addie v Dumbreck* These cases concerned what duty of care was owed to a child trespasser. In *Addie* it was decided that there was only a duty when injuries to a child were caused deliberately or recklessly. *Herrington* overruled this due to the changes in social conditions and made the duty owed stronger. *Herrington* was the first major use of the Practice Statement.
	Pepper v Hart overruled Davis v Johnson These cases concerned the use of *Hansard*. In *Davis* the use of Hansard by a judge as an aid to statutory interpretation was not allowed. *Pepper v Hart* removed this limit.

CONTINUED ▸

	Examples Criminal
What criminal examples highlight the Practice Statement? What problems can be seen with the use of the Practice Statement?	*R v Shivpuri overruled Anderton v Ryan* These cases concerned the criminal nature of attempting the impossible. *Anderton* decided that you could not have criminal liability if what you were doing was impossible. This was contrary to an Act of Parliament. *Shivpuri* therefore overruled *Anderton*. It can now be a crime if you attempt the impossible. This was the first criminal case to use the Practice Statement.

Spider diagram

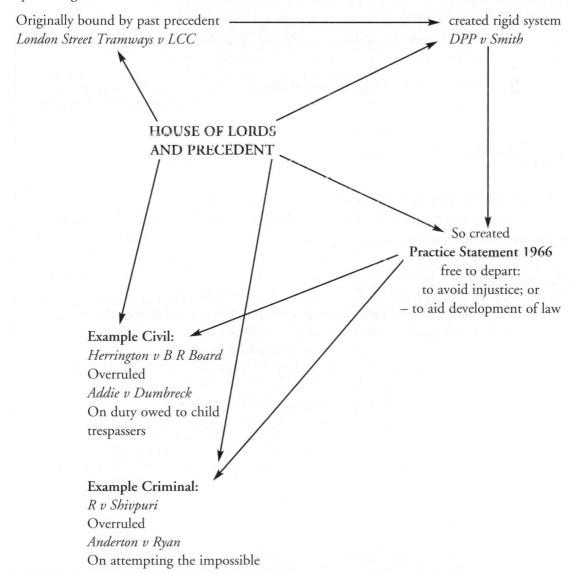

Originally bound by past precedent   created rigid system
London Street Tramways v LCC   *DPP v Smith*

**HOUSE OF LORDS
AND PRECEDENT**

So created
Practice Statement 1966
free to depart:
to avoid injustice; or
– to aid development of law

Example Civil:
Herrington v B R Board
Overruled
Addie v Dumbreck
On duty owed to child
trespassers

Example Criminal:
R v Shivpuri
Overruled
Anderton v Ryan
On attempting the impossible

Chapter 3

Hyde v Wrench	
Rolls Court [1840] 3 Beav 334; Jur 1106; 49 ER 132	
June 6. The defendant wrote to the plaintiff offering to sell his farm for £1,000. The plaintiff's agent immediately called on the defendant and made an offer of £950, which the defendant wished to have a few days to consider.	*Material facts*
June 27. The defendant wrote to say that he would not accept this offer.	
June 29. The plaintiff wrote accepting the offer of June 6.	
The plaintiff brought an action for specific performance.	
The defendant filed a general demurrer.	
THE MASTER OF THE ROLLS (LORD LANGDALE): Under the circumstances stated in this bill, I think there exists no valid binding contract between the parties for the purchase of the property. The defendant offered to sell it for £1,000, and if that had at once been unconditionally accepted, there would undoubtedly have been a perfect binding contract; instead of that, the plaintiff made an offer of his own, to purchase the property for £950, and he thereby rejected the offer previously made by the defendant. I think that it was not afterwards competent for him to revive the proposal of the defendant, by tendering an acceptance of it; and that, therefore, there exists no obligation of any sort between the parties; the demurrer must be allowed.	*Outcome – no contract* *Original law – agreement = offer followed by unconditional acceptance* *A counter offer = a rejection of the offer* *So the offer is no longer open to acceptance*

KEY FACTS

Hyde v Wrench

- An acceptance must be unconditional.
- A counter offer amounts to a rejection of the offer.
- The offer is no longer open to acceptance.

Chapter 4

Grobbelaar v News Group Newspapers Ltd

House of Lords

You should cite the Weekly Law Reports version as this appears above the other versions in the hierarchy

[2002] 4 All ER 732 – All England Law Reports

[2002] 1 WLR 3024 – Weekly Law Reports

[2003] EMLR 1 – Entertainment and Media Law Report

Rees v Darlington Memorial Hospital NHS Trust

House of Lords

You should cite the Law Reports Appeal Cases version as this appears above the other versions in the hierarchy

[2004] 1 FLR 234 – Family Law Reports

[2003] 3 WLR 1091 – Weekly Law Reports

[2004] 1 AC 309 – Law Reports Appeal Cases

MCC Proceeds Inc v Lehman

Court of Appeal

You should cite the All Engand Law Reports version as this appears above the other versions in the hierarchy

[1998] 4 All ER 675 – All England Law Reports

[1998] 2 BCLC 659 – Butterworths Company Law Cases

(1998) 142 SJLB 40 – Solicitor's Journal Law Brief

What does EMLR stand for?	Entertainment and Media Law Reports
What does BWCC stand for?	Butterworths Workmen's Compensation Cases
What is the correct abbreviation for the Criminal Appeal Reports (Sentencing)?	Cr App R (S)
What is the correct abbreviation for the Criminal Law Review?	Crim LR

Chapter 5

What is the Chapter number of the Access to Justice Act 1999?	Chapter 22
What is the title of the act with the official citation 1995 Chapter 50?	Disability Discrimination Act 1995
On what date did the Education Act 2002 receive Royal Assent?	24 July 2002

---

1. How many Acts of Parliament received Royal Assent in 2005 and 2006? *Tip: Use the OPSI website www.opsi.gov.uk/acts.htm*

2005 – 24

2006 – 55

2. What is the title of Section 13 of the Human Rights Act 1998? Which source did you use to find out?

Section 13: Freedom of thought, conscience and religion

Source used: You could use any of these sources: *Westlaw, LexisNexis Butterworths, Lawtel, JustCite, BAILII,* OPSI website, Public General Acts, *Halsbury's Statutes of England and Wales,* Current Law Statutes Annotated.

How many Statutory Instruments were made in 2005 and 2006 *Tip: Use the OPSI website www.opsi.gov.uk/stat.htm*

2005 – 3,601

2006 – 3,511

Look up the case '*Whiston v Whiston*, Court of Appeal, Civil Division, 23 March 1995'. What is this case about? Which database or printed source did you use to find out?

About: Bigamy and financial provision.

Source used: You could use any of these sources: *Westlaw, LexisNexis Butterworths, Lawtel, JustCite.*

> Using *Halsbury's Laws* (either in print or online via *LexisNexis Butterworths*), find out what the punishment is for possessing a live badger.
>
> Punishable on summary conviction with a fine not exceeding level 5 on the standard scale.

> Using the *Legal Journals Index* (either in print or online via *Westlaw*), find out how many articles have been written about the case *Savage v Fairclough*.
>
> Six (at November 2007)

Chapter 6

Answers to exercise on precedent
Answers to the questions on *Bunny v Browning*

1. Jittery J in his judgment indicates that he is bound by the decision of Rough-Justice J in *Berry v Branch*. Consider what you think Jittery J believes to be the *ratio decidendi* of *Berry v Branch*. (Remembering that it is only the *ratio decidendi* of a previous decision which can bind a judge in a later case.)

Answer:

Here we have yet another situation where the judge, Jittery J, has not really made it clear in his judgment either what he believes the *ratio* in *Berry v Branch* to be, or indeed what the *ratio* is in the case of *Bunny v Browning*.

All that we can do is to eliminate those principles which appear to be too tightly tied to the facts of either case to be a *ratio* in both of them.

If we do this then we must eliminate the statement in *Berry v Branch* '. . . *if someone plants a poisonous tree, they must be liable for the damage it does . . .*' because there is no poisonous vegetation in *Bunny v Browning*. This principle then can obviously not be applied. Similarly the statement about firing a gun into a neighbour's garden from *Berry v Branch* cannot be applied. There are no facts in *Bunny v Browning* that would support this as the *ratio* of that case.

What is left then from *Berry v Branch* is the statement about the duty of neighbours living cheek by jowl in cramped suburbia; and also the statement about the obligation imposed on anyone who undertakes a dangerous activity. If we study these two carefully, then the statement about the duty of city-dwelling neighbours towards each other seems to be the most likely that Jittery J has applied. It is the narrowest of the two possibilities; and in Justice Jittery's view there is an underlying similarity between all modes of urban life as compared to life in the country.

2. Consider whether in his judgment Jittery J has in fact widened the application of the principle from *Berry v Branch*.

Answer:

Yes. We are able to suggest that he has. By saying that he considers *Berry v Branch* to be a precedent, he is, at a minimum, widening its authority into situations which do not involve poisonous plants. However, we must also remember that how far he has widened it depends on what we decide is the *ratio* in his own case, *Bunny v Browning*.

3. Identify the *ratio decidendi* of *Bunny v Browning*.

Answer:

Again there are several possibilities:

- If someone fires a gun into his neighbour's garden, the neighbour is entirely innocent and should not suffer a loss. (We can identify this from our answers to Exercise 1 as one of the *obiter* from *Berry v Branch*. Remember that an *obiter dictum* from one case can serve only as a *persuasive* precedent in a later case.)

- People who live cheek by jowl in cramped suburbia must pay due regard to those who live next to them.

- If someone embarks on any activity which is dangerous, then they should take the consequences.

Jittery J does not make it very clear which of these he considers to be decisive in the case (query 'People who live cheek by jowl . . .'?). Therefore, it will once again be left to another judge, dealing with a later case, to define the legal principle on which *Bunny v Browning* was decided.

4. Assuming that *Berry v Branch* is sufficiently analogous to *Bunny v Browning* to serve as a precedent in the case, consider whether it a persuasive precedent or a binding precedent.

Answer:

Both cases were heard in the QBD and therefore, following the principle that respect should be shown for same level precedents, the decision in *Berry v Branch* is very persuasive and probably would be followed by a later judge in the same court who found the situation to be analogous.

Answers to the questions on *Dove v Digger*

1. Consider what you think could be said in favour of using *Berry v Branch* as precedent to be followed in this case.

Answer:

Looking at the facts of *Bunny v Browning* three of Rough-Justice J's propositions in *Berry v Branch* might have some application:

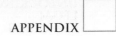

- In cases 'where a man throws acid into his neighbour's property or fires a shotgun over his fence . . . the neighbour is entirely innocent and should not suffer a loss' and if he does 'the miscreant takes the risk, not the neighbour' (clearly here damage has resulted from Dove firing a shotgun).

- 'People who live cheek by jowl with other in cramped suburbia must pay due regard to those who live next to them' (again the claimant and defendant are near neighbours).

- 'if someone embarks on any activity which is dangerous, then they should take the consequences' (even in very controlled circumstances the use of firearms must be seen as intrinsically dangerous).

On this basis, it is reasonable that Mr Dove's counsel should have sought to rely on *Berry v Branch* as a precedent.

2. Consider the reasons that might be used in the case to distinguish it from *Berry v Branch*.

Answer:

Here we might look back to the reasons given by Miss Trigger, the counsel for the defendant in *Bunny v Browning*, for distinguishing that case from *Berry v Branch*:

- She suggested there that the material facts of the two cases were too different for the one to follow the principle in the other (that could equally be said of *Dove v Digger*. Damage to carnations in a greenhouse caused by a missed clay falling through a greenhouse seems to be quite different to a dog being killed by eating poisonous leaves).

- She also suggested that there was no inherent hazard in *Bunny v Browning* which there certainly was in *Berry v Branch* (the yew leaves). Here also we are not looking at a natural hazard.

- She also said that the damage suffered by the claimant was not foreseeable in the way that the death of the dog was in *Berry v Branch*. Again the damage to the carnations may seem a more remote possibility than the death of the dog.

It is therefore also possible for Careless J to distinguish from *Berry v Branch*.

Questions on the judgment in *Blaster v Burns*

1. Identify the *ratio decidendi* of the Court of Appeal in *Blaster v Burns*.

Answer:

In the Court of Appeal in *Blaster v Burns* it is plain from Highman LJ's judgment that he is approving of the proposition of Rough-Justice J's which he refers to in the case that 'if someone embarks on any activity which is dangerous then they should take the consequences'. It is also plain, since he also refers to it in his judgment, that he approves of Rough-Justice J's proposition that neighbours 'living together cheek by jowl in cramped suburbia' should have 'due regard' to one another. Nevertheless, the judgment is insufficiently precise for us to say with absolute certainty which of these propositions he is using to decide the outcome of the case. The one real clue we have that he actually favours the first of the two and therefore the much broader principle, in that he states that even if the experiments had been carried out in open countryside, he would still have found Mr Blaster liable.

2. On the basis of Highman LJ's judgment what do you consider the *ratio* in *Berry v Branch* now to be?

Answer:

Following on from **1.** above this is still not absolutely certain. One thing can be said, however, from Highman LJ's judgment. He is not seeing the decision in *Berry v Branch* being based on the narrowest principle, that of planting poisonous trees leading to duty. So he clearly prefers a broader *ratio* with wider application for further cases. The key feature of the case in fact is that the *ratio* in *Berry v Branch*, whatever it is, is no longer of great significance. This is because we now have a precedent from a higher court which must include any of the possible *ratio* from *Berry v Branch*. The precedent to be carried into further cases is now that in *Blaster v Burns* in the Court of Appeal.

3. Identify anything in Highman LJ's judgment that you consider to be *obiter dicta*.

Answer:

This is not so obvious but there is in fact an *obiter* statement. Highman LJ refers to what the possible outcome of the case would be if the facts had occurred in open country rather than in a built-up town. Since the facts of the case concern town dwellers, this point has no bearing on the outcome of the case and must be *obiter*.

4. Assuming that the essential facts of the cases are sufficiently similar, consider whether Highman LJ is in fact bound to follow the decision in *Berry v Branch*.

Answer:

The answer here is clearly no. Whatever the similarities in the facts of the two cases they are decided by two different courts at different points in the hierarchy. The Court of Appeal is the higher of the two courts so, even though *Berry v Branch* may have been very persuasive, as a High Court case it could never have been binding on the superior court.

Questions on the judgment in *Fly v Porker*

1. Identify the *ratio decidendi* of the case.

Answer:

This is now quite easy to identify: 'if a person undertakes a dangerous activity, whether in the context of urban confines or in the countryside, he or she must bear responsibility for the consequences.'

2. Is the law on responsibility of neighbours now settled and in what way could it be developed or changed?

Answer:

The principle is now a clear precedent for all courts to follow. Since the House of Lords approved of the principle stated by Highman LJ in *Blaster v Burns* when the case reached them, this principle is now binding on all lower courts on cases involving neighbours' liability. This will be the case until either:

- the law is amended by a subsequent House of Lords decision or
- Statute changes or develops the law since Parliament is the supreme legislator.

3. Consider whether any of Clearly J's comments in the case amount to *obiter dicta*.

Answer:

There is an indication of a legal proposition that has no bearing on the case itself and this can therefore be classed as *obiter dictum*: that liability is possible for the 'storage of explosives or volatile substances'.

4. Consider in what way the case is a development from the decision in *Berry v Branch*.

Answer:

We were originally uncertain what the precise *ratio* in *Berry v Branch* was. All we could say for certain was that there was liability for the planting of poisonous trees, a fairly narrow principle of law. *Porker v Fly*, applying the principle accepted by the higher courts, confirms that there is a broad principle imposing liability on anyone in either town or country for the consequences of dangerous activities for which they are responsible.

Answers to the exercise on statutory interpretation

Scenario 3

Eric has been convicted under the Act. Eric lives in a house in the same street as the United football ground. On match days Eric regularly leans out of his open upstairs window and sings abusive songs to the away supporters. Eric is appealing.

Answer to Scenario 3

Again this one is not necessarily as straightforward as it may look at first sight. The clear problem is that Eric is singing inside his house and according to s 4 'The Act shall not apply to private residential properties'.

- He is singing abusive songs so he certainly falls within s 1(1).
- He also lives near to the ground so he is also *'within reasonable vicinity of a football ground'* for s 1(1).
- Using the literal rule technically he cannot be said to fall within the Act because of s 4 – he is in a private residence, not a public place.
- The only category of public place under s 2(1) that might apply is (a) 'any public thoroughfare'.

CONTINUED ▸

- Public thoroughfare is defined in s 2(2) (an interpretation section and therefore an intrinsic aid) as 'any road, pavement, precinct or other similar place along, over or through which vehicles or pedestrians pass'.

- Using a strict literal interpretation, Eric could not be convicted because he is in his residence and does not conform to the definition in s 2(2).

- The words in s 2(2) are not ambiguous so again the golden rule would not be used in its narrow sense (although again public policy may mean that the broad application of the rule is used to add the circumstances into the definition).

- However, if the mischief rule was used then we can see the similarity with the case of *Smith v Hughes* (prostitutes soliciting from a first floor balcony) – Eric's conviction is likely to stand under this rule – he is technically in his house but in effect by leaning out of the window he could be said to be in the 'thoroughfare'

- Similarly use of the purposive approach would mean the conviction would be upheld because the purpose of the Act was to prohibit 'racist, hostile, abusive and provocative singing and chanting' and Eric's behaviour is certainly provocative.

- The conviction would also satisfy the purposes of the EU Directive which the Act was introduced to comply with.

Scenario 4

Freddie runs a portable fast food stand on a piece of waste land five kilometres from the Wanderers' football ground in the north of England. Coaches bringing away fans to the ground regularly pull up in a lay-by near to the wasteland for them to buy refreshments. Freddie has been convicted after a fight occurred when Freddie told some fans from a London football club that he should not have to serve them because 'all cockneys are animals and you should get your food from the pet shop in town'. Freddie is appealing.

Answer to Scenario 4

This one has lots of complicating factors. The key difficulties are that: first, Freddie is speaking to the fans rather than singing or chanting as identified as illegal under the Act, although it would be illegal under the Directive, and secondly he is doing so outside of the two kilometre limit identified in the Directive, although the Act is less specific. He is also on a piece of waste land when the offence occurs and it is questionable whether this can be classed as a public place in the terms in which the Act is drafted.

- Freddie has not been singing or chanting therefore technically this does not fall under s 1(1). If the literal rule is applied on this point then the conviction will be quashed on appeal.

- This is a point on which the Act fails to give full effect to the Directive. Public policy may dictate that the judges include Freddie's spoken abuse as 'other provocative verbal behaviour' under the broad application of the golden rule, thus conforming with the Directive.

- In any case a judge applying the mischief rule or the purposive approach may look to the Commission reports (extrinsic aid) leading to the Directive and decide that the purpose of the

CONTINUED ▶

legislation is fulfilled by covering spoken abuse or provocative speech, as well as singing and chanting.

- It would obviously be useful here to have another extrinsic aid available, *Hansard*, to see why Parliament chose to legislate only on singing and chanting, and maybe the fact that the Act is this restrictive is down to a drafting error. Obviously this could only apply if the criteria in *Pepper v Hart* are met.

- There is still the problem of fitting Freddie into the definition in s 2(1)(a) which is unlikely as he is not on a 'road, pavement or precinct', and even though a language rule, *ejusdem generis,* might be used here it is unlikely that other similar places would include waste land which does not appear to conform to the specific words in the list.

- If the literal rule is used his appeal is likely to succeed on this basis.

- However, the *Smith v Hughes* principle may allow the conviction to be upheld under either the mischief rule or the purposive approach.

- The other obvious possibility is (b) 'any building licensed for the purposes of eating food or for the consumption of alcoholic beverages'.

- The problem is whether a portable hot dog stand could satisfy the definition of building.

- It is generally accepted that a building is a permanent structure so under the literal rule the conviction could not stand.

- Also since the word is relatively unambiguous it is unlikely that the golden rule could be applied, unless it was the broad approach for policy reasons.

- However, once more the mischief rule or the purposive approach might allow the conviction to stand, allowing that the judges take the line in the second bullet above on Freddie speaking provocatively rather than singing or chanting.

- The final problem is obviously that the words 'within reasonable proximity of a football ground or on the route to a football ground' are potentially very wide and ambiguous.

- Within the Act it would seem that, using the literal rule, a conviction might succeed where the offence occurred hundreds of miles from the football ground because of the words 'on the route to a football ground'.

- Judges applying the purposive approach may see that this goes well beyond the very strict wording of the Directive and cannot be what Parliament intended.

Scenario 5

Gregory, a Town fan, is appealing against his conviction for singing abusive songs about the number of foreign players in the City team. The song includes verses of racial and personal abuse to named members of the City team. He did this while he was on his way to a match at the City ground and was walking on the platform in an underground railway station which (at the surface) is only 200 metres away from the City ground.

CONTINUED ▸

Answer to Scenario 5

Again the situation is not absolutely straightforward. Gregory seems to satisfy s 1(1) in general and is certainly engaging in exactly the behaviour the legislation is seeking to prevent. However he is on the platform in an underground train station so the question is whether he satisfies the definition of public place in s 2(1)(a) and s 2(2).

- In relation to what Gregory is doing, the conviction would clearly stand whatever rule of interpretation is used.

- If the literal rule is used, then Gregory is singing racist and abusive songs, exactly what the Act prohibits.

- There is no need for the golden rule to be applied as there is no ambiguity and using the literal rule would not lead to an absurd result.

- Both the mischief rule and the purposive approach would also lead to a conviction since what Gregory is doing is the 'mischief' that the Act was intended to remedy and prohibiting such behaviour is the clear purpose of the Act.

- The key question then is to decide whether or not Gregory is in a public place as defined in s 2(1).

- Again the most likely is 2(1)(a) 'any public thoroughfare'.

- Again we have to examine the definition of 'public thoroughfare' given in s 4, the interpretation section – 'any road, pavement, precinct or other similar place along, over or through which vehicles or pedestrians pass'.

- We can apply the same principles as we did in Eric's situation in Scenario 3 and Freddie's in Scenario 4.

- If a strict literal interpretation of s 2(2) is used then there can be no conviction – Gregory is not in a public thoroughfare as defined in s 2(2).

- However, if we apply either the broad application of the golden rule for public policy reasons, or the mischief rule or the purposive approach, then upholding the conviction should be possible.

- Clearly once again we have to look to the EU legislation to see that the simple definition given there is much broader than that drafted into the Act.

Scenario 6

Henry and 17 members of his staff or members of their families have all been convicted under the Act. Henry manages a call centre, which is not open to the public and which is 100 metres from the Borough football ground. Many of the staff, including Henry, are Borough supporters and on match days Henry allows them to park in the company's car park. They were convicted following a recent match against Athletic when they chanted abusive anti-Athletic chants from the company car park at passing Athletic supporters. Henry believes that they should not have been convicted.

CONTINUED ▶

Answer to Scenario 6

Henry seems to have a point. While what they were clearly doing was prohibited under s 1(1), s 2(1)(b) and s 4 need to be examined carefully. Nevertheless, this is a reasonably simple and straightforward one to finish with:

- Subject to the definition of public place, s 1(1) appears to be satisfied under any of the rules.

- The question then is whether Henry and the others who were convicted engaged in abusive chanting in a public place.

- A very strict literal application of the words of s 2(1)(b), 'car park or coach park open to the public' indicates that the company car park is not a place that the public has access to and is therefore not a public place. Such an interpretation would not be unlike that in *Whiteley v Chappel* so there is precedent for such strict but apparently unrealistic application of the rule.

- Moreover, s 4 states that the Act does not apply to 'business premises not open to the general public' so again applying the literal rule, there is no way that the convictions could stand.

- The words 'open to the public' and 'not open to the general public' are plain and clear with no ambiguity so the narrow approach of the golden rule could not be used.

- However, Henry and his colleagues are doing exactly what the EU and UK legislation was seeking to prevent, antagonising the Athletic supporters, so to apply the literal rule would lead to an absurd result and so a purposive approach is far more acceptable in the circumstances.

- Taking a policy stance under the broad approach to the golden rule, applying the mischief rule or the purposive approach are all likely to ensure that the convictions stand.

INDEX

Upper case headings in italics refer to publications, those in lower case are Latin phrases. Page numbers in italics refer to diagrams and charts